Gendered Talk at Work

Language and Social Change

Series Editors:

Jennifer Coates, Roehampton University
Jenny Cheshire, Queen Mary, University of London
Euan Reid, Institute of Education, University of London

The *Language and Social Change* series explores the relationships between language, society and social change, and encompasses both theoretical and applied aspects of language use. Books in the series draw on naturally occurring language data from a wide variety of social contexts and take a broad view of the relationship between language and social change. They include work on groups that are socially marginalized and that were previously neglected by sociolinguists. They also include books that focus primarily on wider social issues concerning language, such as language ecology. The series takes a critical approach to sociolinguistics. It challenges current orthodoxies not only by dealing with familiar topics in new and radical ways, but also by making use of the results of empirical research which alter our current understanding of the relationship between language and social change. Above all, language will be viewed as constitutive of, as well as reflective of, cultures and societies.

1. *An Introduction to Language Policy: Theory and Method*
   Edited by Thomas Ricento

2. *Gendered Talk at Work: Constructing Gender Identity Through Workplace Discourse*
   Janet Holmes

Gendered Talk at Work

Constructing Gender Identity Through
Workplace Discourse

Janet Holmes

Blackwell
Publishing

BLACKWELL PUBLISHING
350 Main Street, Malden, MA 02148-5020, USA
9600 Garsington Road, Oxford OX4 2DQ, UK
550 Swanston Street, Carlton, Victoria 3053, Australia

First published 2006 by Blackwell Publishing Ltd

1   2006

Library of Congress Cataloging-in-Publication Data

Holmes, Janet, 1947–
    Gendered talk at work : constructing gender identity through workplace
    discourse / Janet Holmes.
        p. cm. — (Language and social change ; 2)
    Includes bibliographical references and index.
    ISBN-13: 978-1-4051-1758-6 (alk. paper)
    ISBN-10: 1-4051-1758-3 (alk. paper)
    ISBN-13: 978-1-4051-1759-3 (pbk. : alk. paper)
    ISBN-10: 1-4051-1759-1 (pbk. : alk. paper)
    1. Language and languages—Sex differences. I. Title. II. Series.
    P120.S48H63 2006
    306.44—dc22
                                                                2005037644

A catalogue record for this title is available from the British Library.

Set in 10/12.5pt Palatino
by Graphicraft Limited, Hong Kong
Printed and bound in the United Kingdom
by TJ International Ltd, Padstow, Cornwall

The publisher's policy is to use permanent paper from mills that operate a
sustainable forestry policy, and which has been manufactured from pulp
processed using acid-free and elementary chlorine-free practices. Furthermore,
the publisher ensures that the text paper and cover board used have met acceptable
environmental accreditation standards.

For further information on
Blackwell Publishing, visit our website:
www.blackwellpublishing.com

For Tony

Contents

Figures

Acknowledgements

While this book is based primarily on research done by the author in her role as Director of the Wellington Language in the Workplace (LWP) Project, it also draws on collaborative work, especially with Meredith Marra, as well as the published and, in some cases, as yet unpublished research of other members of the LWP team. This work is specifically acknowledged in the footnotes and the references, but the LWP Project's collaborative approach means my debt to others in the research team remains a large one. Any errors or infelicities are, on the other hand, entirely my responsibility.

I would particularly like to thank other members of the research team for their invaluable contributions to the research from which this book derives. Bernadette Vine, in her role as corpus manager, has been closely involved in the processing, transcription and archiving of the project data from the earliest stages of the project. She has also been a wonderful proofreader. Maria Stubbe, a former Research Fellow with the Project, has made a large contribution over the years to our research on gender and problematic talk in the workplace. Meredith Marra, a Research Officer with the Project, was a co-researcher for several of the topics covered in this book, especially chapters 3 and 4, and also competently gathered together the reference list, and formatted the many examples and excerpts from transcripts which are included. The contribution of work by team members Jonathan Newton and Nicola Daly is apparent in chapter 5, in particular. My Ph.D. students, Stephanie Schnurr, Angela Chan and Tina Chiles, have helped with examples and references, and my collaborative work with Stephanie is especially apparent from the attributions in chapters 2 and 4.

I also wish to acknowledge the important contribution of the many other individuals who participated in the construction of the unique

LWP Project data set, critiqued our analyses, or debated the various theoretical frameworks on which the research presented in this book is based.

First and foremost, I would like to express our appreciation to the workplace volunteers who did the actual recording, or allowed their workplace interactions to be recorded, and who gave so generously of their time to provide ethnographic information and feedback on our analyses.

I would also like to express appreciation to several Research Associates of the LWP Project, including Harima Fraser and Frances Austin, who facilitated our entrée into the two workplaces where we first piloted our research methodology, and who have continued to provide us with feedback on our analyses from their perspectives as workplace practitioners. In addition, many colleagues have provided valuable input over the years, including Chris Lane, Derek Wallace, Deborah Jones, Jane Bryson and Brad Jackson. Thanks also to Vivien Trott and Emily Major, who provided excellent administrative support.

Over the years of data collection, the Language in the Workplace Project has employed a number of very enthusiastic and competent research assistants, who have helped us to collect, catalogue, transcribe and analyse the data. They include Megan Ingle and Louise Burns who helped analyse some of the data subsets referred to in chapter 4. Thanks are also due to the many other research assistants who have persevered with the often tedious task of transcription and provided various kinds of administrative support: Melanee Beatson, Katie Brannan, Tim Brown, Jacqui Burnett, Margaret Cain, Sasha Calhoun, Tina Chiles, Maiona Fata, Fleur Findlay, Robert Holmes, Kate Kilkenny, Antonia Mann, Fiona Mann, Shannon Marra, Emily Major, George Major, Anthea Morrison, Diane McConnell, Martin Paviour-Smith, Bobby Semau, Rowan Shoemark, Clare Solon, Ben Taylor.

The Project has also had outstanding support with audio and video equipment from Richard Keenan at the Language Learning Centre, as well as very helpful computer advice from Mark Chadwick.

The final version of this book benefited from careful reading and comment by Bernadette Vine and Meredith Marra. I would also like to express appreciation to the three anonymous reviewers who engaged deeply with my arguments and provided many insightful and trenchant comments which greatly improved the text. I did not always follow their advice, however; and remaining flaws are thus entirely my responsibility.

Finally I thank my many supportive friends, and especially Anna Cottrell, who provided the lovely place where I revised this book, and Tony, who, as always, provided encouragement throughout the writing. This book is dedicated to him.

The research for this book was supported between 1996 and 2003 by grants from the New Zealand Foundation for Research, Science and Technology, and more recently by the Victoria University of Wellington Research Fund. The first draft was completed at the beautiful Bellagio Study and Conference Center in northern Italy in May 2004, with the assistance of a Rockefeller Foundation Fellowship, for which I am extremely grateful.

CHAPTER ONE

The Role of Gender in Workplace Talk

How do women and men talk at work? Are there distinctively 'feminine' or particularly 'masculine' ways of interacting in the workplace? If so, who uses them? In what contexts? And to what effect? This book explores the ways in which gender contributes to the interpretation of meaning in workplace interaction, and examines how women and men negotiate their gender identities as well as their professional roles in everyday workplace talk. The analysis demonstrates that effective communicators, both female and male, typically draw from a very wide and varied discursive repertoire, ranging from normatively 'feminine' to normatively 'masculine' ways of talking, and that they skilfully select their discursive strategies in response to the particular interactional context. I argue that their effectiveness derives from this discursive flexibility and contextual sensitivity.

By identifying the diversity in social and linguistic practices enacted by both women and men at work, I also hope to advance the interests of those, especially women, who run up against barriers to advancement as a result of prejudice and stereotyping. There is little doubt that most workplaces are predominantly masculine domains with masculine norms for behaving, including ways of interacting. Consequently, women often find themselves disadvantaged. Moreover, much research in areas such as management, business and leadership has, until relatively recently, tended to bolster such attitudes and misconceptions. The evidence in this book that people's interactional styles at work are anything but uniform, and that stylistic diversity and sensitivity to context are features of the ways in which both women and men interact at work, may help to counter negative stereotypes and undermine the prejudice that affects women in particular in many workplaces.

Having said that, I am not arguing that gender is irrelevant in workplace talk. Gender is potentially relevant in every social interaction, a 'pervasive social category',[1] and an undeniable, ever-present influence on how we behave, even if our level of awareness of this influence varies from one interaction to another, and from moment to moment within an interaction.[2] As Ann Weatherall points put,

> The identification of a person as belonging to one of two gender groups is a fundamental guide to how they are perceived, how their behaviour is interpreted and how they are responded to in every interaction and throughout the course of their life.[3]

The workplace data which provides the basis for the analysis in this book supports the view that gender is always potentially relevant to understanding what is going on in face-to-face interaction. Ignoring it will not make it less relevant. Gender is always there – a latent, omnipresent, background factor in every communicative encounter, with the potential to move into the foreground at any moment, to creep into our talk in subtle and not-so-subtle ways, as I will illustrate.

At some level we are always aware of whether we are talking to a woman or a man, and we bring to every interaction our familiarity with societal gender stereotypes and the gendered norms to which women and men are expected to conform. We orient to norms 'as a kind of organizing device in society, an ideological map, setting out the range of the possible within which we place ourselves and assess others'.[4] In other words, gender is an ever-present consideration, though participants may not always be conscious of its influence on their behaviour. In fact, it seems likely that awareness of the relevance of gender in interaction moves in and out of participants' consciousness.[5]

Consider the following excerpt from an interaction recorded in a small New Zealand IT company:

Example 1.1[6]

Context: Jill, Chair of the Board of an IT company, has had a problem with her computer and has consulted Douglas, a software engineer, for help. Returning to her office, she reports her experience to her colleague, Lucy, a project manager in the company.

1. **Jill:**   [*walks into room*] he just laughed at me
2. **Lucy:**   [laughs]: oh no:
3. **Jill:**   he's definitely going to come to my aid
4.   but ( ) he just sort of laughed at me
5. **Lucy:**   [laughs]
6. **Jill:**   and then I've got this appalling reputation
7.   of being such a technical klutz

Jill makes no overt reference to gender in this exchange, and yet gender stereotypes are a vital component of the scenario she constructs. She draws attention to her reputation as ignorant, a *technical klutz* (line 7), in the area of the organization's specialization, computer technology. And she also describes how her ignorance elicited laughter from the male expert who assisted her (lines 1, 4). In this self-deprecating construction of herself, Jill is undoubtedly drawing on the well-established stereotype of feminine incompetence around technology. Moreover, she makes use of normatively 'feminine' linguistic features in doing so: e.g. emphatic intensifiers *just, definitely, such a* (see next section). We have abundant evidence from further recordings to suggest that *technical klutz* is an identity she regularly adopts, milking it for humour and playing up her role as inept and ignorant in the IT area.[7] This a simple example of how gender may contribute to the social meaning of an interaction, and be relevant to a full understanding of what is being conveyed, but in an understated and subtle way rather than in a foregrounded and emphatic manner.

In fact Jill is a very able and confident woman manager in this workplace, and in the larger context of her workplace role, this exchange can be interpreted as having elements of ironic parody of the stereotypical role associated with women around computers.[8] In other words, by refusing to treat lack of IT technical knowledge as a serious matter, she implicitly 'troubles',[9] or parodies, 'traditional norms about feminine behaviour',[10] and questions the validity of stereo-typically discounting the competence of women who are technically unsophisticated.

Of course, men may be technically ignorant too, but the equivalent exchange between two men would, I contend, equally exploit the 'feminine' stereotype of the technical *klutz*. In other words, a male incompetent in the area of computer technology would play out such an interaction aware that he was invoking a normatively 'feminine' role in doing so.[11] Gender stereotypes contribute differently in different contexts, but they are omnipresent and always available to make a contribution to socio-pragmatic meaning.

Women in leadership positions in many New Zealand workplaces still need to prove themselves: the double bind of 'damned if you do and damned if you don't' regarding women's ways of talking, which was identified by Robin Lakoff in the 1970s,[12] has characteristically transformed into a demand that women leaders talk in ways perceived as appropriate both to their gender identities and their (often stereo-typically masculine) professional identities. The business management literature provides extensive testimony to the pervasiveness of these conflicting requirements of senior women.[13] Different women respond in different ways to these demands, as I will show.[14] Furthermore, people's ways of talking are typically strongly influenced by specific features of their workplaces, and by the particular type of interaction in which they are involved – a crucial point, and one which is central to the argument in this book.

Management research suggests that, like other countries, many New Zealand workplaces are still male dominated, and a substantial number operate with stereotypically masculine or 'masculinized'[15] norms with regard to particular aspects of behaviour, including verbal interaction.[16] Using questionnaire data collected from the corporate sector, for example, Hofstede identified New Zealand managers as relatively high in individualism, and above average in masculinity, although his study also suggested that differentials in power and authority tended to be played down in New Zealand.[17] In such workplaces, '[t]he masculine model is considered to be the professional model: this applies to communication, standards of behaviour, processes and practices in an organization. The cultural view is that men's ways of doing things are the standard or norm.'[18] In other workplaces – usually those where women are better represented in the workforce – relatively feminine or 'feminized discourse'[19] and ways of interacting may be more typical. These differently gendered expectations, and norms for appropriate ways of talking, influence perceptions of individual contributions to workplace interaction, and not surprisingly people respond to them in different ways. And while much of the management literature treats such patterns as established behaviours (despite their status as self-report data), I draw on them rather as evidence of ideologically produced norms which are useful for interpreting the complexities of workplace interaction, and especially for understanding the pressures on women and men to conform to particular ways of speaking at work.

In this book, then, I explore some of the diverse ways in which women and men in a number of mainly white-collar, professional, New Zealand organizations manage workplace discourse, and illustrate how they respond to the varied contextual conditions and communicative demands of their different 'communities of practice'.[20] The rest of this chapter first identifies features of feminine and masculine ways of talking, or 'feminized' and 'masculinized' discourse,[21] and then discusses the concept of the 'gendered' workplace. The analytical concepts and frameworks drawn on in the book are then outlined, followed by a brief description of the database and the methodology which was used to collect the data drawn on in the analysis. The chapter ends with an outline of the contents of subsequent chapters.

Gendered Ways of Talking

One dimension on which we are constantly, if generally unconsciously, assessing people's behaviour is that of contextual appropriateness in relation to gender norms. As with all social norms, this is often most evident when a person breaks or challenges the taken-for-granted assumptions about the way women or men 'should' behave. In a professional meeting I attended recently, for instance, a middle-aged American woman used a strong expletive to emphasize a point. The responsive facial expressions of several others present clearly indicated that she had challenged one of their norms for appropriate language in a white-collar, professional, formal context. While it is possible that the same word from a male would have elicited a similar reaction, it seemed to me that gender norms contributed to the emphatic effect.

In any conversation, people bring to bear their expectations about appropriate ways of talking, including appropriately gendered ways of talking. These expectations derive from our extensive experience of the diverse meanings conveyed by language in context. Gender is one particular type of meaning or social identity conveyed by particular linguistic choices, which may also concurrently convey other meanings as well.[22] So, for example, a compliment such as *nice jacket*, conveys positive affect, but may also convey an admiring or a patronizing stance, depending on who says it to whom and when. And it may also (indirectly) convey femininity in communities where compliments on appearance are much more strongly associated with women than with

Table 1.1 Widely cited features of feminine and masculine interactional styles (adapted from Holmes 2000a)

Feminine	Masculine
• facilitative	• competitive
• supportive feedback	• aggressive interruptions
• conciliatory	• confrontational
• indirect	• direct
• collaborative	• autonomous
• minor contribution (in public)	• dominates (public) talking time
• person/process-oriented	• task/outcome-oriented
• affectively oriented	• referentially oriented

men. In fact, it is well-accepted by linguists that 'the relationship between language and gender is almost always indirect'.[23] Ways of talking are associated with particular roles, stances (e.g. authoritative, consultative, deferential, polite), activities, or behaviours, and to the extent that these are 'culturally coded as gendered . . . the ways of speaking associated with them become indices of gender'.[24]

Features of interactional styles which may index femininity and masculinity in different social contexts have been identified in extensive research on language and gender over the last 30 years. Table 1.1 summarizes some of the most widely cited of these features.[25]

It is self-evident that

> a list such as this takes no account of the many sources of diversity and variation (such as age, class, ethnicity, sexual orientation, and so on), which are relevant when comparing styles of interaction. It largely ignores stylistic variation arising from contextual factors, including the social and discourse context of an interaction, and the participants' goals. And there is no consideration of how such differences develop: fundamental underlying issues such as the social distribution of power and influence are inevitably factored out.[26]

What the list *does* provide is a useful summary of discursive strategies strongly associated with middle-class white men and women in the construction of their normative and unmarked gender identity; strategies which instantiate and reinforce 'the gender order'.[27] These form the discursive resources from which such individuals construct or interactionally accomplish the kind of gender identity they want to convey.[28] A list is unavoidably crude, and hence the particular social meanings indexed by these features can only be interpreted in the specific communities of practice and discourse contexts in which they occur. Moreover, as noted, this particular list of features is class-based, and also obviously limited in terms of the relevance of such features to different ethnic groups.[29]

Extensive research throughout the last three decades has established some of the ways in which these strategies are expressed linguistically in a range of social settings, including professional, white-collar workplaces.[30] Facilitative devices, for instance, include tag questions (*isn't it? haven't they?*) and pragmatic particles (*you see, you know*) which may encourage the addressee's participation in the conversation. Encouraging supportive feedback often takes the form of positive minimal responses (e.g. *mm, yeah*). Indirect strategies include interrogatives (*could you reach that file?*) rather than imperatives (*pass that file*) for giving directives, and conciliatory strategies include mitigating epistemic modals (e.g. *might, could*), and attenuating pragmatic particles (e.g. *perhaps, sort of*) to soften and hedge requests and statements. These strategies are indexed as feminine in many social contexts.[31]

Similarly, the features listed as characteristic of masculine interactional style(s) are substantiated by a good deal of empirical research. In interviews, team discussions, classrooms, and department meetings, patterns of domination of talking time, disruptive interruption, competitive and confrontational discourse, have been noted as characterizing authoritative, powerful and assertive talk, and interactional styles conventionally associated with men rather than women, indicating why such features are so widely regarded as indexing masculinity, and associated with relatively masculine rather than feminine ways of speaking.[32] These are just some of the well-documented means of indexing gender and constructing a particular gender identity in many white-collar, professional workplaces.[33]

This wide-ranging research has thus established the broad parameters of what are widely regarded as normative, appropriate, and unmarked means of signalling gender identity in the workplace. These parameters provide a useful starting point for analysing specific instances of workplace talk. They constitute implicit, taken-for-granted norms for gendered interaction against which particular performances are assessed. As Swann (2002: 60) says, '[l]ocalized studies are framed by earlier research that established patterns of gender difference'.[34]

Example 1.2 illustrates some of the features (indicated in bold) indexing normatively feminine discourse.

Example 1.2[35]

Context: Meeting of 6 women in a government department. They have identified a problem with their recruitment processes. Leila is the section manager. [XF is an unidentifiable female voice.]

1. Lei: it's **a bit more of** a mess than what any of us thought . . .
2. Em: I've got Meredith's note about what she left behind . . .
3.   so I should be able to work it out from there
4. XF: mm but it's **just** time consuming **isn't it**
5. Lei: **well** it's more than time consuming because it **does look as if**
6.   **you know** when we went through those folders the other day
7.   and got all of those bright ideas for names
8.   **it looks** from looking at that **as if um**
9.   there's a lot of recruitment that **probably** hasn't happened
10.   **the problem is that** nothing's annotated to say
11.   whether the recruitment has actually occurred or not
12. XF: so that's you're stressing note keeping this /morning\
13. Lei: /yeah\
14. Em: we can check what recruitment letters Meredith sent out though
15.   cos they'll be in the system
16. Lei: but **I mean it's** /may- it maybe\
17. Em: /it's just a matter of someone\ going /and finding it\\
18. Lei: **it may be** /easier to\ write brand new recruitment letters saying **you know**
19. Em: we apologize if we wrote to you three months ago
20. Lei: yeah /( )\
21.   /[laughter]\
22. Ker: we **probably** won't be able to find them on the file ( )
23. Lei: Pauline will be able to find them
24. XF: um Meredith asked me not to keep quite a few letters

25.		she said once they were gone off the thing not to keep them so
26.	Lei:	mm they would have to they'd be in hard copy ( )
27.		**I'm not going to worry too much /about that**
28.	XF:	/[laughs]\
29.	Lei:	/**I think we might\ find a way of** doing a letter
30.		/so what have we got\
31.		**now I'm happy look shall we** make some decisions

This is a complex excerpt and I will not analyse it in detail here. However, it is clear from the components in bold type alone, that much of the exchange is expressed in terms that conform to relatively feminine norms for speaking. Focusing just on Leila, we see her criticizing the fact that the section's records are inadequate (lines 1, 9–11), and advocating a solution which others initially resist (line 18), two unwelcome discursive moves. In accomplishing these moves, she uses a high proportion of hedging devices (e.g. *well, um, looks as if, probably*), she uses passives, as well as *it* and *there* constructions which avoid allocating blame (e.g. lines 5–6, 8–9), and she uses the solidarity-oriented pronouns *we* and *us*, thus characterizing the problem (lines 1, 6), and especially the solution (lines 29, 30, 31) as shared. Moreover, she implies rather than asserts that she wants things to change; as XF correctly infers, *you're stressing note keeping this morning* (line 12).

This is perhaps the most unmarked way in which people do gender at work – through apparently unconscious choices which index gender identity by association with normatively gendered ways of talking. This is ordinary, appropriate talk between those who belong to this workplace: in this context it is not regarded as especially polite or particularly feminine. This is how people speak to each other for much of the time in this community of practice.[36] Well-established and familiar gendered discourse patterns are resources used to construct or display an appropriate professional identity in this workplace. If gender is omni-relevant, then familiarity with what is *unmarked* in relation to doing gender identity is a necessary basis for engagement in any social interaction, including talk at work. Identifying norms of interaction, including gender norms, is thus an important starting point in interpreting the social meanings encoded in workplace talk, and especially in identifying the significance of strategically marked vs. unmarked usage in signalling gender identity.[37]

Gendered workplaces

The notion of the gendered workplace, though an obvious simpli-fication, is a useful starting point for analysis. As mentioned above, research in areas such as management and leadership has established that many New Zealand workplaces are perceived to be dominated by relatively masculine norms of interaction, and by masculine attitudes and values. So, for instance, Maier describes the cultural system that predominates in many New Zealand organizations as marked by 'an emphasis on objectivity, competition and getting down to business. Being hard-nosed and adversarial is taken for granted. Managers are expected to be single-mindedly devoted to the pursuit of organizational goals and objectives, to be competitive, logical, rational, decisive, ambitious, efficient, task- and results-oriented, assertive and confident in their use of power.'[38] Adopting a term from Sinclair, Su Olsson, Director of the New Zealand Centre for Women and Leadership, labels this an image of 'heroic masculinism', and analyses how it contributes to the dominant organizational mythology which marginalizes women in many workplaces.[39] We could describe such workplaces as gendered masculine.

Assigning a label such as 'masculine' or 'feminine' to a workplace is then a matter of how the dominant values and attitudes are perceived and enacted, a cultural, perceptual and structural issue, and, as dis-cussed in earlier research, a matter of interactional style, rather than a reflection of the sex of those who work there.[40] The criteria are attitudinal, structural and stylistic rather than biological. More feminine workplaces, for instance, are characterized by 'openness of feelings, supportive social relationships, and the integration of private and work life';[41] by more democratic and non-hierarchical structures, and 'by a marked orientation towards collaborative styles and process of inter-action, together with a high level of attention to the interpersonal dimension'.[42] Some men can and do interact at times and in ways that contribute to the perception of a workplace as more feminine, just as the behaviour of some women reinforces the view of their workplaces as particularly masculine. Moreover, different workplaces can be characterized as more or less feminine, and more or less masculine in different respects, and different contexts. So, in a particular workplace, meeting structures and interactional processes may conform to more masculine styles of interaction, while the way small talk is distributed and its frequency may fit more conventionally feminine styles. Even the amount of pre-meeting talk tolerated after the scheduled starting time for the meeting may contribute to the construction of a more feminine vs. a more masculine community of practice. Furthermore, individuals may, of course, behave in ways indexing masculine or feminine ways of speaking at different points within the same interaction.[43]

At one end of the spectrum, gendered talk may be a quite explicit and conscious feature of workplace interaction. Kira Hall describes, for instance, how fantasy-line operators, offering telephone sex services, deliberately exploit stereotypical features of feminine talk in the enactment of their professional roles. In order to 'sell to a male market, women's pre-recorded messages and live conversational exchange must cater to hegemonic male perceptions of the ideal woman'.[44] At a different level, some workplaces may be perceived as more or less hospitable to women and to female values.[45] Other workplaces may be more masculine or even 'macho' in certain aspects of the workplace culture, making them uncomfortable places to work for those with different values, attitudes and preferred ways of interacting.[46] To a greater or lesser extent, then, people 'do gender' in the workplace; they engage in gender performances which have the potential to strengthen the 'gender order'.[47] Hence, although professional identity may be the most obviously relevant social identity in workplace interaction, the analyses in this book will demonstrate that gender identity is also an important component of workplace performance.

In concluding this section, it is worth noting that in many societies it is more masculine styles of interacting that tend to be more highly valued in workplace interaction, especially in more public and formal contexts. Luisa Martín Rojo and Conception Estaban comment on the fact that in Spain 'male style and norms are so deeply rooted in organizational culture', and they point to the perception of 'women's communicative behaviour as deviant'.[48] This is, of course, largely due to the fact that men have been in a majority in most workplaces until relatively recently, occupying nearly all the influential and powerful positions. Male models of success and masculine definitions of what is required to make progress at work have dominated in many work spheres.[49] Hence, unsurprisingly, masculine ways of interacting are strongly associated, especially in the business and management research literature, with effective workplace communication. The analyses in the chapters which follow offer an alternative model of successful workplace interaction.

It is also important to bear in mind that, despite the prevalence of this 'male-as-norm' model in much of the organizational communication literature, workplace interaction appears very much more complex when we examine the specific interactional norms of particular communities of practice in different organizations. Whether these are more authoritarian styles, indexed as masculine, or more collaborative and supportive styles, indexed as feminine, they provide the background or context within which individual women and men operate. The identification of the implicitly gendered, taken-for-granted, interactional norms of different communities of practice is thus a valuable exercise. But just as important is the analysis of the ways in which these norms are adhered to, exploited, or flouted from moment to moment in specific interactions.

A Dash of Theory

In analysing workplace interaction, my colleagues and I have consistently drawn on a variety of theoretical frameworks, and made use of a number of analytical concepts from socio-linguistics, pragmatics and discourse analysis. The material drawn on in this book was collected using an ethnographic approach (see next section), and the dominant paradigm adopted in the analysis is social-constructionist combined with an interactional socio-linguistic framework. The concept of 'face', and especially the notions of positive and negative face, have also proved valuable.[50]

Both interactional socio-linguistics and social-constructionist approaches emphasize the dynamic aspects of interaction, and the constantly changing and developing nature of social identities, social categories and group boundaries, a process in which talk plays an essential part. Individuals are constantly engaged in constructing aspects of their interpersonal and intergroup identity, including their professional identity and their gender identity.[51] The words we select, the discourse strategies we adopt, and even the pronunciations we favour may all contribute to the construction of a particular social identity. Penelope Eckert's analysis of American high school adolescents, for instance, indicated how certain phonological variables functioned as distinguishing linguistic resources for those who engaged in 'cruising' urban centres and parks.[52] And lexical items such as *dude*, *man*, *cuz* and *bro'* used as address terms in interaction play a part in constructing the socio-cultural identity of 'cool' young men in some New Zealand contexts.

Social constructionism is also basic to the notion of the *community of practice*, a concept which emphasizes process and interaction.[53] Workplace interactions tend to be strongly embedded in the business and social context of a particular work group, the community of practice, as well as in a wider socio-cultural or institutional order. This concept has proved very valuable in examining the way language contributes to the construction of gender identity as one aspect of social identity in the workplace. Penelope Eckert and Sally McConnell-Ginet define a community of practice (CofP) as follows:

> an aggregate of people who come together around mutual engagement in an endeavor. Ways of doing things, ways of talking, beliefs, values, power relations – in short, practices – emerge in the course of this mutual endeavor. As a social construct, a CofP is different from the traditional community, primarily because it is defined simultaneously by its membership and by the practice in which that membership engages.[54]

The notion of 'practice' is central. The CofP approach focuses on what members do – the practice or activities which indicate that they belong to the group, and also the extent to which they belong. It takes account of the attitudes, beliefs, values and social relations which underlie their practice. Hence, the CofP model encourages a focus on 'not gender differences but the difference gender makes'.[55] It has proved very valuable in examining the issue of what people mean when they talk about a 'feminine' or 'masculine' workplace or gendered workplace culture. Using a CofP approach, the analysis focuses on gendered behaviours, or the ways in which people exploit gendered resources, rather than examining behaviour based on the gender of the speaker.

By focusing on 'practice', the detailed management of face-to-face interaction, a community of practice approach illuminates how language is used in the construction of salient social boundaries. So, for example, how do people include or exclude others from a discussion, or more subtly, how do they signal that someone is a member of the in-group or not. In-group humour can function to include or exclude people from a CofP, and nicknames and in-group language function similarly. In the following exchange, a group member refers to a recently coined phrase, 'the Len factor', a piece of jargon which subsequently develops as a marker of membership of their CofP.

Example 1.3[56]

Context: Meeting of three work colleagues in a government department. They are discussing the fact that eliciting a response to a proposal or request for advice is a slow process in their organization.

1. **Cli:** let's go let's go and talk to someone else
2.   we'll get a <u>completely</u> different story about what to do
3. **Ser:** [laughs] /[laughs]\
4. **Cli:** /you know the whole thing will just sort of\ grow in/to a\ soap opera
5. **Val:** /[laughs] yeah\
6.   this is Christina came up with a good phrase before
7.   I think we should just adopt it the of- in in the office
8.   she said you need to account for the Len factor
9. **Sio:** [gasps] the Len factor I love it oh brilliant
10. **Val:** [laughs] /laughs]\
11. **Sio:** /I think Alex and I were talking about\ the Len factor yesterday [laughs]
12. **Cli:** /[laughs] oh yeah\
13. **Val:** exactly thank you Siobhan that's great

In lines 1–4, Clive describes how the same problem frequently elicits completely different advice from different individuals. Val tells the others about the phrase, 'the Len factor', coined to describe the unavoidable delay which must be built into any estimate of how long obtaining a response will take. Len is a colleague who is well known for always seeing difficulties and identifying problems, rather than facilitating the speedy resolution of an issue or the smooth passage of a proposal. 'The Len factor' is an amusing, succinct means of referring to the inevitable delays that such behaviour generates, and is quickly adopted as a useful piece of in-group jargon.

At different points in this book I discuss differently gendered *styles* of workplace interaction, with attention to a number of the characteristics that Etienne Wenger identifies as important in distinguishing different communities of practice, including shared ways of engaging in doing things together, and discursive ways of sustaining relationships and displaying group membership, such as social talk, small talk, and the use of humour. Focusing on complex interactional practice at the micro-level, I analyse how gender is 'produced and reproduced in differential forms of participation in particular CofPs'.[57]

As mentioned above, this approach draws attention to the dynamic nature of talk. Interaction in the workplace can be productively viewed as social practice in action. Interacting participants are constantly negotiating meaning, and in the process reproducing or challenging the larger social structures within which they operate. As Sally McConnell-Ginet notes:

> Whether a particular person's talk and other actions affect many or few, it is the unfolding over time of a structured totality of situated acts that creates meaning in and for society.[58]

In this way, the culture of a workplace is constantly being instantiated in ongoing talk and action; it develops and is gradually modified by large and small acts in regular social interaction within ongoing exchanges. Larger patterns are established through the accumulation of repeated individual instances, and each instance gains its significance against the backdrop of the established norms. From this perspective, people simultaneously perform a number of different aspects of their social identity, including gender, in their ongoing talk.[59]

Workplace culture is a multi-dimensional, complex concept, and one of those dimensions is often the masculine–feminine dimension. As they talk to others throughout the working day, people enact their ethnicity, their professional status, and their gender identity.[60] A female Pākehā[61] manager, such as Penelope in example 1.4 (below), may 'do power', as one way of enacting her professional identity in an interaction with a lower-status colleague, but she is simultaneously constructing her identity as a Pākehā in New Zealand society, and a woman in a particular community of practice. Different aspects of these various identities may be more or less salient at any particular point in the interaction, and this may be signalled by 'shifts in talk'.[62] Example 1.4 illustrates Penelope doing both collegiality and power within a very brief time span.

Example 1.4[63]

Context: Strategic planning meeting of three women and three men in a national organization. Penelope is the CEO.

1. **Pen**: /and yes and and\ stood our ground
2. **Het**: /mm yeah yeah\
3. **Pen**: [inhales] strode up the street /[laughs]
4. letting fly a number of expletives\ . . .
5. **Het**: /[laughs]: I'm sure that you get the general gist:\
6. [others laugh]
7. **Pen**: and she felt exactly the /same we'd both been feeling like this\
8. **Het**: /yep [laughs]\
9. **Pen**: I mean that's of course what happens when people abuse you
10. that's what you do feel angry and and uncooperative
11. and all of the things that we were feeling

Penelope and Hettie are describing their reaction to being treated dismissively and disrespectfully at a meeting with another organization. Lines 1–8 illustrate the two women constructing a genuinely collaborative floor with much infectious laughter. They work together discursively to convey their shared experience, with Penelope, in particular, using language which constructs them as assertive and strong (e.g. *strode up the street . . . letting fly a number of expletives*). It is clear from the tone of this very high-spirited interaction that Penelope and Hettie are on the same wave-length, a point made explicitly at line 7, *and she felt exactly the same we'd both been feeling like this*. Penelope constructs herself as a supportive and sympathetic colleague in this section; she is doing solidarity.

In concluding their account of the treatment they received, however, Penelope reverts to a more powerful style with a more distancing tone, bringing the narrative to a close with a very overt statement of the 'moral' (lines 9–11). Note, for instance, the use of the distancing pragmatic particle *of course* (line 9). By stepping back to reflect on the wider implications of their experience, Penelope here subtly asserts her powerful role, using features of a style conventionally coded as masculine, and constructing herself as a leader, someone with the right to evaluate the significance of the interaction.

In analysing workplace talk, it is important to take account of the many and various influences on how social meaning is encoded and interpreted. These embrace the wider situational context of interaction, including the contribution of ideology to interpretation, the role we are enacting, the social setting in which we are operating, who we are talking to, and what about – these are all crucial for understanding the discourse, and for defining our social identity in any particular encounter.[64] As Deborah Cameron says, 'language is *radically* contextual' and 'meaning is radically indeterminate and variable'.[65] As discourse analysts we must take note of these complex realities. Interactional socio-linguistics provides a starting point; it is concerned with what John Gumperz describes as the 'situated interpretation of communicative intent', and with 'discourse as the basic research site'.[66] This approach emphasizes the contextual relativity of the concept of 'appropriateness', and the importance of attending to the wider socio-cultural context in interpreting discourse at a local level.[67] As Deborah Schiffrin notes, 'social identity is locally situated: who we are is, at least partially, a product of where we are and who we are with'.[68] And whether gender is foregrounded, or an aspect of the taken-for-granted background, is similarly contextually relative.

Moreover, participants always bring to any interaction a great deal of background knowledge which enables them to understand what is going on and assists them in making effective and appropriate contributions to the interaction. So, for example, an accurate interpretation of the intended meaning of an utterance such as *it's time you went home* will differ according to the relevant background knowledge brought to bear. As part of an interaction with a work manager in work time, it might be an indication that the manager is concerned about the addressee's ability to properly manage her work. If uttered with the knowledge that the addressee's child was ill, the utterance could serve as permission to leave early or perhaps an indication that the speaker felt that maternal or domestic duties were being neglected. Background knowledge about the role relationships involved, as well as the kind of talk appropriate in each setting, are obviously relevant to how participants interpret utterances in their sequential context. An utterance may be interpreted as significantly 'gendered' in one context but as unmarked in another.

Both social constructionism and interactional socio-linguistics also emphasize the dynamic nature of interaction. Most obviously, every utterance must be interpreted in its discourse context: what precedes and follows contributes to a full understanding of what is going on. To give a very simple example, the significance and implications of a statement such as *it's time you went home* will be very different if it follows an utterance such as *that's the second time you've bitten my head off* as opposed to *you've done more than enough for today Mary*. This is a particularly clear example of the way the local discourse context contributes to an accurate interpretation of an utterance's meaning, but most interactions offer many more subtle examples of the ways in which particular meanings are conveyed through their placement in relation to the preceding and following discourse. Indeed, our workplace data provided a number of examples where the same utterance recurred at several different points in a discussion, but with different 'meanings' each time according to its placement. So, for instance, a proposition which on first mention introduced a tentative proposal might, by its fourth appearance, function as the affirmation of a firm decision.[69] This is clearly crucial for interpreting the contribution of an utterance to gender identity construction.

In addition, through their behaviour, and especially their discourse, participants in an interaction are continuously engaged in the process of constructing relatively masculine or feminine social identities.[70] Doing gender identity work involves constantly performing masculinity and femininity; these are 'on-going social processes dependent upon systematic restatement'.[71] The sequential structures in an interaction provide the means by which participants jointly construct a particular social order, and come to a shared interpretation of what is going on.[72] So speakers are regarded as constantly 'doing' gender, ethnicity, power, friendship, and so on, in interaction in a range of social settings.[73] Using this approach, any particular utterance may be analysed as contributing simultaneously to the construction of more than one aspect of an individual's identity, whether social (enacting gender identity), institutional (such as their professional identity as a manager), or personal (such as their wish to be considered friendly, well-informed, and so on). As Deborah Cameron and Don Kulick note, often 'the same way of speaking signifies both a professional identity and a gendered identity, and in practice these are difficult to separate: the two meanings coexist, and both of them are always potentially relevant. The actual balance between them is not determined in advance by some general principle, but has to be negotiated in specific situations.'[74]

A dynamic model of a communicative event which can accommodate these different aspects of identity construction in ongoing interaction, is provided by Miriam Meyerhoff and Nancy Niedzielski.[75] Each utterance contributes to the social and personal identity construction of speakers, as well as modifying the perceptions of the addressee in an interaction in a dynamic, ongoing way. Meyerhoff and Niedzielski note that linguistic choices (of language, dialect, style or register), and at every level (from phonetic, through syntactic, lexical, pragmatic, discursive and paralinguistic), are constantly being made in the light of participants' ongoing assessment of the relative weight of a wide range of social factors such as the formality of the setting, the seriousness or familiarity of the topic, the role relationships involved, and so on. Hence, in any interaction, while all facets of an individual's social identity are potentially relevant resources, individuals tend to present or focus on particular aspects of their social identity, sometimes emphasizing gender, sometimes ethnicity, sometimes power, authority or professional status, and sometimes organizational or institutional identity. Roz Ivanic makes a similar point, noting that an individual's multiple identities or, as conceptualized here, different aspects of their complex social identity, are unlikely to be equally salient at any particular moment in time.[76] Different aspects of identity will be foregrounded at different moments. The approach is a dynamic one, allowing for constant flux and interplay between aspects of an individual's diverse social and personal identities in response to contextual influences. For instance, Penelope's discourse in lines 1–7 of example 1.4 simultaneously constructs her as Hettie's colleague and as a strong, assertive person, while in lines 9–11, by providing an interpretation, she begins to wind up the story, responding to contextual pressures to move on with the agenda, and simultaneously doing power as discussed above.

In the workplace, power is obviously a very relevant consideration, requiring careful analysis as a dynamic and systemic aspect of interaction, though not always a very overt one.[77] Both power and gender relations may be constructed unobtrusively, through taken-for-granted, 'naturalized' conversational strategies, and reinforced in everyday, unremarkable, workplace interactions.[78] It is those who are in positions of power who decide what is correct or appropriate in an interaction: who may talk, for instance, and for how long; what counts as a relevant contribution, and what is considered a digression. They also have 'the capacity to determine to what extent . . . [their] power will be overtly expressed'.[79] Fairclough has argued that in recent years the overt marking of power has been declining, and that power is increasingly enacted in subtle and covert ways – but it is no less influential in affecting how people's behaviour, including their talk, is classified and perceived. This is very important in the context of an analysis of gendered talk at work. What counts as 'marked', or as 'normal' and unremarkable from a gender perspective, will be influenced by the regulatory norms established by the dominant group – in a society, an organization, and a community of practice. How then do we identify implicit interactional norms and unpack their social significance? One useful place to start is by describing the discursive patterns which instantiate power and gender relations at work, and the specific ways in which both women and men draw on gendered discourse resources to enact a range of workplace roles in different communities of practice.

Database and Methodology[80]

The workplace talk analysed in this book is taken from a large database of authentic recorded data collected over seven years by members of the Wellington Language in the Workplace (henceforth LWP) Project. This database currently stands at around 2,500 interactions, involving more than 500 people from a diverse range of backgrounds. These recordings are supplemented by detailed ethnographic notes, interviews and, in some workplaces, with focus group meetings discussing issues of particular interest. The different kinds of contributing workplaces are identified in figure 1.1.

The white-collar professional workplaces which are the main focus of the analysis in this book include government departments and commercial organizations of various kinds.[81] Most New Zealand businesses are small to medium in size by international standards, and the commercial organizations which feature in this book mainly conform to this pattern. There are 2 multinational companies among the 22 workplaces represented in our database, but within these larger organizations we focused on specific workplace teams for our data collection. The data collected from workplaces was as diverse as

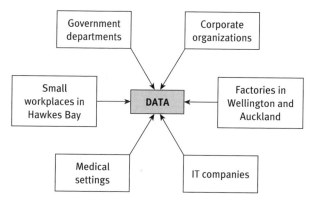

Figure 1.1 The Language in the Workplace Project data set

possible. For instance, from larger commercial and semi-public organizations, we audio-recorded and video-recorded sets of more formal meetings, typically involving project teams who met regularly over a period of time, and sometimes for several months. In the factories, we recorded team meetings, briefing sessions, one-to-one interactions between individuals on the factory floor and in the white-collar workers' offices, communications over the factory intercom system, and conversations in the control room. In small businesses, in addition to typical work-related interactions, more social conversations at morning tea-time and lunchtime were a particular focus. The complete data set thus comprises a wide variety of different types of interaction, from small, relatively informal, work-related discussions between two or three participants, ranging in time between 20 seconds and 2 hours, to more formal meetings ranging in size from 4 to 13 participants, and in time from 20 minutes to 4 or 5 hours. The corpus also includes telephone calls and social talk as it occurred, for example, at the beginning of the day, at tea and coffee-breaks, and at lunchtime.

Groups of volunteers from each workplace were provided with tape recorders and were asked to record a range of their everyday interactions at work over a period of one to two weeks. Some kept a recorder and microphone on their desks, others carried the equipment with them as they moved around the workplace. In the factories, data was collected by 'key' individuals who carried radio microphones for 2–3 hours at a time, transmitting to a recorder in a suitable location, and monitored by a participant observer fieldworker. Over the recording period, people increasingly ignored the microphones and (where used) the video cameras, which were relatively small and fixed in place. They simply came to be regarded as a standard part of the furniture, and there are often comments indicating people had forgotten about the recording equipment. Also over time the amount of material they deleted, or which they asked us to edit out, decreased dramatically. As a result we collected some excellent examples of workplace interaction which were as close to 'natural' as one could hope for.

Most of the data analysed in this book was recorded in organizations where talk was integral to the core business of the workplace. As described in more detail elsewhere,[82] we deliberately chose one workplace where there was a high proportion of women, one where there was a predominance of men, and one with a high proportion of Māori[83] workers, in addition to a number of other workplaces where we expected the ethnic and gender balance to be roughly 'normal' for the New Zealand workplace. Ethnographic data of various kinds was also collected via a number of channels including workplace observation, informal contacts with participants, pre- and post-recording briefings, follow-up interviews and contextual notes (written or on tape) provided by the participants at the time of recording. Except in the factories, the great majority of people recorded were native speakers of English, and they came from a range of ages and professional levels within each organization.[84]

Finally, in discussing the methodology, it is important to note that the LWP team consists predominantly of female researchers. In a book written by a woman and focused on gender, the possibility of gender bias in the interpretation of the data is an obvious issue. Hopefully this is mitigated to some extent by the use of extensive samples taken from our transcriptions of the recorded interactions in our database to illustrate the arguments in each chapter. In this way, readers have at least some means of checking the credibility and plausibility of the interpretations proposed.

Outline of the Content of Book

Each chapter of this book approaches the issue of gendered talk at work from a different perspective. Chapter 2 focuses on the relationship between leadership, gender and discourse, and explores, in particular, the traditional association of leadership with masculinity, including masculine styles of discourse. The analysis questions the claim that in order to succeed, women (and men) *must* adopt normatively masculine ways of doing things at work by illustrating the complexities of leadership talk in different workplaces. Two specific aspects of managerial discourse, namely the way managers give directives and the way they manage the opening of meetings, are used to illustrate differently gendered management styles. The examples indicate that contextual considerations are always fundamental in analysing discourse choices, including the relevant community of practice. The chapter includes a case study of a very effective woman leader in a relatively masculine community of practice, illustrating the ways in which she integrates communicative skills regarded as normatively masculine with those traditionally regarded as more feminine. The complex realities of talk at work illustrated in this chapter suggest that the barriers that women often face in attaining senior positions are rather the result of prejudice and stereotyping than due to limitations on their ability to enact leadership appropriately in diverse contexts. The chapter concludes by suggesting ways in which people may challenge, and hopefully slowly change, ideologically based regulatory discourse norms concerning appropriate ways of doing leadership which may subtly disadvantage some people (and especially some women) when senior positions are under consideration.

Chapter 3 examines the proposition that 'relational practice' is a gendered concept and explores its realization in discourse. Using a framework introduced by Joyce Fletcher in her book *Disappearing Acts*, the analysis explores the varied ways in which relational practice is enacted in workplace interaction to ensure projects stay on track, to empower colleagues and facilitate their work, and to maintain solidarity and enhance team relations. Fletcher used only observational and interview data in her study, and focused on the behaviour of women in an engineering company. Drawing on our recorded data, this chapter illustrates how such functions are actually instantiated by a range of women and men in their everyday workplace talk.

Fletcher argues that relational practice is associated with women's behaviour at work and is gendered 'feminine'. The material in our database indicates, however, that relational practice may also be expressed in distinctly unfeminine ways. The constraints of different workplace cultures and the norms of different communities of practice also impact on acceptable and appropriate ways of doing relational practice. The chapter concludes by noting the implications of such norms, both for the options available to those who wish to advance to senior positions, and for the comfort levels and effectiveness of those who find themselves in workplaces where the dominant interactional style is not one they feel at ease with.

Chapter 4 explores the ways in which humour serves as a subtly gendered resource in workplace interaction. The analysis demonstrates how people use humour in normatively gendered ways (supportive/challenging, collaborative/non-collaborative) to construct different aspects of their gender identity at work, and in some cases to integrate the potentially conflicting demands of different aspects of their workplace identity. A wide range of examples illustrate how participants in workplace interaction use humour to support or challenge the claims of their colleagues, using features of a collaborative or alternatively a competitive interactional style. The analysis also demonstrates that humour may serve as a vehicle through which gender issues, and even sexism and sexist stereotypes, may subtly invade workplace interaction in ways that are sometimes difficult to challenge without losing face. A number of instances of this process are examined, and the analysis illustrates the ways in which both women and men exploit the entertainment value of sexual humour at work, as well as how sexist comments can be contested and managed through humour.

Managing workplace conflict is always challenging, requiring complex and multi-dimensional skills which respond sensitively to the specific discourse context within a particular community of practice. Progress may depend on constructive confrontation in some contexts, while avoidance may be a more effective strategy in others. Negotiating through instances of problematic discourse (rather than confronting and challenging one's 'opponents') is most useful in other contexts. Chapter 5 demonstrates that conventionally gendered conflict management strategies, such as avoidance and negotiation, may be accomplished using a range of differently gendered styles at the micro-level of face-to-face interaction. As in other areas of interaction, gender lines are anything but clear-cut: in managing conflict, both women and men draw extensively on masculine and feminine discursive resources and gendered norms to achieve their transactional and relational objectives in different workplace contexts.

Narrative is a useful means of instantiating diverse aspects of a person's complex social and professional identity in the workplace, including gender identity. Chapter 6 explores how workplace narratives contribute to the construction of gendered workplace identities. Narratives are one of the ways in which people make use of gendered discursive resources to achieve an integrated workplace identity, exploiting feminine and masculine stances as appropriate in pursuit of both relational and transactional goals. The analysis examines the extent to which narratives contribute dynamically to differently gendered styles of interaction, and thus to the gendering of different workplace contexts and cultures.

What are the implications of the analysis of gender as a component in workplace discourse for women's employment opportunities? To what extent does the expectation that women should portray or adopt a feminine as opposed to a more masculine social identity exert pressure on women at work – especially on those in senior management positions in organizations? And is it possible that we could convert such expectations from constraints into advantages? Chapter 7 takes a more explicitly political stance, and surveys the evidence provided in previous chapters, not only that there is enormous diversity in discursive practices at work, but also that features of normatively feminine styles are not inappropriate at work, but rather essential components of effective workplace interaction in many contexts. Indeed, effective workplace talk often involves a sophisticated integration of features from both feminine and masculine interactional styles. The book concludes with a discussion of how research on gendered discourse in the workplace may make a contribution to improving the position of women at work.

Conclusion

This chapter had laid the groundwork for an analysis of gendered talk in the workplace. In every aspect of this analysis it will become apparent that talk is deeply embedded in its socio-cultural context, and that in order to interpret the significance of what people say we need to have a thorough understanding of the social setting, the discourse context, and the community of practice and workplace culture in which the talk was produced. In addition, ideology inevitably plays a fundamental role in any examination of the relevance of gender as a component in workplace interaction.[85] Taken-for-granted assumptions about the place of women and men in society legitimize the status quo and existing workplace relationships. Assuming gender is always relevant at some level in every interaction, the following chapters address in a variety of ways the questions of where, when, and especially how, gender is relevant in workplace communication.

The dangers of over-reliance on stereotypes in this enterprise are quite apparent, although it is also important to recognize, as Sara Mills points out, that hypothesizations of stereotypes make a vital contribution to our notions of what is appropriate in relation to male and female discourse.[86] Interaction is typically viewed through 'gendered' spectacles much of the time.[87] Gender is a salient dimension in everyday life, and a key social category for most people.[88] Our discourse is drenched in gender. Assumptions about what constitutes more feminine as opposed to more masculine ways of talking are constantly being reinforced in everyday interaction, and the process of 'gendering' individuals is clearly an ongoing, dynamic one. Denying this is misleading, and potentially damaging to the feminist enterprise. Exposing sexist assumptions and challenging covert patterns of male domination is important, and the workplace is a significant location for such taken-for-granted assumptions.

Finally, it is important to bear in mind that though gender is the focus of the analysis in this book, many other factors impact on workplace discourse, and some may be much more important than gender in particular situations, contexts and communities of practices. Discourse contributes to our construction as people of a particular social class, ethnicity, sexual orientation, and age, as well as gender. Gender 'never exhibits itself in pure form, but in the context of lives that are shaped by a multiplicity of influences which cannot be neatly sorted out.'[89] Reflecting on this issue, Joan Swann emphasizes the importance of being clear about the class, ethnicity, age and so on, of those whose speech we are describing.[90] So while gender is my focus, I also point to these other intersecting and layered influences when they are relevant in contributing to an understanding of what is going on in an interaction.

I hope that the analysis in this book will contribute to a richer and more complex picture of the ways in which women and men draw on gendered discourse resources in their everyday interactions at work. Hopefully, too, the contextually-based, analytical approach adopted in this book will help erode traditional associations between femininity and ineffectiveness on the one hand, and masculinity and seniority on

Figure 1.2   'Do you think the directors ever pretend to be us?' © Hector Breeze

the other, and thus make a contribution to 'the development of gender ideologies that offer and encourage positive experiences for women'.[91]

NOTES

1   Weatherall (2000: 287).
2   See, for example, West and Fenstermaker (1995), Stokoe and Weatherall (2002), Stokoe and Smithson (2002), Kitzinger (2002), and from a canonical Conversational Analysis perspective, Garfinkel (1967).
3   Weatherall (2000: 287). The issue of whether the appropriate term in this quotation should be 'sex' rather than 'gender' is discussed by Freed (2004).
4   Eckert and McConnell-Ginet (2003: 87).
5   Martín Rojo (1998).
6   Transcription conventions are provided at the end of the book immediately before the reference list. This example is taken from a longer excerpt which is discussed more extensively in Holmes and Schnurr (2004, 2005).
7   Trauth (2002) suggests IT is a particularly masculine domain.

8 Holmes and Schnurr (2004).

9 Butler (1990).

10 Eder (1993: 25).

11 In the rest of this book I do not put the words 'feminine' and 'masculine' in scare quotes unless I am making a particular point, as their frequency would inevitably irritate readers. I hereby give notice, therefore, that I am aware that these terms invoke stereotypes and I use them recognizing that they have many limitations.

12 Lakoff (1975).

13 For evidence of this in New Zealand, see Olsson and Stirton (1996), Parry (2000), Olsson and Walker (2003).

14 Bunker (1990) notes, for example, that 'the latitude for acceptable behaviour for women executives appears to be very narrow'. See also Brewis (2001).

15 Baxter (2003: 167).

16 Kendall and Tannen make the same observation about US workplaces: 'styles of interaction more common among men have become the workplace norm' (1997: 85). Berryman-Fink (1997) similarly comments that 'the culture of most [US] organizations is still based on male norms and assumptions'. And Wood (2000) describes behavior and communication patterns that are familiar and comfortable for men but not women.

17 Hofstede (1980). An Australasian phrase, 'the tall poppy' syndrome, is relevant here. It describes the tendency for New Zealanders and Australians to try to 'cut down to size' those who excel in any way – whether intellectually, in status or in wealth. Jackson and Parry (2001: 27) comment that 'it would be difficult to find a nation that has institutionalized and ritualized . . . wealth and status envy' or 'lack of reverence for big business' to the extent that Australasians have.

18 Still (1996: 71).

19 Baxter (2003: 172).

20 This term is discussed below. See also Eckert and McConnell-Ginet (1992), Wenger (1998).

21 Baxter (2003).

22 See Holmes (1997a) for further discussion.

23 Cameron and Kulick (2003: 57), summarizing Ochs' (1992) argument on indexing function of language.

24 Cameron and Kulick (2003: 57).

25 A version of this table was first published in Holmes (2000a).

26 Holmes and Stubbe (2003a: 574–5).

27 Eckert and McConnell-Ginet (2003: 32), Connell (1987).

28 Heritage (1984), West and Fenstermaker (2002).

29 Mills (2003) notes that these stereotypes are often inappropriately extended to other classes and racial groups when judgements of 'politeness' are made by those in positions of power and influence.

30 See, for example, Aries (1996), Coates (1996), Crawford (1995), Holmes (1995), Romaine (1999), Talbot (1998), Tannen (1993, 1994a, 1994b), West (1995), Wodak (1997).

31 Ochs (1992).

32 See Eakins and Eakins (1979), Edelsky (1981), West (1984), Case (1988, 1991), Woods (1989), Ainsworth-Vaughn (1992), Holmes (1992, 2000a), James and Drakich (1993), Tannen (1994a, 1994b), Swann (1992), Stanworth (1983), Nelson (1998),

33 See also Holmes, Stubbe and Vine (1999), Kendall (2003), Holmes and Stubbe (2003a), McElhinny (2003a), Wodak (1995). As Cameron (1996) points out, the patterns identified in such research have proved remarkably robust.

34 Swann (2002) provides an excellent and very thorough discussion of the problems facing those undertaking the analysis of gendered talk. Her position explicitly endorses my own view (Holmes 1996), namely that quantitative analyses of the kind referred to here, can serve as a basis for more detailed qualitative analyses of specific instances of discourse in context. They provide the ground in the context of which we can attempt to interpret the figure or detail. Interestingly, in the light of her post-modernist orientation, Mills (1999: 93) also advocates a 'combination of quantitative and qualitative research methods'.

35 This example has been slightly edited to reduce its length and improve its readability: for instance, minimal feedback from participants who do not make any other contribution has been omitted.

36 The notion of a 'community of practice' with shared norms of interaction is clearly important here; the concept is discussed in the next section.

37 While I have drawn attention to the normatively feminine discourse features of the women's speech in example 1.2, it is important to note that there are also many direct and unmitigated assertions in the excerpt, e.g. most of what Emma contributes is direct and unmitigated (lines 2–3, 14–15, 17), and Leila actually uses a skilful mix of mitigation and appeals to solidarity on the one hand, together with direct, unmitigated assertion on the other, especially when contradicting something with which she disagrees: e.g. *it's more than time consuming* (line 6), *Pauline will be able to find them* (line 23). The important implications of this point are explored in later chapters.

38 Maier (1997), cited in Olsson (2000: 183).

39 Sinclair (1994: 188), Olsson (2000: 178).

40 This discussion is developed from that in Holmes and Stubbe (2003a).

41 Alvesson and Billing (1997: 116).

42 Holmes and Stubbe (2003a: 587–8).

43 Mills (1999) argues for the concept of the 'discursively competent speaker' to displace the concepts of 'masculine' and 'feminine' speech styles.

This is essentially an androgynous conception (though Mills repudiates this term too (1999: 90)), and hence, although her chapter is subtitled 'How to Theorize Strong Women Speakers', implying women are her focus, she provides no indication of how a 'strong woman speaker' might be distinguished from a discursively competent male speaker. Case (1988, 1993) made this point 20 years ago and supported it with empirical data.

44 Hall (1995: 190). See also Cameron (2000).

45 See Beck (1999), Holmes and Stubbe (2003a), Holmes and Marra (2004a).

46 See Beck (1999: 205).

47 Connell (1987), Eckert and McConnell-Ginet (2003).

48 Martín Rojo and Esteban (2003: 268).

49 See, for example, Sinclair (1994), Beck (1999), Jackson and Parry (2001), Martín Rojo and Esteban (2003).

50 Goffman (1967), Brown and Levinson (1987). I am well aware of the limitations of Politeness Theory, and especially its relative neglect of important aspects of the social context, including the extended discourse context, in interpreting the social meaning of components of an interaction. Watts (2003) and Mills (2003) provide valuable summaries of some of the most frequently identified criticisms of Politeness Theory. The interactional socio-linguistic framework provides a counter to these limitations.

51 See, for example, Butler (1990), Hall and Bucholtz (1995), Bergvall, Bing and Freed (1996), Holmes (1997a), Bucholtz, Liang and Sutton (1999), Eckert (2000), Litosseliti and Sunderland (2002), Eckert and McConnell-Ginet (2003).

52 Eckert (2000: 139–53).

53 Wenger (1998).

54 Eckert and McConnell-Ginet (1992: 464); see also Eckert and McConnell-Ginet (2003).

55 Cameron (1992: 13).

56 This example is from Holmes and Marra (2004a: 384).

57 Eckert and McConnell-Ginet (1995: 491).

58 McConnell-Ginet (2000: 263).

59 This section is a revised and updated version of material from Holmes, Stubbe and Vine (1999).

60 See Sarangi and Roberts (1999).

61 Pākehā is a Māori word used widely in New Zealand to refer to people of European (mainly British) descent.

62 Sarangi and Slembrouk (1996: 61).

63 This example is from Holmes (2005a).

64 Gumperz (1982, 1992, 2001a, 2001b).

65 Cameron (1992: 192); italics in original.

66 Gumperz (2001b: 223, 215).

67 See also Spencer-Oatey (2000).
68 Schiffrin (1996: 198).
69 See, for example, Vine (2004), ch. 6.
70 See Butler (1990), Hall and Bucholtz (1995), Bergvall et al. (1996).
71 Johnson (1997: 22).
72 Drew and Heritage (1992).
73 See, for example, Johnstone (1990), McElhinny (1995), Cook-Gumperz (1995), Bergvall (1996), Holmes (1997a).
74 Cameron and Kulick (2003: 58).
75 Meyerhoff and Niedzielski (1994).
76 Ivanic (1998: 11).
77 See, for example, Fletcher (1999), Fairclough (1989, 1992), Wodak (1996, 1999).
78 See Fairclough (1989, 1992).
79 Fairclough (1989: 72).
80 We have published a wide range of materials based on the rich corpus described in this section; see our website: www.vuw.ac.nz/lals/lwp/. See especially Holmes and Stubbe (2003b) for an account of some of the main findings of the project. For further detail on the database and methodology, see Holmes and Stubbe (2003b: ch. 2), and Stubbe (2001).
81 Interestingly, Martín Rojo, who collected interviews and life histories from male and female professionals and upper-level managers in Madrid and Barcelona, working, like those in our sample, either for the public administration or for large multinational corporations, describes them as 'individuals who work in sectors with a high degree of competitiveness between genders . . .' (1997: 233).
82 Holmes and Stubbe (2003b: ch. 2), Stubbe (2001).
83 The Māori people are New Zealand's original Polynesian inhabitants, now comprising approximately 15 per cent of the population.
84 The factories employed a number of Polynesian workers for whom English was a second language. The few examples from factories used in this book involve people who were fluent speakers of English, whether as a first or second language.
85 See McElhinny (2003a), Philips (2003), Talbot (2003).
86 Mills (2003: 184).
87 Eckert and McConnell-Ginet (2003).
88 Holmes and Meyerhoff (2003b: 9).
89 Bordo (1990: 114). Referring to the same phenomenon, Johnson (1997: 19) talks of the 'pluralization of gender', while Ivanic (1998: 11) argues similarly for the concept of a multiplicity of identities.
90 Swann (2002: 48).
91 Phillips (2003: 272).

CHAPTER TWO

Gender and Leadership Talk at Work

'The ceiling isn't glass – it is a dense layer of men!'
Anne Jardim, The New Yorker, *1996*

Introduction

With few exceptions, women have only begun to occupy roles with real power, status, and responsibility in professional white-collar organizations in the last two decades. In the past, most women in the workplace were typically restricted to relatively menial roles, supporting the men who did the 'real' work. Women were cleaners and tea-ladies, and then secretaries and librarians. Their roles were circumscribed and their interactions restricted. Even in recent times, they have more often been deputies than chiefs. And even when they make it to more influential positions, it has been argued that their contributions are often underestimated and undervalued. Cynthia Berryman-Fink comments that in the USA, for instance, there are 'a variety of gender and communication issues affecting contemporary organizations' which 'stem from increasing numbers of women entering the workforce but encountering barriers of equal opportunity compared to men'.[1] This chapter challenges the stereotypical conception of effective leadership as necessarily masculine in style. Different conceptions of leadership and different ways of discursively doing leadership are illustrated, with particular attention to the gendered features of leadership discourse.

The term 'leader' is used to include people who range in status and levels of responsibility from CEOs of large government and commercial organizations to team leaders of groups as small as eight people. All have leadership responsibilities, and their communicative behaviour provides useful insights into the issue of whether and how gender influences the way people enact leadership in New Zealand workplaces. Following a discussion of the relationship between leadership and gender, and the notion of gendered styles in leadership discourse, the analysis focuses on two specific aspects of managerial discourse: firstly, some of the varied ways in which leaders get people to do things are examined, and then a particular aspect of meeting management is analysed, namely how leaders manage the opening of meetings. This is followed by a case study, illustrating how one woman leader integrates communicative skills indexed as normatively masculine with those conventionally coded as feminine in doing effective leadership in a relatively masculine community of practice. The chapter concludes by considering the restricted range of models available to aspiring women leaders, and discusses ways in which women may challenge, and thus perhaps slowly change, the gendered norms which often disadvantage them when senior positions are under consideration.

The analysis in this chapter also pays attention to the ways in which gendered norms of workplace talk can subtly contribute to excluding women from positions of power and influence. In other words, the relegation of women to peripheral or marginal roles may be supported by the uncontested preponderance of masculine ways of talking in particular communities of practice. Even though people draw on styles indexed as both masculine and feminine in different contexts and for different effects, the absence of women in senior roles in many workplaces, means the association of masculine styles with men is constantly reinforced. Even more serious, because they are so difficult to challenge, are the taken-for-granted systemic assumptions about the way things are most effectively done. In a study of an American engineering company, for example, Joyce Fletcher, identified what she labelled 'a masculine logic of effectiveness operating in organizations that is accepted as so natural and right that it may seem odd to call it masculine. This logic of effectiveness suppresses or "disappears" behaviour that is inconsistent with its basic premises.'[2] In other words, she argues, ways of talking and interacting conventionally associated with women are unappreciated, devalued and even erased from the organizational screen. Our New Zealand data certainly supports the view that some workplaces promulgate a more masculine ethos, with leaders who encourage contestive and challenging interactional styles, and devalue more feminine styles of talk. However, as the examples discussed in this chapter illustrate, our data also includes communities of practice where ways of talking indexed as feminine predominate, and where different conceptions of leadership have developed.

I am not suggesting that patterns of workplace talk are the only factors, or even the most important factors, involved in the systematic discrimination against women in leadership roles in many workplaces. Talk alone cannot account for the density or impermeability of the glass ceiling.[3] But interactional patterns and, more subtly, what Berryman-Fink calls 'the climate of interaction for women and men in their jobs'[4] can certainly play a part in defining the ways of 'doing leadership' which are considered appropriate and acceptable in different communities of practice. I begin with a brief discussion of the relationship between the concepts of gender and leadership, and the problems raised by the double bind facing women who aspire to leadership positions.

Leadership, Gender and the 'Double Bind'

Leadership is a gendered concept. Although an increasing number of workplace leaders and managers are female, until relatively recently, the prevailing stereotype of a leader, chief executive officer, and even senior manager has been decidedly male.[5] In New Zealand, in particular, despite the fact that in recent years the positions of Prime Minister, Governor-General, Chief Justice, Chief Executive of Telecom, and CEO of a number of government Ministries have been held by women, many people continue to 'think leader, think male'.[6]

It is not only popular conceptions of leadership which have a decidedly male bias.[7] A good deal of research in the area of leadership also indicates a remarkably masculine conception of what makes an effective leader, especially among male respondents, and the standard measures seem embedded in an authoritarian and masculine perspective on the way it is accomplished.[8] Leaders are typically characterized as authoritative, strong-minded, decisive, aggressive, competitive, confident, single-minded, goal-oriented, courageous, hard-nosed, and adversarial.[9] And even research which takes a more dynamic approach, and which analyses leadership as a process or an activity, rather than a set of identifiable characteristics, tends to present a rather masculine conceptualization of how leadership is ideally performed.[10] Leadership qualities within this framework include willingness to challenge, ability to inspire, problem-solving in approach, toughness, and willingness to take risks.[11] In terms of norms and stereotypes, these undoubtedly favour the masculine end of the scale.

In addition, as noted in chapter 1, the norms for behaviour in many workplaces, including norms for interaction, are often predominantly masculine norms,[12] and in many workplace contexts men's discourse styles have been institutionalized as ways of speaking with authority.[13] As Susan Gal says, institutions are 'organized to define, demonstrate, and enforce the legitimacy and authority of linguistic strategies used by one gender – of men of one class or ethnic group – while denying the power of others'.[14] Although this situation is gradually changing, as I discuss in the final section of this chapter, men's ways of doing and saying things are still strongly associated with authority and leadership in the minds of many people, including influential 'captains of industry'.[15] For these people, 'what counts as leadership, the means of gaining legitimacy in leadership, and so on, are male dominated'.[16] Indeed, Deborah Tannen claims that 'the very notion of authority is associated with maleness',[17] and consequently normatively masculine ways of talking are associated with authority and leadership. As a result, women are less likely to be perceived as potential leaders, and those who do move into leadership positions face a double bind 'regarding professionalism and femininity'.[18] Deborah Jones summarizes:

> If she talks like a manager she is transgressing the boundaries of femininity: if she talks like a woman she no longer represents herself as a manager.[19]

Supporting this view, Joanna Brewis cites research on senior women who trod a tightrope of impression management, giving signals that, while they were masculine enough to do the job, they had not 'in any way abandoned or compromised their femininity'.[20] The model presented in figure 2.1 suggests that the scope of acceptable behaviour for women executives is very narrow.

How do New Zealand leaders who are women deal with this issue? How do they negotiate the construction of their professional identities in everyday workplace talk, without this involving unacceptable levels of conflict with their gender identities?

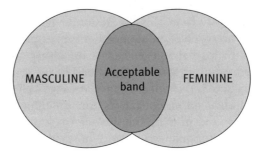

Figure 2.1 Model of the overlap between masculine and feminine styles of leadership (adapted from Morrison, White, Van Velsor and the Center for Creative Leadership 1987)

Leadership Discourse and Gender

It is useful to start by considering what it means to 'talk like a manager' or to discursively 'do leadership' in traditionally and conventionally masculine ways. Researchers in the organizational communication area tend to sum this issue up in terms of normative male-as-standard features:

> The male-as-standard norm affects notions of leadership which are typically linked with masculine modes of communication – assertion, independence, competitiveness and confidence. Deference, inclusivity, collaboration and cooperation, which are prioritized in women's speech communities, are linked with subordinate roles rather than leadership.[21]

This is a useful starting point but a more complete analysis involves considering the very diverse range of activities in which leaders engage, including planning how to meet objectives, giving instructions, running meetings, and evaluating the performance of others. As suggested in chapter 1, there are many different discursive features which may characterize such activities as more or less masculine in style, but my interest here is in features which are currently perceived as incompatible or at least dissonant with female gender identity, and features which result in potential leaders who are women feeling excluded or uncomfortable in professional workplaces. Secondly, the wide range of broadly contextual influences on a person's choice of how to encode meaning encourages caution in identifying a particular expression as an instance of a specifically gendered choice. The way someone gets cooperation on a task or discursively accomplishes a meeting opening or closing is often the result of their skill in assessing what is required on that specific occasion in that specific context, as opposed to the instantiation of a more general pattern. Bearing such caveats in mind, it is none the less worth examining the discourse of workplace leaders in order to better understand why the interactional styles which characterize some workplaces appear uncompromisingly masculine, and to see how some women manage to contest the view that the term 'woman leader' is an oxymoron.

Giving Instructions and Getting Things Done[22]

Masculine ways of giving directives

Being decisive and getting things done are key requirements of effective leadership. Leaders issue directives and give instructions; these are intrinsically social acts which are generally considered constitutive of the professional identity of a manager.[23] The discussion of masculine and feminine interactional styles in chapter 1 indicated that more direct ways of speaking typically index masculinity, while more indirect styles tend to be culturally coded as feminine. Hence, linguistic forms such as imperatives and *need* statements, as exemplified in the following instances from our workplace corpus, index a normatively masculine style of giving instructions or getting someone to do something.

- *check that out*
- *ring the applicants and say . . .*
- *go right through this*
- *send them back to us*
- *make some notes*
- *you finish doing it*
- *get rid of them now*
- *get a printout*
- *get him to make the changes*
- *I need these by ten*
- *I need to see that file*
- *you need to get that to me soon*

Forms such as these index masculine rather than feminine styles of leadership largely because they are forms which are commonly used by more powerful to less powerful people.[24]

Women in powerful roles are a relatively recent phenomenon in many workplaces, and when women in leadership positions use such forms to subordinates, they are making effective use of an authoritative style.[25] Ginette, for example, a team manager in a New Zealand factory, is typically direct and assertive in running team meetings, using many imperative forms: *check those boxes, fill out the forms properly, when you do these sheets do them properly.* Example 2.1 is taken from an early morning team meeting. Ginette is giving her team their instructions for the day's activities.

Example 2.1

Context: Ginette, the team manager of a factory production team, gives instructions at the 6.00 a.m. briefing meeting of the packing line team. There are 3 women and 9 men present.

1.	**Gin**:	the very last 25 cases that you take off that line I want them put
2.		aside the very last 25 cases put them on a pallet
3.		get them stretch wrapped
4.		they're going to be a momentum for everybody
5.		so make sure you er remember that . . .
6.		so just remember the last the very last 25 cases put them on a pallet
7.		get them stretch wrapped
8.		put them aside for X . . .
9.		send them through with no glue [laughs]

Example 2.2 illustrates a middle-level manager in a white-collar workplace using the same authoritative style.

Example 2.2

Context: Manager to her administrative assistant in a government department.

1. **Kate**: okay here's the list
2.   ring all the people on it and tell them the meeting is ten tomorrow

In another organization, the CEO addressed a firm imperative, *settle down*, to the team when the discussion was getting rather raucous. Such direct and conventionally masculine discourse strategies clearly contribute to the construction of these managers as confident and authoritative leaders.

Feminine ways of giving directives

By contrast, as the language and gender literature has extensively demonstrated, normatively feminine ways of getting people to do something involve the use of less direct discourse strategies.[26] These typically include such features as interrogative rather than imperative forms; modal verbs such as *may, might, could, would*; hedges, such as *probably, perhaps*, and *sort of*; and paralinguistic features such as hesitations and pauses – all linguistic forms which soften and attenuate the directive. The following list provides instances from our database where a hedged directive was addressed to a subordinate. The hedging devices are italicized.

- *perhaps* you *could* bring me that file now
- *I wonder if* you *could* find that number for me
- *we might* need some more help
- *what we might need to do is* send down a confirmation note
- *if we just* tell them exactly where it is
- *can* you *just* write that up *a bit* neater
- *I think* it needs revising *don't you*
- and *um I think that* you need to look at this
- *we want to* get this up to [place] *fairly* soon

In addition to attenuating words like *perhaps* and *just*, modals such as *might* and *could*, and the hedging phrases *I wonder if, a bit, I think*, and *don't you*, these examples also demonstrate the softening effect on a directive of the inclusive pronoun *we*. In all these examples *we* means *you*; there was no doubt that it was the addressee alone who was to undertake the task.

Such mitigated, hedged and indirect forms for giving directives downwards index a more feminine style of doing leadership. And while such forms are unsurprising and unmarked when people want to get their equals to comply with them, or when they try to persuade their superiors to a particular course of action, they are often perceived as gendered when used downwards. Hence, out of context, the following exchange between Sonia and Ana could be regarded as markedly feminine in style (though it was not marked in the context in which it was produced, a point developed further below).

Example 2.3

Context: Senior manager to administrative assistant in a government department.

1.	**Son**:	you'll be out here by yourself
2.		and I wondered if you wouldn't mind spending some of that time
3.		in contacting while no one else is around
4.		contacting the people for their interviews
5.		and setting up the the appointment times for their interviews

Indirect forms such as *I wondered if you wouldn't mind* contribute to the construction of a manager as considerate, other-oriented and empathetic, i.e., normatively feminine in leadership style.

The relevance of context on perceptions of gendered leadership styles

The discussion so far has suggested somewhat indirectly that the perception of a particular way of expressing a directive as gendered depends very much on contextual factors, namely, who is speaking to whom, and in what kind of setting and discourse context. In other words, the impact of a leader's choice of particular directive forms is always context dependent. This point is so fundamental and important that it deserves more explicit discussion.

Any leader's linguistic choices depend for their effect on where, when and to whom they are uttered, as well as what has preceded them. Imperatives used in formal contexts such as meetings, as illustrated in example 2.1, are more likely to be perceived as exemplifying authoritative and masculine leadership styles, than imperatives used in an informal context with a person one knows well. Talking to Beth, the administrative assistant with whom she has worked for several years, Sonia, a senior manager, uses a relatively direct and decisive style, but this is a component of their well-established close working relationship, rather than an instantiation of a masculine, authoritative style.[27] On the other hand, Sonia can also use a very elliptical and indirect style with Beth, confident that Beth will pick up what needs to be done without needing things spelled out explicitly.[28]

Even more interesting is the fact that direct imperative forms and *need* statements may be used without any suggestion of a masculine, authoritative style when the actions required are embedded in surrounding utterances which have the effect of softening them. Bernadette Vine, for example, provides many instances of imperative directives from the LWP corpus that are modified by preceding or following reasons or explanations (labelled 'grounders').[29] In example 2.4, the italicized directives are both in imperative form, but they are softened by the surrounding utterances which include an explanation of why the staffing lists are required. This is the same senior manager who featured in the previous example.

Example 2.4[30]

Context: Senior manager to administrative assistant in a government department.

1. **Son:** *check with Beth i- [voc] about the um + the new [drawls]: staffing: list*
2. which they should have copies of I'm not sure whether they do have
3. *but take some extra ones with you*
4. and that's the staffing list it's sort of got [voc]
5. what w- areas of work people are covering

Vine also demonstrates that the softening effect of context may be even more subtle. So, for example, a required action, which has been negotiated and discussed using relatively indirect strategies at an earlier point, may be conveyed in a much more direct way in the final wrapping-up stages of the interaction. And in some cases, this effect carries over more than one interaction, so the mitigating effect of an earlier negotiation sanctions the use of a direct form in a later meeting. The directive has been prepared for and is expected, and so does not require the same degree of attenuation that it would if uttered without any advance signalling.[31]

Clearly, assessing directive force is not a simple matter, and identifying particular strategies as instances of gendered behaviour requires careful attention to contextual factors. Just as an assessment of Sonia's management style as relatively feminine requires attention to the length and closeness of her relationship with her administrative assistant, as well as the discussion which has occurred earlier in their interaction, so the evaluation of Ginette's style in example 2.1 as direct, authoritative, and hence relatively masculine, takes account not only of the imperative forms, but the fact that she uses a barrage of imperatives, addressed to the whole team in a relatively formal meeting context. Furthermore, it is equally apparent that there is no simple way of equating the preponderance of particular forms with particular interactional styles. All leaders use a wide range of linguistic forms to give directives, negotiating their choices according to contextual factors.

All the same, one of those factors is gender; gender identity is constructed dynamically and responsively in specific contexts. The strategic choice of appropriate ways of giving directives is one skilful and salient means of constructing either an authoritative masculine style or an empathetic feminine style, each of which serves male and female leaders well in particular situations. These choices also accumulate as contributions to the construction of the relatively masculine vs. feminine communities of practices in which they operate. Hence, the predominant choice of more direct forms to subordinates, for example, especially in more public or formal contexts, can contribute to the construction of relatively masculine styles of discourse, and to the subtle gendering of the workplace environment in ways inimical to some women's (and some men's) comfort levels.

Managing Meeting Discourse

Gendered leadership styles in workplace meetings

There is a large research literature on meetings and meeting management encompassing a wide range of disciplines from organizational communication, through business studies, to discourse analysis.[32]

Within language and gender research, a good deal of attention has been paid to features such as the amount of talk appropriated by different participants, and the number and kind of disruptive inter-ruptions which occur in meetings – both features which have been regarded as manifestations of power or dominance in interaction.[33] There is also related research on the extent to which politeness consid-erations appear to influence participants' contributions to meetings.[34]

This previous work identifies features of interaction which may contribute to the construction of gendered leadership styles in meetings in the communities of practice in which we collected data. So, for instance, more masculine meeting management styles often entail the domination of the talking time by the leader, as well as the use of relatively disruptive interruptions of other participants' talk. Focusing on discursive strategies, other aspects of meeting management may also be accomplished in gendered ways: e.g. opening and closing the meeting, managing the agenda, ratifying topics for discussion, labelling a discussion as a digression, bringing the meeting 'to order', indicating that a digression has proceeded long enough, summarizing, ratifying decisions, and so on.[35]

In the next section, then, while recognizing that the ways in which these aspects of meeting talk are achieved are typically complex and context dependent, I explore how aspects of this achievement may also be perceived as gendered: i.e. more authoritarian and normatively masculine as opposed to more consensual and conventionally feminine. Focusing on ways of opening meetings, I provide examples of gendered styles of 'doing leadership' in these respects, illustrating in the process some of the ways in which a workplace might prove interactionally uncomfortable for some women (and men), and why women may find it difficult to break through the glass ceiling to senior management status.

Opening meetings[36]

Meeting openings have attracted attention from a number of re-searchers, especially by those working within a Conversation Analysis framework.[37] This research indicates that meeting openings are highly structured, and thus prime sites for both enacting and contesting power. And, not surprisingly, analysis of the ways in which different leaders accomplish the opening of a meeting provides interesting insights on the issue of the relevance of gender in leadership practices.

The amount of time allowed for people to gather and chat before the start of a meeting was very variable in different workplaces, and depended on a number of factors such as the scheduled length of the meeting, the purpose of the meeting, and even the relevance of the topics of the pre-meeting talk to official, ratified business. For meetings with long and diverse agendas, pre-meeting talk time might extend up to 15 minutes after the scheduled start time – especially if participants were talking 'shop'. Nevertheless, the amount of pre-meeting talk permitted or tolerated after the scheduled starting time for the meeting was certainly one factor which contributed to the impression of more masculine vs. more feminine ways of interacting at work. Starting the meeting as close to the appointed time as possible, and cutting off small-talk relatively abruptly, were very overt ways of doing gendered leadership in masculine communities of practice. (I return to this point below.) In addition, chairs differed in terms of the precise ways in which they started a meeting.

The opening of a meeting is a crucial juncture for establishing the chair's control and ensuring that participants orient to the chair's authority throughout the meeting. As the 'authorized starter', the chair has the right to discursively mark the opening of the meeting. Our data provided examples of many different styles of starting meetings, including some features associated with gendered leadership styles.[38] The most authoritative and normatively masculine style of opening a meeting involved using a number of relatively explicit strategies for attracting attention, including rapping on the table in some cases, and a more or less formal statement of various kinds, usually at higher volume than the concurrent talk, as illustrated in examples 2.5 and 2.6.

Example 2.5

Context: Large formal meeting of 18 high-level managers, 10 female and 8 male, in a government department.

1. **Har:**   okay well formally let me open the meeting

Example 2.6

Context: Meeting of team of 12 people, 6 female and 6 male in a large commercial organization.

1. **Cla**: [rising volume]: okay + thank you ++ stop talking now +
2. we're going to start ++:

In example 2.7, Victor waits till people hand back the forms consenting to be recorded. He responds *thanks* as he receives the last one, then allows a two-second pause and opens the meeting using louder volume and with a formal grammatical construction which notes explicitly that the conditions have been fulfilled for beginning the meeting.

Example 2.7

Context: Formal meeting of 4 men and one woman, the senior management team in a medium-sized commercial IT organization.

1. **Vic**: thanks ++ so having got the documentation we need
2. and er all the participants here
3. then we can make a start

More subtly, effectively establishing one's authority at this crucial point was often skilfully accomplished by attending to less overt interactional signals which indicated that people would be receptive to such a declaration. These included (a) waiting till a sufficient number (including key people) of those expected to attend were present; (b) choosing a lull in the talk to announce the start of the meeting; (c) using a number of discursive features to give the announcement weight, and ensure it attracted attention: e.g. preliminary drawled *mm*, discourse markers such as *okay, right*, use of a 'standard marker'[39] such as *we might as well start, time we got underway*. Examples 2.8 to 2.10 illustrate meeting openings in different communities of practice in our data, which make use of these lower-key strategies.

Example 2.8

Context: Meeting of senior management group of 4 men and 4 women in private organization.

1. **Pen**: okay well now we'll start properly +

Example 2.9

Context: Regular reporting meeting of 2 men and 2 women in government department.

1. **Jan**:   okay + um shall we just start with our agenda ++

Example 2.10

Context: Meeting of project team of 6 men and one woman in large commercial organization.

1. **Bar**:   + okay that's great + so what do we want to talk about + release six

The initial *okay* and the pauses (marked + per second) are attention-attracting devices that typically characterize such opening statements. In some cases, especially with smaller groups, the discourse marker *okay* followed by a pause was a sufficient opening signal. These less 'in-your-face' ways of opening meetings were perfectly effective in many contexts, and contrasted markedly with the more overtly authoritative style illustrated in examples 2.5 and 2.6.

In general, the size of the group was the most obviously relevant factor in accounting for the adoption of more authoritative and on-record opening moves. More formal opening statements and higher volume were generally required to bring large groups to order at the beginning of a meeting. By contrast, as mentioned above, smaller, less formal meetings often opened with utterances such as *well let's get started shall we, let's get underway, let's go, okay we'll start, okay*. However, another factor that could result in the use of a more authoritative style was an attempt by another person to challenge the chair in some way at this crucial point of the opening of the meeting. Subversive moves of this kind tended to elicit a firm response.

Example 2.11 illustrates an authoritative and direct style of dealing with a challenge to the chair's authority. Renee is not so much trying to open the meeting as challenging Clara's role as chair by suggesting she should be taking the minutes instead.

Example 2.11[40]

Context: Meeting of 6 women and 5 men, members of a project team in a multinational white-collar commercial organization. The meeting is chaired by Clara, a senior manager, since the usual chairperson is absent. Seth has gone to collect the minutes from the previous meeting, which he hadn't realized he was supposed to circulate.

1. **Cla**: okay well we might just start without Seth
2.   he can come in and can review the minutes from last week
3. **Ren**: are you taking the minutes this week
4. **Cla**: no I'm just trying to chair the meeting
5.   who would like to take minutes this week . . .
6. **Cla**: okay shall we kick off and just go round the room um doing an update
7.   and then when Seth comes in with the the minutes
8.   we need to check on any action items from our planning
9.   over to you Marlene

Clara begins with a relatively low-key opening move, *we might just start* (line 1); note the inclusive *we*, the modal *might*, and the minimizer *just*. However, she then adopts a more authoritative style to deal with Renee's subversive move *are you taking the minutes this week* (line 3). Renee's enquiry is clearly not guileless, since Clara has provided a number of non-verbal signals that she intends to chair this meeting, and the chair does not take the minutes in this group. Clara answers with an uncompromising *no* followed by a clear statement that she is taking the role of chair. Her use of the phrase *just trying to chair* could be interpreted as a reproof in response to Renee's unhelpful question. In lines 6–8, she sets the agenda for the first part of the meeting and then she allocates the first turn, *over to you Marlene* (line 9). Enacting the chairing role in this way, she firmly establishes her authority.

By contrast in example 2.12, Barry responds in a much less confrontational and low-key style to an attempt by Callum, the minute taker, to abrogate Barry's right to open the meeting.

Example 2.12

Context: Regular weekly meeting of an IT project team in a large commercial organization. There are 5 male participants at this meeting. Barry is the meeting chair. Callum is the minute taker.

1.	**Bar**:	okay
2.	**Call**:	o/kay (we)\
3.	**Bar**:	/we're gonna\ do a focus session and
4.	**Call**:	yeah we're um it's a focus session this week
5.		so we haven't got any formal minutes to go through er
6.		the subjects on the [drawls]: agenda: data release +
7.		release five progress
8.		release bat and training + um progress update on the s- s l a
9.		and progress update on p g m two point one
10.		plus any other matters that er might need to be discussed +++
11.		I've got some handouts
12.	**Bar**:	[clears throat] (5) (one of those)

Barry starts the meeting with a standard marker *okay* (line 1). Callum immediately follows with another *okay* and is about to say more but is interrupted by Barry who provides a statement of the agenda (line 3). Callum than effectively takes over the floor (lines 4–11), identifying the topics on the agenda, and indicating he has material to discuss. Barry's response to this blatant takeover of the role of chair is to leave a marked 5 second pause when Callum finally stops speaking (line 11); he then follows up quietly with a throat clearing indicating he is about to speak and a long pause before he begins to discuss the first item on the agenda. Thus Callum is effectively silenced by a lack of appropriate response as indicated by the long pause (line 10). Barry's method of re-asserting control is very low key, and, indeed, in this very masculine community of practice of contestive males, his strategies for keeping control of the meeting sometimes appear discordantly feminine and unassertive. Nevertheless, in this example he does succeed in re-establishing control of the agenda.

Example 2.13 is from another meeting opening where the chair is subject to pressure from others, but retains control and manages the opening successfully despite this. Ann has been appointed to replace the regular chair, Donald, while he is away, and in this meeting she is having a trial run while Donald is still around. Jane, the person who usually takes over the chair while Donald is away, is also present.

Example 2.13[41]

Context: Regular weekly meeting of IT project team of 4 men and 3 women in a small commercial organization. Will has not yet arrived.

1.		+++
2.	**Jane**:	right ( )
3.		shall I get Will or
4.	**Ann**:	he's on the phone.
5.	**Jane**:	okay
6.		( ) . . .
7.	**Lucy**:	yep I'm not sure I could get it polished
8.		/(erm)\ depending on how long this takes
9.	**Don**:	/yeah\
10.		/(I'm sure you can)\
11.	**Ann**:	/it's gonna be\ the shortest meeting ever.
12.	**Lucy**:	cool +++
13.	**Ann**:	okay let's start ++ /sales\
14.	**Jane**:	/sales?\

Following a three-second pause, Jane's utterance *right* (line 2) could be seen as a signal to Ann that Jane thinks the meeting should get under way. Similarly her offer to go and get Will (line 3), who is still missing, suggests that she considers it is time to get started. However, the video of the meeting shows that Ann is not yet ready; she is still preparing the computer to take the minutes. (Interestingly, in this company the chair *does* take the minutes on computer, and they are shown on screen as they are composed throughout the meeting). While they are waiting for Ann, Donald initiates a work-related topic with Lucy, asking her how her writing up of something is going (omitted from the transcript). In lines 7–8 Lucy responds and her utterance *depending on how long this* (the meeting) *takes* could be seen as putting further pressure on Ann in terms of time. In response, Ann promises that *it's gonna be the shortest meeting ever*. A few seconds later following another pause she declares the meeting open (line 13) and firmly announces the first agenda item, sales, overlapping with Jane's querying utterance (line 14).

In this example, Ann is put under some pressure by the others to get the meeting started, but she resists until she is ready. On the other hand, when an indirect comment suggests that people are under pressure from other demands on their time, she responds sensitively and with humour *it's gonna be the shortest meeting ever*. Hence, despite her relative inexperience in the role, Ann manages to resist attempts by Jane to get the meeting started, and asserts her role as chair. Her strategies are laid back and low key, but firm, and she makes good use of a light tone to avoid causing offence.

The final example in this section is similarly low key, but Tricia, the chair in this meeting, is not at all firm and authoritative. Her laid-back, hands-off style of chairing meetings would have been unremarkable and unmarked in most of the more feminine communities of practice in which we recorded. In the rather more masculine context in which Tricia worked, however, it seemed to be a source of frustration for at least some staff members. Example 2.14 is a typical meeting opening from our set of recordings of this team.

Example 2.14[42]

Context: Meeting of IT management team of 4 women and 2 men in a government organization.

1.	**Tri:**	[drawls]: mm: Tracey is er not here so she's disappeared
2.		Isabelle of course has got her foot up +
3.		/she had an operation on her foot on Thursday so she's at home\
4.	**Gar:**	/oh she was she ( ) + mm\
5.	**Tri:**	with her foot up
6.	**Gar:**	yeah I got some emails from her some time ago about that too
7.	**Tri:**	yeah
8.	**Ser:**	oh are you sure we've got a quorum Tricia
9.	**Tri:**	yes but it'll be a quick meeting [laughs]
10.		we're just waiting for Carol now

11.		do you want to just give her a ring [*provides Carol's number*]
12.	**Gar:**	[laughs] has Wendy spoken with you
13.	**Tri:**	no
14.	**Noe:**	she's back today I saw her today /so\
15.	**Tri:**	/I believe\\ she's got a meeting though
16.	**Gar:**	yes +
17.	**Tri:**	mm yes she is back er not sure how long for
18.	**Gar:**	mm no
19.	**Ser:**	mm ([clears throat])
20.	**Tri:**	have you got the little trolley by the way [*Discussion about trolley for 10 seconds. Then two conversations at once for almost two minutes, followed by laughter for 9 seconds. Carol and then Evelyn arrive. A conversation develops about email for a further 50 seconds.*]
21.	**Tri:**	okay well Tracey's not here and Isabelle's laid up +
22.		so there's only [voc]
23.	**Noe:**	is everything running?
24.	**Tri:**	is everything running?
25.	**Noe:**	is the camera on and running is it or (are we) [*Two conversations at once for 38 seconds including a discussion about the setting up and source of the recording equipment.*]
26.	**Tri:**	/what we've got\ here /is a little\ thing
27.		[*Two other people are talking through this.*]
28.	**Tri:**	that Garth and I put together
29.		for training managers and team leaders

It is difficult to convey with only a transcript how extremely 'hands-off' this opening appears compared with those from similar teams in different organizations in our data set. There is no evidence of time pressure or anxiety to get underway from most of those present. Rather than starting on time, Tricia waits for those who should be attending to turn up, and even sends someone to phone and remind one of them. She makes three attempts to begin the meeting before she succeeds, and even then begins somewhat informally by simply starting to discuss the first agenda item rather than by declaring the meeting open in any way.

Tricia first attempts to begin the meeting (lines 1–3) with a verbal headcount, noting those who have a reason not to be there. Garth subverts this (whether deliberately or not we cannot know) by responding with small-talk comments about one of those mentioned (lines 4, 6), and Serena contributes to the subversion by asking *are you sure we've got a quorum Tricia* (line 8). Serena's contribution seems more overtly intended to delay the opening; her initial *oh* registers surprise that Tricia is attempting to start when so many people are missing. Two more people arrive but there is another couple of minutes of small-talk before Tricia tries again *okay well Tracey's not here and Isabelle's laid up + so there's only* (lines 21–2). This time Noel disrupts the attempt by asking if the cameras are running, and this leads to another diversionary conversation for just over half a minute. Finally Tricia introduces the first agenda item and eventually gets the floor to herself (lines 26–8).

Under Tricia's leadership, this community of practice has clearly adopted a relaxed attitude to many of the formalities of meeting management. At the start of other meetings in this workplace there is discussion of penalties for lateness, but they are humorous and refer to imposing chocolate fines rather than serious reprimands. One possible explanation for this tolerant attitude is that group members are aware in this client-centred section that people often have a good client-based reason for being late for routine meetings.

However, there is evidence that at least some members feel irritated by the casual attitude which the section leader takes to the starting time of meeting, and especially by the fact that people have to sit around waiting for others to arrive. One person comments, for example, in another meeting, about a cake that has been provided: *this isn't a fine this is a payment it's a reimbursement to the rest of the committee for that lost time*. And when the final two team members eventually arrive the following exchange takes place.

Example 2.15

Context: Meeting of IT management team of 4 women and 2 men in a government organization.

1.	**Eve:**	good afternoon
2.	**Ser:**	sorry we're late
3.	**Eve:**	it's been noted chocolates expected next meeting
4.		[laughter]

5.	**Ser:**	cos I was considering whether you'd notice if we didn't turn up
6.		[laughter]
7.	**Tri:**	we noticed +
8.	**Tri:**	okay Andrew
9.	**And:**	oh this one is real basic it's just network cables

It is noteworthy that the sardonic formality of Evelyn's greeting *good afternoon* (line 1) can be interpreted as conveying a degree of implicit disapproval, an interpretation which is further supported by the apology which it elicits from Serena. Moreover the humorous exchange which follows suggests the need to re-establish good relations in the light of this rather cool reception. It is also worth noting that again Tricia's opening is very low key and simply consists of handing the floor to the person who is to introduce the first agenda item, *okay Andrew* (line 8).

Our analysis of a large number of her interactions indicates that Tricia consistently adopts a relaxed, good-humoured and conventionally feminine approach to management, and this is especially evident in formal meetings which she runs in a relatively loosely structured way. She rarely puts a firm decision on record at an early stage, for example, but rather allows others to come up with suggestions, and waits for a consensus to emerge. The openings are thus consistent with her leadership style throughout the meetings. This approach was also found in other relatively feminine communities of practice, where it was unmarked and clearly expected by other participants. As indicated, however, there was some evidence of a degree of frustration over this approach among some members of Tricia's staff. It is possible that Tricia's normatively feminine leadership style is not a good fit with all members of this community of practice, some of whom adopt a rather more contestive approach to interaction. Mismatches such as this are among the hazards that all leaders face in the workplace (cf. Barry in example 2.12 above), but where the dominant workplace culture is relatively masculine, they are likely to be a more frequent problem for aspiring females than for males.[43]

To sum up, then, our data indicates that meeting management may be accomplished in a wide range of different ways, including ways that can be regarded as differently gendered. At the more masculine end of the spectrum of gendered talk, leaders tend to set the agenda very explicitly and keep to it very strictly; they explicitly assign turns of talking, and provide on-record directives as to the way the meeting will proceed. As illustrated, meetings are opened with discursive moves which explicitly assert the leader's authority, and challenges are firmly squashed. At the more feminine end of the spectrum, the agenda may emerge much more organically, digressions tend to be tolerated, and voluntary contributions from the floor are treated as acceptable. As illustrated, meeting openings are accomplished in a relatively relaxed and low-key way, and those who challenge the authority of the chair are dealt with using relatively unconfrontational strategies of different kinds, including humour (a topic explored further in chapter 4).

I have discussed examples of particular discursive processes involved in 'doing leadership' in some detail to illustrate that the complexities of gendered talk are often evident only at the micro-level of interactional analysis. The discussion has indicated the importance of taking account of the situational, professional, and immediate discourse context in interpreting the social meaning of talk. The next section illustrates some of the ways in which one very successful manager instantiated effective leadership practices within one particular community of practice. For exemplification purposes I focus on instances of talk which presented Clara with some kind of discursive challenge.

Clara: A Case Study

Clara was identified by her superiors, peers and subordinates as an effective leader, and subsequent promotions and career advances confirmed these assessments. At the time of our recording, she was a senior manager in a very masculine, multinational commercial organization whose core business relates to petroleum products. However, within this larger masculine institutional culture, she headed a large, client-oriented section of around 50 personnel concerned with communication and client relations. Her staff was pretty evenly distributed between female and male personnel at different levels (a distribution which was not characteristic of the larger organization, which was more male-dominated at the higher levels, with more females in lower-paid support positions). As a community of practice, Clara's team had some characteristics which placed them towards the feminine end of the spectrum and others which were distinctly and stereotypically masculine.

Most participants in this workplace interacted daily in different kinds of meetings and work contexts, and some also socialized with each other outside work, though Clara did not do much out-of-work socializing. The hierarchical structure of the organization as a whole was reflected within the team, and each team member had a specific area of responsibility. Roles and responsibilities were very explicitly articulated, and people were clear about lines of accountability and who they reported to. Moreover, despite a very relaxed and informal tone, and much friendly social talk, in the interchanges at the beginnings and ends of meetings, the meetings themselves were run relatively formally, with authoritarian decision-making very evident (and clearly regarded as unmarked and acceptable) at points of controversy. So, while face-to-face communication was valued and patterns of talk were relatively 'high-involvement' – features consistent with the feminine end of the style continuum – there were also a number of features of more masculine communication styles. These included the level of formality of larger meetings, the fact that the high energy and enthusiastic engagement were often adversarial and combative in content and highly competitive in making claims on the floor. Especially, there was a very strong emphasis on authority and hierarchy.

In this organization, roles were allocated rather than negotiated. Different team members were responsible for different aspects of the team's work, and so there was a complex relationship with the 'joint enterprise',[44] with different sub-teams working on different aspects of the overall project. This often led to conflicts as sub-teams argued through their different positions. Such differences of opinion were typically thoroughly discussed, but the section leader had the final say, and everyone recognized this authority. Finally, while personal topics were discussed, often quite extensively, around the edges of business talk, the boundaries between business talk and social talk were relatively firm and clear-cut.

Clara had developed an interesting way of dealing with the double bind of the conflicting demands of gender identity and professional identity. She had adopted a slightly ironic and distant, but very functional, 'queenly' persona, which resolved the problems of authority, but also allowed her to express her femininity when appropriate. Indeed, her team had nicknamed her 'Queen Clara', an overt, if somewhat double-edged, recognition of the gracious but firm and authoritative way in which she wielded authority.[45] This queenly identity was clearly an excellent resolution of the potential identity conflict from the viewpoint of her team, since it allowed them to exploit this role with humour at times, while also providing a face-saving reason for deferring to Clara and respecting the authoritative demeanour she used to perform her role as section leader.

Clara was well aware of her nickname and was happy to exploit it for entertainment purposes at times, as the following excerpt illustrates. As background, readers need to be aware that the British Queen Mother had recently damaged her hip.

Example 2.16

Context: Beginning of a regular project team meeting involving 7 women and 6 men in a multinational white-collar commercial organization. Participants have all arrived. Smithy is about to open the meeting.

1.	**Smi**:	how's your mum?
2.	**Cla**:	sorry?
3.	**Smi**:	she broke her hip didn't she?
4.	**Cla**:	my mother?
5.	**All**:	[laugh]
6.	**Cla**:	what are you talking about?
7.	**XF**:	[laughs]: the queen mother:
8.	**Dai**:	[laughs]: the queen mother:
9.	**Cla**:	oh
10.	**All**:	[laugh]
11.	**Cla**:	my husband and I [*using a hyperlectal accent and superior tone*]
12.	**All**:	[laugh]
13.	**Cla**:	are confident that she'll pull through
14.	**All**:	[laugh]

While Clara is initially taken aback (lines 2, 4, 6) at the apparent reference to her personal life – which she generally does not bring to work – it is clear, once she decodes Smithy's reference, that she is happy to play along with the charade and ham up her role as Queen Clara with a parody of queenly style: *my husband and I are confident that she'll pull through* (lines 11, 13). This is typical: she consistently responds positively and collaboratively to humour when appropriate, and the quick wits which are evident here serve her equally well in more serious contexts.

Clara's recorded interactions also provide extensive evidence that she is a self-confident, authoritative, goal-oriented and task-focused manager, consistently adopting very effective strategies for achieving her workplace objectives. She participates in social talk at appropriate points, such as the margins and boundaries of meetings, but she runs meetings in ways that challenge traditional gender stereotypes: she is direct and often very succinct, for example, and, while short digressions are tolerated, she frequently guides her team back to the agenda and the meeting objectives, often uttering in a humorous but firm tone the phrase *moving right along*. Typically, then, Clara plays an important role in keeping discussion on track once a meeting is underway (even when not in the chair!), and she makes a noticeable contribution to moving the discussion systematically through the items on the agenda.

Clara's willingness to be explicitly authoritative when required is well illustrated by the way she resolves a conflict when a sub-team wants to bend the rules established at the beginning of the project. In example 2.17, the team is discussing how best to provide instructions to other members of their organization about a specialized computer process. The discussion revolves around a request to allow people to print off material from the computer screen (i.e. to 'screendump').

Example 2.17[46]

Context: Regular weekly meeting of project team in a multinational white-collar commercial organization. There are 4 women and 4 men at this meeting.

1.	**Har**:	look's like there's been actually a request for screendumps
2.		I know it was outside of the scope
3.		but people will be pretty worried about it
4.	**Cla**:	no screendumps
5.	**Matt**:	we-
6.	**Cla**:	no screendumps
7.	**Peg**:	[sarcastically]: thank you Clara:
8.	**Cla**:	/no screendumps\
9.	**Matt**:	/we know\ we know you didn't want them and we um er /we've\

10. **Cla**: /that does not\ meet the criteria\
    [*several reasons provided why screendumps should be allowed*]
11. **Cla**: thanks for looking at that though
12. **Smi**: so that's a clear well maybe no
13. **Cla**: it's a no
14. **Smi**: it's a no a royal no
15. **Cla**: did people feel disempowered by that decision
16. **Peg**: [sarcastically]: no:

Clara here gives a very clear directive that under no circumstances will people be allowed to print material from their screens. She states her position clearly and explicitly: i.e. *no screendumps*. And she does so three times (lines 4, 6, 8) without any modification, thus conveying her message in very strong terms indeed. Moreover, when Matt suggests this is simply a matter of what she wants, *we know you didn't want them* (line 9), she follows up with an explicit reference to the previously agreed and ratified criteria (line 10). In other words, this is a very clear instance of Clara doing leadership in an authoritative and conventionally masculine way.

As mentioned, this close-knit team has developed ways of 'managing' the inherent contradictions of responding to someone who is both authoritative and female. Humour is their consistent resource when things get tense. Here they skilfully respond to Clara's peremptory veto in a way that preserves good working relations. Peggy's sarcastic *thank you Clara* (line 7) provides an initial tension-breaker. However, the sub-team members proceed to provide further reasons for allowing screendumps, leading Clara to respond (line 11) with a more conventionally polite dismissal of their suggestions *thanks for looking at that though*. Smithy's internally contradictory suggestion that Clara may be wavering *so that's a clear well maybe no* (line 12) is deliberately humorous, but it leads Clara to restate her position quite explicitly *it's a no* (line 13). Again Smithy defuses the tension with a humorous hyperbolic comment *it's a no a royal no* (line 14), referring to Clara's queenly persona. Finally, Clara too relents with a tongue-in-cheek comment which draws explicit attention to feelings which people usually conceal in a business context *did people feel disempowered by that decision* (line 15). The team's well-established good relationships thus enable them to ride out Clara's 'bald, on-record' directives, without irreparable damage to the face needs of team members.[47]

Example 2.18 illustrates again how Clara's team makes use of her queenly persona to demystify a potentially problematic point. In this meeting Clara is laying out the different roles that she and Smithy have in relation to a specific project that the group is undertaking. She is the overall manager of the section and responsible for delivering the outcome of the project on time to the organization as a whole. Smithy is the day-to-day project manager, and at times their roles may overlap. She holds the floor uninterrupted for well over a minute and a half explaining the situation, and then after the brief exchange illustrated in lines 11–22, again for another two minutes. The excerpt below gives something of the flavour of her contribution as a lead-in to the tension-breaking reference to Clara as Queen.

Example 2.18

Context: First of a series of regular weekly meetings of a project team of 6 men and 6 women in a multinational white-collar commercial organization.

1.	**Cla:**	+ then a just a couple of words about role and that is
2.		clearly um + Smithy and I have roles that may seem to overlap
3.		and we just wanted to make it clear where they did overlap
4.		and where they didn't overlap [drawls]: um:
5.		Smithy's the project manager
6.		he's responsible for coordinating the project . . .
7.		and: he's there to make sure that <u>everything</u> we you do
8.		while on on the project fits into that big picture . . . <u>my</u> role is . . .
9.		I'm responsible I need to deliver to the rest of [*name of organization*] . . .
10.		so in a way I'm the person you're doing this for ( )
11.		/[general laughter]\ . . .
12.	**Smi:**	because in effect you're working for for /two different +\
13.	**Cla:**	/two masters\
14.	**Smi:**	two different masters

15.	**Cla**:	so when you're on the project where you're working for the master
16.		and when you're working on your normal job you're working for <u>me</u>
17.	**Smi**:	yes
18.	**Mar**:	the queen
19.	**XF**:	the queen
20.		[general laughter]
21.	**Smi**:	/the queen is a customer for the project\
22.		/[laughter]\ [laughter]
23.	**Cla**:	I realize for those of you that have got two roles
24.		and working on the project . . .
25.		don't want y- people worrying about these things
26.		really want you to get them out on the table so we can resolve them + [tut]
27.		although I'm the one who's accountable . . .
28.		so I'm the person who has the final say on stuff that goes on . . .
29.		I'm the one whose gonna make that final decision . . .
30.		because it's my butt on the line okay?
31.		so that's make that clear as well the differentiation between Smithy and me

This rather long excerpt has been much edited in the interests of saving space, but even in this truncated form it illustrates well some of the points made above. On the one hand, Clara is clear and explicit about relative responsibilities (lines 1–10, 15–16), and about her authority (lines 27–30), which is characterized, interestingly, using the masculine term 'master' (lines 13, 14, 15). On the other hand, she is sensitive to potential causes of tension and anxiety (lines 23–5), and she addresses these quite explicitly. Moreover, she makes it clear that she expects people to bring their worries up for discussion (line 26). In this community of practice, contestation and challenge is acceptable and unmarked, and so is discussion of problems, worries and concerns.

One interpretation of the laughter, interjections and humorous, overlapping contributions represented in lines 11–22, is that it is a reaction to the explicitness with which Clara is discursively doing power in this meeting. Both the content and the form of her discourse emphasize her authority: e.g. her long, uninterrupted speaking turns, together with the explicit direct language: *we just wanted to make it clear where they did overlap and where they didn't overlap* (lines 3–4), *Smithy's the project manager, my role is . . .* (lines 5, 8), *I'm the one who's accountable* (line 27), and so on. She uses short, clear clauses with the minimum of modification. All this contributes to the construction of a very authoritative and normatively masculine leadership style. Her team's reference to her queenly identity can thus be seen as one satisfactory way of managing the potential contradictions raised by any woman who adopts such an authoritative style.

Finally, it is important to mention the range of ways in which Clara performs a more feminine identity within this relatively masculine workplace. Firstly, she participated fully in her team's high-involvement interactional style, contributing to the general social talk, and to the humour (see also example 4.15). Before and after meetings, she typically took time to express interest in her team members' personal lives (see example 3.6). Secondly, it is very noticeable how generous she is in giving praise, and expressing appreciation for people's contributions to the team's work. Her discourse is liberally peppered with approving and appreciative words and phrases: *good, great, that'll be great, great so we're on target, things are going really well, good stuff, very good, that's good, excellent, thanks, thank you* (it is very apparent from our analyses that her favourite appreciative word is *great*). Her authoritative style is always modified by her acknowledgement and appreciation of the expertise of her team members, and her recognition of its contribution to her decisions. So, while, as she says above, she will make the final decision, she also says that she will do that in the light of the arguments she has heard, and the recommendations of her team members. Thirdly, she believes in the value of discussion and explanation, and especially the importance of making things explicit so that people understand complex issues. Her reasons for this are at least partly relational; she does not want *people worrying about these things* (example 2.18, line 25). We have many more similar examples of her revisiting issues which people need to understand in order to ensure that they have got the point. Indeed, she often uses a spiral approach to complex issues, coming back to them from different directions if she suspects they need further clarification.[48] These features are normatively associated with a more feminine discursive style; though, of course, they are found in the discourse of both men and women in our data.

The role of 'Queen Clara' thus enables Clara to resolve the inherent conflict between her role as manager and her feminine gender identity. This persona allows her to behave in ways which are authoritative and indexed as masculine, without causing discomfort to or attracting resentment from her team members. It allows her to maintain a certain social distance, and contributes to the impression of dignified graciousness and status. But it also allows her to act in conventionally feminine ways, attending to interpersonal aspects of workplace inter-action by participating fully in the team's high-involvement interac-tional style, contributing to the general social talk and collaborative humour, giving generous praise and approval, and encouraging thorough discussion and exploration of problematic issues.[49] In this way, Clara successfully creates a satisfactory space for herself as an effective leader in a masculine workspace, a way of doing leadership that does not involve negating her feminine gender identity.

Focusing on one particular leader has allowed relatively detailed discussion of exactly how leadership is discursively accomplished in a specific community of practice. There are many other examples which could have been used to illustrate the skills with which effective leaders integrate authoritatively masculine with relationally feminine discourse strategies in the accomplishment of their leadership role in different communities of practice. In a much more feminine CofP, for example, Leila, a manager discussed in detail in earlier publications,[50] adopts a predominantly collaborative style, paying a great deal of attention to the interpersonal dimension, and selecting less direct discourse strategies to achieve her goals in a consensual way. While she is willing to act authoritatively when required to make a decision, or to resolve a conflict, her generally consultative approach fitted well with the democratic, egalitarian and participatory culture of her CofP. In many ways, as our earlier analyses demonstrate in detail, she can be described as a 'maternal boss', another acceptable model for leaders who are women.[51] There is not space to illustrate this in detail here, but several interactions indicate that adopting this 'motherly' role proved a useful strategy for resolving the inherent contradictions of taking a senior and powerful leadership role in her relatively feminine community of practice. (See chapter 4 for further discussion.) Len, the leader who features in examples 5.3, 5.5 and 5.9, takes a similar approach in his relatively feminine community of practice.[52]

By contrast, Ginette, a leader in a stereotypically masculine CofP, mentioned above and discussed extensively elsewhere,[53] adopted a much more directive and authoritarian style, especially in team meetings, as illustrated in example 2.1. In contexts where she needed to assert her authority, she used in-your-face insult and jocular abuse, matching her team members' contestive, normatively masculine style.[54] In other words, she plays the tartar or the battle-axe. In less public and more informal interactions, Ginette's attention to the negative face needs of individuals, and orientation to their need to understand issues, were more evident.[55] In addition, she would regularly tell jokes, and even play practical jokes on team members.[56] None the less, Ginette's walk along the tightrope between professional leader and female identity appeared to frequently require a lean to the authoritative and assertive side in order to maintain a convincing professional identity in a demanding and very masculine workplace context.[57] Her interesting solution to the leadership and femininity conflict is to adopt the persona of the 'good joker' (a role usually associated with men).[58]

Possible Models for Women Leaders

In the discussion above, I have suggested that effective leadership involves a balance of skills. Good leaders, female and male, pay attention both to the objectives of the organization they work for, and to the interpersonal needs of those they work with in a specific community of practice. In other words, they integrate authoritatively masculine with relationally feminine discourse strategies in ways that are responsive to the features of their particular workplace culture. Recent research in the management area confirms this view of leadership as a performance in which an effective leader successfully integrates the achievement of transactional objectives with more transformational and relational aspects of workplace interaction.[59] A *transactional* style of leadership tends to focus on getting things done by following established routines, rewards people according to their level of performance, and motivates them by appealing to self-interest.[60] The focus is on meeting objectives, and avoiding or correcting mistakes. A *transformational* style of leadership, on the other hand, focuses on a positive vision of what can be achieved, is characterized by enthusiasm and optimism, and encourages innovation, creativity, and the questioning of old assumptions. Adopting this style involves orienting to each individual's specific needs, listening effectively, and using a personalized approach. Transactional behaviours 'focus on the task to be achieved, the problem to be solved, or the purpose of the meeting'.[61] Relationally oriented behaviours concentrate on fostering workplace relationships, 'creating team',[62] and developing a productive working atmosphere (see chapters 3 and 4 for further discussion of these concepts). It will be apparent that these styles also have features in common with gendered conceptions of leadership. The parallels with more masculine (or transactional) and more feminine (or transformational) styles of interaction are obvious, though not exact, since, for example, 'charisma' and vision are features of a more transformational style which are not usually associated with women and femininity.

None the less, the increasingly widespread recognition that effective leadership entails aspects of both styles has been associated with a more positive attitude to the skills that women bring to the workplace. Indeed, some researchers go further. Berryman-Fink for instance, reports a range of organizational communication research which claims to show that

> a woman's leadership style is transformational and interpersonal while a man's style is based on command and control. Women managers promote positive interactions with subordinates, encourage participation, and share power and information more than men do. . . . women leaders use collaborative, participative communication that enables and empowers others while men use more unilateral, directive communication in their leadership.[63]

As I have indicated, and illustrated in this chapter, my view is that such generalizations oversimplify the complex reality of language in context; both males and females in leadership positions make use of a range of gendered discursive resources according to their contextual needs. The advantage of such research is that it has created a climate in which more normatively feminine communicative strategies are increasingly recognized as valuable, and perceived positively, rather than regarded as superfluous and irrelevant.

In the light of such research, it is worth reflecting on the range of acceptable ways of doing leadership which are currently available to women in western society. While welcoming such attitudinal changes, a number of feminist researchers have questioned the extent to which leaders who are women are permitted to behave in other than stereotypically acceptable gendered ways.[64] The 'gendering' of the leadership role means that a number of unexamined cultural assumptions present barriers to women with leadership ambitions.[65] Thus, it is suggested, women in leadership positions are typically confined to a rather narrow range of stereotypical roles and, even as leaders, women are expected to conform to society's expectations of the ways in which (in this case powerful) women should behave. The analysis in this chapter has provided some support for this view. Despite the success of many women in breaking through the glass ceiling, the available positive models for powerful women remain relatively restricted – the roles of mother and queen are among the more obvious in western society.[66] Adopting the role of 'good joker' in a very masculine CofP, Ginette presents a more radical challenge to the acceptable stereotypes of women in powerful positions.[67] Women like Clara, Leila and Ginette provide an indication of a way forward. They are in their different ways broadening the notion of what counts as acceptable leadership behaviour: i.e. they are combating the erasure of women's ways of leading by making it to the top and integrating their diversely gendered discourse skills into effective leadership practices.

Conclusion

The data discussed in this chapter suggests that effective leaders make use of a wide range of styles, expressing themselves and interacting in ways that instantiate many different points on the masculine–feminine dimension. The material has illustrated how people enact both their professional identities and their gender identities, as they talk to others throughout the working day. While often locatable on a masculine–feminine stylistic dimension, discursive choices reflect a range of complex socio-pragmatic influences, including the speaker's ongoing dynamic assessment of the relative weight of factors such as the formality of the setting, the nature of the topic, and the role relationships involved. In the examples discussed, it is clear that responsiveness to the specific demands of the particular interaction is an important aspect of the management skills displayed by effective managers. People construct their identity at work in response to a wide range of contextual factors. Gender identity is just one aspect of an individual's social identity, and in the workplace context, it is often not the most salient dimension. Nevertheless, I have argued that gendered norms are always covertly relevant influences on how people behave, and on how their behaviour is interpreted, and these norms are available as resources for effective leaders to draw on.

As suggested in the opening sections of this chapter, many of the traditional measures of leadership seem to be embedded in a very authoritarian view of the way management and leadership is most effectively accomplished, and consequently a relatively masculine profile of the 'best' leaders is what seems to emerge. In many organizations, women with aspirations to leadership are thus faced with a dilemma – unless they learn to operate in the masculine gendered styles which dominate in so many workplaces, they will not be taken seriously. On the other hand, more feminine ways of interacting at work, although often paid lip-service, and apparently valued when men adopt them as aspects of their management style, are often regarded negatively when used by women in many organizations.[68]

The data from the LWP Project suggests some alternative avenues for women faced with this dilemma. Some of the effective leaders in our database opted to work in women-friendly communities of practice, where feminine styles of interaction were non-deviant and unmarked. The contextual factors which influenced their ways of giving directives and running meetings, for instance, included membership of a community of practice where less authoritarian and more other-oriented ways of doing things were regarded as normal and standard. Feminine styles of discourse were acceptable and unremarkable in such contexts, so that, for example, pre-meeting talk topics included personal and family topics without attracting comment (see chapter 3), humour tended to be collaborative and non-abrasive (see chapter 4), and it was acceptable to instantiate leadership in more negotiative and less authoritarian ways (see chapter 5). Clearly, these women could do leadership using more forceful, conventionally masculine strategies when appropriate. In many of their interactions, however, the norms of gendered discourse which prevailed in their CofP meant that they could frequently choose to operate in more normatively feminine ways, ways which gave weight to relational as well as transactional considerations.

Many women in leadership positions, however, work in a world which is far from woman-friendly. As Berryman-Fink says, 'for the most part, workplace organizations operate on masculine assumptions and approaches to life and women are expected to adjust to this male model if they are to be successful in the workplace'.[69] Kendall argues similarly that a female technical director who created a 'non-traditional' (i.e. not normatively masculine) demeanour of authority in her radio station workplace risked not having her 'excellent work and job skills recognized'. She suggests that the relational strategies adopted by this woman 'may be perceived as indexing a stance of insecurity and incompetence, rather than authority, from the perspective of those who expect someone in her position to take a one-up position within a hierarchical alignment'.[70]

The range of possible responses to the problems that such attitudes raise are varied and interesting. The leadership research identifies women who appear to conform to a greater or lesser extent to the expectation that leaders should use predominantly masculine and authoritarian styles of behaviour in the workplace. These women often dress in ways that indicate they wish to be identified with the corporate, male-dominated business world. Moreover, it is claimed, their ways of talking are often largely indistinguishable from those of the men they work with.[71] More interesting, and much more encouraging from a feminist perspective, are the kind of women (and men) identified in our research – people whose behaviour, including their communicative behaviour, challenges the existing gendered discourse norms of their workplaces in a variety of interesting ways. In order to be treated with respect, women often need to prove they can foot it with their predominantly male colleagues in many aspects of the way they do their jobs, but many of them also effectively integrate aspects of more feminine discourse styles in their workplace talk. Their talk is characterized by the skilful meshing of transactional and relational discourse features. It could be argued that by adopting normatively masculine strategies to do some aspects of leadership, and especially to construct an authoritative persona, women leaders reinforce the association of leadership with masculinity. I take a more positive perspective. By appropriating such strategies, women contribute to de-gendering them and make it clear that they are tools of leadership discourse, and not exclusively of male discourse. (Similarly, men, like Len, discussed in chapter 5, who adopt more feminine strategies in the workplace, have the same potential effect.) Using another strategy, some senior women even 'do femininity' quite explicitly and con-fidently in a variety of discursive ways in their workplace interactions, creating 'feminine' spaces within masculine workplaces.[72] In a range of ways, and to differing degrees, such women contest and trouble the gendered discourse norms which characterize so many workplaces, and which contribute to the glass ceiling they are trying to break through.

As mentioned above, current research in the leadership and organizational communication literature suggests that ways of interacting associated with femininity are gradually being identified as important by those assessing effective leaders in business contexts. Indeed, a balance of gendered interactional skills is increasingly recognized as desirable: 'Leaders perceived as transformational, whether male or female, exhibit gender balance – displaying characteristics traditionally regarded as masculine and feminine.'[73] Effective leadership thus involves communicative behaviours conventionally associated with both male and female styles of interaction.[74] Judy Rosener draws attention to leadership research that highlights women's participatory style of leadership, and their willingness to share power and information, but also notes that women leaders tend to be stylistically flexible and recognize that there are times when they need to be decisive.[75] On the basis of a national survey of New Zealand managers, while he noted that distinctions were always a matter of degree, Ken Parry reported that 'women were rated higher than men on the most effective leadership qualities . . . and lower than men on some of the transactional qualities of leadership'. And that 'women are better able to identify and empathize with the various messages they receive through interactions with their co-workers'.[76] While generalizations based on people's sex alone are obviously questionable, the change in attitude indicated by the results of such surveys can none the less be welcomed.

Such results also suggest that at least some women are contesting, challenging and troubling institutional boundaries, and stereotypical expectations about the way successful leaders behave. The material discussed in this chapter provides some detailed micro-level support for this suggestion. People often respond creatively to the specific demands of the situation in which they find themselves, and such responses may be the source of new ways of doing things which become more widespread. Interaction is a dynamic process. At least some women in leadership positions in some New Zealand workplaces appear to be making use of interactional opportunities to effectively trouble stereotypes of good leadership, and to contest established gender boundaries in the area of leadership. These women are helping to accelerate change.

Finally, in this chapter, it is important to re-emphasize the fact that, while it is satisfying to identify patterns and draw out general trends from the data we analyse, it is also important to remember that reality is never as neat as such generalizations suggest. The patterns identified in this chapter can only be suggestive; they provide a very simplified map of the many diverse resources available to women struggling to integrate professional and gender identity in a range of different workplace contexts. One of my aims has been to demonstrate that people do leadership in a range of diverse ways, influenced by many different factors, from the broader organizational or institutional setting and their particular community of practice, to the specific interaction in which they are participating. Many factors impinge on the specific choices individual women make – factors such as ethnicity, social class, relative seniority and age, workplace experience, and so on. Very specific contextual factors are also relevant, as indicated at times in the discussion above: e.g. the size, purpose and relative formality of the meeting, and the composition of the meeting in terms of the status, roles and gender of participants. In any interaction the threads of doing power or leadership and doing gender are only two of many potentially relevant dimensions.

The discussion of gender and leadership has covered a great deal of ground, some of which, as indicated at various points in the discussion

Figure 2.2 'You must be new around here. That woman you called a "broad" this morning would like a word with you in her office!' © Joe Kohl

above, is explored further in subsequent chapters. In the next chapter, I examine the concept of relational practice, a concept which has been developed precisely to make visible a particular dimension of gendered workplace interaction. As Fletcher says, ' "nice", "helpful" and "thoughtful" are not found on many lists of leadership characteristics';[77] none the less, these gendered attributes can be regarded as key characteristics of those who contribute to the achievement of workplace goals.

NOTES

1 Berryman-Fink (1997: 259).
2 Fletcher (1999: 3).
3 But see McConnell-Ginet (2000) for an incisive analysis of the contribution that talk often does make to the process of excluding women from senior and responsible positions.
4 Berryman-Fink (1997: 263).
5 See, for example, Marshall (1984, 1993, 1995).
6 The tendency to 'think leader, think male' is discussed by a number of feminist analysts: e.g. Hearn and Parkin (1989), Sinclair (1998), Kendall and Tannen (1997), Holmes (2000a), Gunnarsson (2001). References to 'hero' leaders (e.g. Jackson and Parry 2001) reinforce this tendency.
7 This discussion is based on material in Holmes (2005b).
8 See, for example, Schein (1973, 1975), Heilman et al. (1989).
9 See Maier (1997), Sinclair (1998), Bass (1998: 78), Harris (2002).
10 For example, Northhouse (2001), Heifertz (1998). But see the discussion below of more nuanced conceptions of effective leadership, including *transformational* leadership.
11 Heifertz and Laurie (2001), Harris (2002), Parry (2001).
12 Kendall and Tannen (1997), Sinclair (1998).
13 Pearson, Turner and Todd-Mancillas (1991).
14 Gal (1991: 188).
15 Jackson and Parry (2001).
16 Hearn and Parkin (1989: 27). See also Kendall and Tannen (1997), Sinclair (1998), Holmes (2000a), Gunnarsson (2001).
17 Tannen (1994: 167).
18 Kendall and Tannen (1997: 92). See also Chase (1988: 276), Lakoff (1990: 206), Bergvall (1996), Coates (1998: 295), Alvesson and Billing (1997), Brewis (2001), Martín Rojo and Esteban (2003, 2005), and Wodak (1995).
19 Jones (2000: 196).
20 Brewis (2001: 299).

21 Still (1996: 71).

22 See Holmes and Stubbe (2003b: ch. 3) and Vine (2004) for a thorough discussion of the factors influencing the forms of directives. This section draws to some extent on these sources.

23 Ochs (1993), Harris (2003), Vine (2004).

24 Weigel and Weigel (1985); West (1990), Holmes and Stubbe (2003b), Vine (2004).

25 Alternative reasons and contextual conditions for using imperatives are discussed later in this chapter.

26 See, for example, Bellinger (1979), Bellinger and Gleason (1982), West (1990, 1995), Hanak (1998).

27 See Vine (2004).

28 For examples of interactions between Sonia and Beth see Holmes, Stubbe and Vine (1999), and especially Vine (2004: 157).

29 Vine (2004: 117–18, 161–4). The term 'grounders' is taken from Blum-Kulka et al. (1989).

30 Example from Vine (2004: 117).

31 Vine (2004: 164).

32 See Marra (2003) for a thorough review.

33 See, for example, Swacker (1979), Edelsky (1981), Holmes (1992), Sollitt-Morris (1996) on amount of talk, and Edelsky (1981), Woods (1989), Craig and Pitts (1990), James and Clarke (1992), Bargiela-Chiappini and Harris (1996), on interruptions.

34 See, for example, Pearson (1988), Scheerhorn (1989), Morand (1996a, 1996b). See also the LWP analysis, based on 80 meetings from 9 different workplaces, of the ways in which power and politeness are manifested in meetings in New Zealand workplaces. In Holmes and Stubbe (2003b: ch. 4).

35 See Holmes, Stubbe and Vine (1999), Holmes and Stubbe (2003b).

36 The material in this section draws on Holmes (2000a).

37 See Boden (1994), Sollitt-Morris (1996), Marra (1998), Barretta-Herman (1990), Cuff and Sharrock (1985), Dwyer (1993), McLaughlin (1984), Robert (1967), Schwartzman (1989). See also Chan (forthcoming) for a thorough review.

38 Holmes (2005c) discusses ways of opening less formal meetings.

39 Turner (1972: 373). See also Atkinson (1979) and Bargiela-Chiappini and Harris (1997) for relevant discussion of such markers.

40 This example is abridged from Holmes and Stubbe (2003b: ch. 4), where it is discussed more fully. See also Marra (2003) where it is analysed from a different perspective.

41 This example, from which I have edited out material irrelevant to the point discussed, is analysed in more detail in Chan (forthcoming).

42 A shorter version of this example is discussed in Marra, Schnurr and Holmes (forthcoming).

43 For an interesting contrast with Tricia see the discussion of the leadership style of Ginette in Holmes and Stubbe (2003a: 589–93, 2003b: 126–30).

44 A 'joint enterprise' is one distinguishing component of a community of practice (Wenger 1998).

45 See Holmes (2005a). Since a man who behaved as Clara did would not have attracted comment, this label could be regarded as a sexist indication that Clara was resented for exercising authority without apology. We explore this issue further in Holmes and Marra (forthcoming). In other contexts the label *queen* has certainly been used quite disparagingly of women in powerful roles, with the suggestion that they were 'putting on airs' or behaving in ways 'above their station' (e.g. Sinclair 1998: 226). Acknowledging this ambivalence, it is nevertheless clear that women who attract such a term are behaving in authoritative ways, and that others recognize that they expect to be treated with respect and deference. Here we note only that there was no indication in this particular case that the title was used with anything other than humour and respect as its basis.

46 We have used this example many times in earlier publications because it is such a succinct illustration of such a wide range of points.

47 These terms are components of Brown and Levinson's (1987) politeness theory, which incorporates Goffman's (1967) notion of 'face'.

48 See Holmes and Stubbe (2003b: 68–71) for further discussion and illustration of linear vs. spiral approaches in meetings.

49 See Holmes and Marra (2005a) for an example of a contrasting normatively masculine strategy, namely, repressing discussion of an issue which at least one participant clearly wished to explore further.

50 See Holmes (2000a), Holmes and Stubbe (2003a, 2003b).

51 Martín Rojo and Esteban (2003: 263), and Holmes (forthcoming).

52 This is *not* the Len of 'the Len factor' referred to in example 1.3.

53 See Holmes and Stubbe (2003a, 2003b), Stubbe (2000a).

54 See Daly et al. (2004), Stubbe (1999) for further exemplification.

55 See Stubbe (2000a).

56 See Holmes and Stubbe (2003b: 126ff).

57 Compare Baxter (2003: 152ff). On the basis of her analysis of discourse in a dotcom organization, Baxter (2003: 179) describes the 'profile of a more powerful or effective speaker [as] likely to be an IT specialist, a founder member and a supporter of the firm's historical belief in open dialogue, but who was versatile enough to use masculinized speech strategies when a more assertive or confrontational style was deemed necessary' (2003: 179). She identifies one woman in her data, pseudonymed Sarah, who fits this profile.

58 The term 'joker' in New Zealand English may be used like the term 'guy' in American English or 'bloke' in British English. Since it can also refer to someone who plays jokes, its ambiguity in this proposition is an advantage.

59 See Dwyer (1993), Gardner and Terry (1996), Heifertz (1998), Parry and Meindl (2002), Smith and Petterson (1988), Stodgill (1997), Proctor-Thomson and Parry (2001: 169), Bass and Alvolio (1994), Vera and Crossan (2004).

60 Bass (1998), Proctor-Thomson and Parry (2001: 171).

61 Dwyer (1993: 572).

62 Fletcher (1999).

63 Berryman-Fink (1997: 269).

64 See, for example, Martín Rojo (1997), Martín Rojo and Esteban (2003), Sinclair (1998), Baxter (2003).

65 Philips (2003: 267).

66 See Fletcher (1999), Philips (2003), Martín Rojo and Esteban (2003).

67 It is possible to see this as a mature version of the 'tomboy', an identity which allows young girls to escape some of the constraints of gendered expectations.

68 Martín Rojo and Estaban (2003). See also Holmes (1984) for a fuller discussion of this issue, i.e. how the 'same' behaviour is often evaluated differently according to the sex of the performer.

69 Berryman-Fink (1997: 266); see also Martín Rojo and Estaban (2003).

70 Kendall (2004: 75).

71 Sinclair (1998: 226) describes such masculine-style female leaders as 'Queen Bees', women who seem 'more macho than all the other men in the senior management team put together', and she discusses reasons for the negative attitudes that their behavior attracts from other women in particular. In the New Zealand context, Jackson and Parry (2001: 175) note that the Chief Executive of the National Museum, Dame Cheryll Sotheran, was nicknamed 'rottweiler chief executive' by those who disliked her aggressive management style.

72 See Holmes and Schnurr (2004), Schnurr (forthcoming).

73 Hackman and Johnson (2000: 327).

74 See also Grant (1988), Rosener (1990), Goleman (1995), Bass (1998), Sinclair (1998), Parry (2003).

75 Rosener (1990: 122).

76 Parry (2000: 26).

77 Fletcher (1999: 115).

CHAPTER THREE

Relational Practice – Not Just Women's Work

Introduction[1]

The term 'relational practice' is widely used by people interested in workplace communication to refer to 'the ability to work effectively with others, understanding the emotional contexts in which work gets done'.[2] This capacity has also been called 'emotional intelligence',[3] and it has been associated predominantly with feminine ways of interacting, and especially with women's talk at work.[4] Little work has been undertaken, however, in identifying how people actually do relational practice. The first section of this chapter examines some of the functions of relational practice in the workplace, and identifies a range of specific ways in which this gendered concept is expressed in workplace discourse.

While, in its original conception, relational practice has been presented as feminine both in function and style, it is interesting to consider the possibility of expanding the concept to encompass more masculine ways of doing relational work. In the second section of this chapter, evidence for alternative ways of doing relational practice is examined.

In the final section, the constraints of different workplace cultures and the norms of different communities of practice, some of them distinctly gendered, are considered, in terms of their impact on acceptable and appropriate ways of doing relational practice. Not surprisingly, mismatches in this area, as in others, have implications for the comfort levels and effectiveness of people at work.

What is Relational Practice?

Relational practice is people-oriented behaviour which oils inter-personal wheels at work and thus facilitates the achievement of workplace objectives. Despite its value, such behaviour often goes unnoticed. In our LWP research, following Fletcher, we have analysed 'relational practice' (henceforth RP) in the workplace as having three crucial components:

1) RP is oriented to the 'face needs' of others[5]
2) RP serves to advance the primary objectives of the workplace
3) RP practices at work are regarded as dispensable, irrelevant, or peripheral.

As its name suggests, doing RP at work involves attending to workplace relationships, including both peoples' need to feel valued, their rapport or 'positive face needs', and the requirement that their autonomy be respected, their 'negative face needs'.[6] In other words, RP may entail being friendly or supportive, as well as being considerate and allowing people space to get on with their work. In the workplace, RP is often appropriately oriented to people's desire to be appreciated both for their special skills or distinctive expertise, and for their contribution as a team member.

To this obvious and common-sense interpretation of the meaning of RP (i.e. any aspect of workplace behaviour oriented to an individual's relationships with work colleagues), Fletcher adds, as specified in (2) and (3) above, that RP is behaviour which actually furthers organizational objectives (i.e. serves transactional functions), but that is, none the less, typically regarded as superfluous or marginal to the main focus of workplace interaction. It is these criteria which distinguish Fletcher's conception of RP from more popular uses of the term.[7] Moreover, while criterion (1), the relational and interpersonal function of RP, is widely indexed as feminine in the gender and communication literature, as indicated in chapter 1, Fletcher also emphasizes the importance of criterion (3), its off-record and background status, as a defining characteristic of RP as gendered (feminine) behaviour. In other words, RP is gendered behaviour, both in function and in style.

Fletcher's research encompassed a wide range of workplace behaviours, both verbal and non-verbal. Her data, however, was restricted to self-report materials rather than recorded interactions. Thus there is as yet very little information on the ways in which RP is actually expressed in face-to-face workplace exchanges. The first section of this chapter addresses this gap. Drawing on our Wellington Language in Workplace (LWP) Project database, I examine how RP, as defined by Fletcher, is instantiated as gendered *discourse* in specific workplaces, exploring first her claim that RP is manifestly feminine workplace behaviour.

Different Aspects of RP in the Workplace

In analyzing different manifestations of RP, Fletcher identifies four categories or 'themes' which she labels *preserving, creating team, mutual empowerment* and *self-achieving*.[8] In this chapter I illustrate three of these themes, showing how they function as gendered workplace talk in specific communities of practice.[9] For the purposes of illustration, each theme is treated separately, although in practice their realizations are often concurrent. People are very skilled in exploiting the multifunctional aspects of human communication systems, including language: one utterance typically serves several functions. An expression of approval, such as *that's really good, exactly right*, for instance, in response to a suggested way forward on a project, may simultaneously

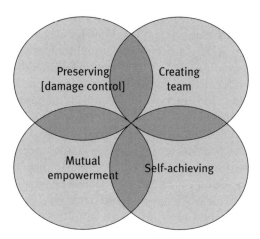

Figure 3.1 The four themes of relational practice (based on Fletcher 1999).

advance the project's objectives (*preserving*) and pay attention to the interpersonal dimension of team relationships (*creating team*) – as indeed the defining criteria suggest. In practice, then, RP provides yet another instance of the complex integrational skills that people demonstrate in managing and reconciling the competing demands of transactional and interpersonal objectives in face-to-face workplace interaction. For analytical purposes, however, I separate out the distinguishing aspects of different kinds of RP.

Preserving

Preserving focuses on relational practices that are primarily aimed at advancing the project's objectives. Preserving activities include doing boring and tedious but necessary tasks, even if they are not strictly speaking your responsibility; it includes taking steps to make sure the project is not held up by misunderstandings or disputes. To a greater or lesser extent, preserving is concerned with damage control: it includes RP which is oriented to constructing and maintaining the dignity of people at work, to saving face and reducing the likelihood of offence being taken, to mitigating potentially threatening behaviour, and to minimizing conflict and negotiating consensus: i.e. culturally coded as conventionally feminine behaviour.[10]

Fletcher emphasizes the *background* nature of preserving activities, an equally gendered feature, as mentioned above. In Fletcher's analysis, preserving typically entails the use of off-record, unnoticed behaviours which keep a project on track, enhance its progress, and prevent it being derailed or delayed. Facilitation and mitigation thus qualify perfectly as verbal means of doing preserving. In our data these strategies contributed in many subtle ways to the achievement of project goals. There are numerous instances where individuals take steps to manage potentially conflictual situations, to smooth ruffled feathers, or to anticipate problems and head off possible challenges. Two brief examples must suffice to illustrate just one preserving strategy, namely, skilful, off-record, facilitative work used in the interests of avoiding conflict and nurturing important team relationships, and thus preserving or furthering the organization's goals.[11]

In example 3.1, Smithy, the leader of a project team in the customer service centre of a large commercial organization, reports on how some off-record, background work that he has undertaken indicates that the team should proceed cautiously with the next stage of their current project.

Example 3.1

Context: Regular project team meeting in a multinational, white-collar commercial organization. There are 5 men and 5 women at this meeting.

1. **Smi**: um I've had a few discussions with people er in the corridor
2. which [*quietly*]: is where I do my best work:
3. um /+ people are\ saying that no
4. **Ben**: /(if we can get your attention)\
5. **Smi**: they're er they're not confident that on day one they're gonna be able to go
6. and and I think it's a little bit of–
7. **Cla**: people are saying they're not confident
8. **Smi**: yeah and I had a discussion with someone who said
9. you know that er it it's taken two years to get up to speed . . .
10. and I just wonder um hopefully that we can channel through the different
11. having the team leaders here and stuff

Smithy's 'corridor work' has picked up rumbles of concern among those responsible for actually implementing the project which this team is managing. This is precisely the kind of invisible, off-record discussion which Fletcher identifies as canonical RP: the relational work involved in anticipating problems, having antennae tuned for potential disaster or failure, and thus 'preserving' the project and increasing its chances of success. Smithy's observations lead to a discussion of what can be done to re-assure and support the implementation group.

Discussions in the corridor, such as Smithy describes, provide an acceptable and off-record means for those most directly involved to express their worries about the project timetable. Smithy's behaviour thus functions as classic RP: on the relational dimension he provides reassurance to those who are worrying, while in transactional terms his covertly facilitative behaviour serves to warn those higher up the authority structure of potential implementation problems, so that preventative action can be taken.

The second instance, example 3.2, involves a project manager, Jock, setting up the department manager to provide approving feedback for a valuable contribution to the discussion and the project. Jock is providing a report on exactly what the various team members have accomplished since the last meeting.

Example 3.2

Context: Regular project team meeting in a large commercial organization. There are 4 men and 4 women at this meeting.

1. **Joc**: um service levels team to produce a strategy document they've done +
2. um Vita was to meet with IS to determine er
3. an implementation plan for the recording device
4. **Vit**: yes done it +
5. **Joc**: [*parenthetical tone*] Vita's done a um work plan just for that
6. um implementation and that
7. **Chr**: great that'll make the plan easier
8. **Joc**: we can feed /(out what) you want\
9. **Vit**: /haven't actually\ (heard anything . . .)
10. **Joc**: Vita's going to meet with Stewart
11. to determine [*the next stage*]

In lines 1–3, Jock reports on what the team agreed Vita should do by this meeting, and in line 4, Vita confirms that she has indeed accomplished the specified task. Since the department manager Chris makes no immediate response, Jock proceeds in lines 5–6 (*Vita's done a work plan just for that implementation*) to 'prime' Chris to provide positive feedback to Vita. Chris responds appropriately in line 7 with a positive and appreciative comment, *great that'll make the plan easier*, and Jock then continues with the next item. The facilitative move is made extremely discreetly, and Chris picks up Jock's cue without missing a beat. This is excellent RP – subtle, backgrounded, relational work, attending to workplace relationships in the interests of the project's progress.

In another organization where we recorded extensively, we observed that the manager of one section regularly engaged in a good deal of off-record RP around the edges of the more on-record transactional interactions which dominated the official record of the department's outputs. And the skilful negotiation of consensus, documented in detail elsewhere,[12] includes many further instances of covert facilitative strategies used to minimize conflict.

Closely related to these more obvious instances of preserving activities are examples where one team member defends another from face attack in the form of teasing or jocular abuse by other team members. Such protective behaviour may function to subtly underline the importance of good team relations in furthering project goals; the covert message is 'don't undermine team members – we all need each other'. Indeed humour can itself be used as a damage control strategy, as illustrated in chapter 4.[13]

Like facilitative behaviour, damage control, especially in the form of the mitigation of negatively affective speech acts, has been identified in the language and gender literature as a distinctive feature of feminine ways of interacting.[14] Research in many different contexts indicates that feminine interactional styles tend to involve frequent and varied mitigating devices to attenuate negatively affective speech acts and maintain good relations. Hence, there seems to be a *prima facie* case for regarding this type of RP in the workplace as gendered workplace talk, and indeed as the kind of talk that supports Fletcher's claim that RP is predominantly regarded as feminine behaviour. As the examples have demonstrated, however, such behaviour is clearly not confined to women in the workplace. Both women and men in the workplaces where we recorded engaged in RP which subtly facilitated project goals, and which preserved team relations and thus prevented delays in achieving objectives.

Mutual Empowering or Off-record Mentoring[15]

Mutual empowering is another type of RP which, like preserving, is very obviously aimed at furthering workplace goals. Mutual empowering includes such activities as making connections or putting people in touch with others who can assist them to achieve their goals, effective networking for the benefit of others, and 'empathic teaching', i.e. providing support and guidance in a fashion which is responsive to the addressee's 'intellectual and emotional reality'.[16] Fletcher regards such activities as gendered, and argues that they are typically associated with women in the workplace, especially when they are performed 'backstage' and discreetly.

There are many examples in our database of people providing support and guidance to others at work. Not all qualify as RP, however. Some are relatively 'on-record' and official activities, authorized and even required by the organization: e.g. performance review interviews, and formal evaluation and advice sessions. During a weekly meeting between a manager, Leila, and her subordinate, Zoe, in a government department, for example, the manager explicitly refers to *thinking about your future* and comments that *there's a couple of quite exciting looking things* coming up. Later in the same meeting Leila promises to think about relevant material which may help Zoe develop her career in a new direction.

Example 3.3

Context: Weekly meeting between a senior manager and the library section manager in a government department. They are discussing the future direction of Zoe's career.

1. **Lei**: um I'm just trying to think + I'll have a wee think
2.   there's probably some decent things to read about that actually
3. **Zoe**: oh okay that would be useful

Leila's offer of help is expressed in an informal and unpushy way, as indicated by the hesitations, pauses, hedges and reflective, colloquial expressions (*I'm just trying to think, I'll have a wee think*), and the mitigating hedges (*just, probably, actually*). The preceding and following discourse also make it clear that this is an integral part of a very positive and supportive interaction in which both participants engage fully. Nevertheless, given the context, namely a discussion of Zoe's future career direction, this could not be described as 'backstage' behaviour in Fletcher's terms. This is relatively explicit mentoring, rather than RP. I return to this point below.

Our database also provides many instances of people giving support and advice to colleagues using off-record and indirect strategies which clearly *do* qualify as classic instances of RP, both in function and in style. These less explicit ways of empowering others include modelling appropriate behaviours, allocating responsibilities which will 'stretch' a colleague, telling anecdotes from which others can draw inferences about appropriate ways of behaving, asking thought-provoking questions of relevance to career development, and providing indirect feedback or advice on another's workplace activities from the perspective of career enhancement.[17]

Examples 3.4a and 3.4b are excerpts from an interaction which involved a much less direct and more off-record approach to assisting others at work. The excerpts are taken from a regular meeting between a senior manager, Jan, and one of the section managers, Kiwa. Throughout the interaction, rather than providing explicit directives, Jan asks questions which encourage Kiwa to think his own way through to effective solutions, and which assist him in identifying the most relevant strategies for managing problematic situations.

Example 3.4a

Context: Weekly meeting between a female senior manager and a male section manager in a large government department.

1.	**Kiw**:	yeah it just i- it's just um it's just knowing
2.		when the thing is actually completed
3.		and how we know it's completed
4.		for example w- when we p- pulled together
5.		those maths resources you know ...
6.		[*detailed description of how the maths resources had been dealt with*]
7.	**Jan**:	god that must have been a long time ago wasn't it ...
8.	**Kiw**:	[*further description of what happened*]
9.	**Jan**:	yeah
10.		/and in actual fact\
11.	**Jan**:	/so it could have fallen\ into a
12.		/black hole and\ no one would have known
13.	**Kiw**:	/right right\ exactly and there were a couple of things I think ...
14.		like like that um (which I'm a bit) concerned about

15.	**Jan:**	okay ++
16.	**Kiw:**	so we need to have a kind of a way of signing off
17.		or finishing off and all that
18.	**Jan:**	yep (well) we'll need to think about
19.		have you got any ideas about how we could do that
20.	**Kiw:**	well normally um . . .

In this excerpt, Kiwa states at some length the problem he is concerned about, i.e. *knowing when the thing is actually completed* (lines 1–2). Jan encourages him to explore the issue very thoroughly and he provides a specific example, *the maths resources*. Jan sympathetically indicates that Kiwa's point has been taken with supportive feedback throughout (e.g. lines 9, 11–12, 15). But, most relevantly for the analysis of this as an instance of RP is the fact that, rather than suggesting a solution, Jan encourages Kiwa to address the issue by asking him for his opinions *have you got any ideas about how we could do that* (line 19), and as a result he proceeds to explore possible responses to the issue. Example 3.4b shows Jan using similar strategies at a later point in the same interaction.

Example 3.4b

Context: Weekly meeting between a female senior manager and a male section manager in a large government department.

1.	**Jan:**	well what are you going to do with this information?
2.	**Kiw:**	well um I think we'll have to use the information now
3.		in our in our discussions with the Ministry of [*name*]
4.		about what policies what you know more/ interventionist\
5.	**Jan:**	/right\
6.	**Kiw:**	type /policies\
7.	**Jan:**	/you'll be\ bri- briefing the Minister of- the Ministry of [*name*]
8.	**Kiw:**	yep
9.	**Jan:**	and what about our Minister . . .

Jan again gently prods Kiwa to think along lines which will be useful for him as a section manager, and improve his performance. Following Kiwa's description of the interesting results and implications of materials that his section has been analysing, Jan poses a propositionally challenging question, though it is expressed in a gentle tone, *well what are you going to do with this information?* (line 1). Kiwa's responds (line 2) in a way that suggests he is thinking on his feet, with the classic introductory 'fumble' or time-claiming pragmatic particle *well*, followed by a hesitation *um*, and the pragmatic particle *I think*, which also indicates tentativeness.[18] Jan provides a positive response, *right* (line 5), which reinforces the procedure that Kiwa has outlined as appropriate, repeating more explicitly what Kiwa has suggested (line 7), and thus reinforcing an assessment of his proposed action as correct. This is followed, however, with another question *and what about our Minister* (line 9), suggesting that, in Jan's view, Kiwa needs to think through further the steps that are required, and pointing to the direction she considers he should be taking. Thus Jan nudges rather than directs Kiwa to think along lines which will be helpful to him in meeting his managerial responsibilities. Both examples 3.3 and 3.4 illustrate helpful and supportive mentoring, but they contrast in directness and the extent to which they can be classified as on-record behaviours. Unlike example 3.3, example 3.4 is low key and indirect, an example of RP both in function and style.

Example 3.5 provides a further contrast. An IT manager, Neil, and his subordinate, Kevin, are working together to solve an IT problem. In this excerpt, Neil provides Kevin with feedback on the ways in which he should operate in order to enhance and extend his learning on the job.

Example 3.5

Context: An IT manager and a team member in a government organization working together on a problem in Neil's office.

1. **Nei**: archive security's ( ) isn't it
2. **Kev**: I'm not sure
3. **Nei**: my gosh what do you mean you're not sure?
4. **Kev**: well Gar- Gary and Robert are the ones
5.   that are involved with sending off tapes
6.   and bringing them back so
7. **Nei**: well if they weren't here what would you do? ++
8. **Kev**: I would most probably find their notes that don't exist

9. **Nei**: okay that's quite surprising you don't know that +
10.   it's quite a critical one don't you think?
11. **Kev**: yeah

Like Jan in example 3.4, Neil clearly intends to provoke Kevin to reflect on his approach to a problem, but he uses a very different discourse strategy. Neil expresses astonishment that Kevin cannot confidently answer a question in an area in which he is expected to be developing expertise, *my gosh what do you mean you're not sure?* (line 3). The question is challenging, boosted by the intensifying pragmatic device *what do you mean* (cf. the much less face-threatening unmodified question *aren't you sure?*) and by the exclamation *my gosh.* When Kevin defends himself by indicating that the relevant knowledge is related to tasks that others are responsible for (lines 4–5), Neil adopts an explicitly 'teacherly' tone with another challenging question *well if they weren't here what would you do?* (line 7). Like Jan, Neil is using a standard coaching strategy – forcing the mentee to think through the consequences of his ignorance in an area where he is expected to be knowledgeable. He uses a more explicit, contestive and on-record approach – in fact, a more conventionally masculine strategy (arguably the most effective way to achieve the organization's goals in this context).

When Kevin replies semi-facetiously and defensively that he would have to find notes that don't exist (line 8), Neil does not respond to his attempt at humour. Rather he maintains the mentoring tone with an explicitly critical comment *that's quite surprising you don't know that* (line 9), followed up with the challenging *it's quite a critical one don't you think?* (line 10). A tag such as *don't you think* often has the effect of softening a critical comment, but in this context, it rather serves to challenge and confront Kevin and to force – rather than invite – him to respond.[19]

Neil's approach to guiding Kevin in addressing gaps in his knowledge can thus be regarded as a classic example of a 'corrective' transaction, or of 'management-by-exception', an approach which entails monitoring errors, mistakes, and deviations from standards.[20] It is certainly not a low-key, backstage strategy, and it contrasts markedly with Jan's demonstration of off-record RP in example 3.4.

Some, but (using Fletcher's criteria) clearly not all, styles of empowering others through mentoring can thus be regarded as ways of instantiating RP. Can we also characterize mentoring as gendered behaviour? While the traditional literature in this area clearly associates mentoring predominantly with men,[21] and often identifies respected male models who have guided the careers of male protégés, the 'nurturing' aspect of mentoring, especially in its more 'backstage' manifestations, has obvious feminine associations. And Fletcher, of course, identifies the empowerment of others as standard RP, gendered as feminine. This difference of viewpoint, I suggest, is in the first instance a matter of whether the empowering or mentoring is undertaken as backstage vs. onstage relational work. Performance review processes and official mentoring programmes require and officially give credit to mentors for undertaking supportive and advisory behaviours. Less overt, indirect and off-record mentoring is not generally recognized as such. Fletcher goes as far as claiming that 'in a culture of independence and self-promotion – where individual achievement is prized and competition means beating the other guy and finishing on top – voluntarily helping others achieve is deviant behaviour'.[22]

One important factor which contributes to the backstage–onstage contrast, and to perceptions of the differently gendered nature of different mentoring behaviours, is the *way* in which empowerment is undertaken, or the style of mentoring adopted between colleagues. This is most obvious in the contrast between examples 3.4 and 3.5. Neil's explicit, on-record mentoring cannot be regarded as an instance of RP, and this classification is further accentuated by the confrontational and contestive questions which approximate the masculine end of a continuum of stylistically gendered behaviour. By contrast, Jan's less direct approach more obviously qualifies as RP, and by the same token her more supportive, mitigated and normatively feminine style of interaction is consistent with Fletcher's conception of RP. Example 3.3, on the other hand, indicates that RP and a more feminine interactional style need not completely correspond. Mentoring can be done explicitly and on-record, yet in a supportive, empathetic and conventionally feminine style. And the converse is also possible, as I will suggest below. Off-record, backstage RP can be accomplished in normatively masculine as well as feminine ways.

Creating Team

Creating team is the term Fletcher uses to discuss activities aimed at 'creating the background conditions in which group life [can] flourish'.[23]

It includes all the typically unobserved behind-the-scenes behaviours which foster group life and the development of team *esprit de corps* – activities such as taking the time to listen and respond empathically to non-work-related information, creating opportunities for collaboration and cooperation, and facilitating productive interaction. This is RP oriented to constructing and nurturing good workplace relationships, to establishing and maintaining solidarity between team members, and to networking and creating new work relationships. In Fletcher's terms, these are obvious ways of 'creating team'.

People at work use a wide variety of discourse strategies to construct and maintain good relations with their co-workers. These include engaging in small-talk and social talk, introducing humour into workplace discourse (see chapter 4), telling entertaining stories or anecdotes (see chapter 6), and paying compliments or giving approval. This section focuses on just one such strategy as a manifestation of discursive RP in the workplace, a strategy regarded as stereotypically feminine, that is, small-talk.

Small-talk and social talk at work clearly serve the function of establishing and nurturing workplace relationships; and the label 'small-talk' itself explicitly signals the perceived status of this type of talk as trivial, and irrelevant to serious workplace business.[24] In fact, most social and interpersonal talk in the workplace is typically discounted, or in Fletcher's terms 'disappeared', from the organizational record. Thus small-talk clearly meets two of the criteria for RP. Not all social talk at work, however, meets the third criterion, namely, serving to advance the transactional objectives of the workplace, except in the rather indirect respect that fostering good relationships at work generally facilitates the achievement of workplace goals. Nevertheless, we did identify a number of interesting instances of classic, conventional social talk in our data which met this third criterion. Example 3.6 is typical; it occurred at the end of a meeting as people were gathering up their papers.

Example 3.6

Context: Peg and her manager, Clara, belong to a multinational white-collar commercial organization. They are chatting at the end of a meeting of their project team. Peg is pregnant.

1. **Cla**: how is the baby?
2. **Peg**: [drawls]: good: still just a baby though
3. **Cla**: right not a boy baby or a girl baby
4. **Peg**: no can't tell /its legs crossed\
5. **Cla**: /haha you\ gonna have to wait . . .
6.   are you feeling tired?
7. **Peg**: yes but I just think it's summer too
8.   because I didn't you know because been in summer
9.   cos I wasn't pregnant last time or AS pregnant in the summertime
10.   so it was much easier cos I didn't know +
11.   um I had help (until) December last time (so it was easier)
12. **Cla**: hey you you're hoping you're gonna work [drawls]: through: /(what)\
13. **Peg**: /well + my\ plan is is to work full time up until the end of May
14. **Cla**: right
15. **Peg**: and then come back as we need as I'm needed after that
16.   just dependent on what happens with Daisy and Matt's group . . .

This conversation moves very clearly but very smoothly from social talk to work talk, from a discussion of non-work topics, Peg's baby's health and sex (lines 1–5) and Peg's own health (lines 6–11), to the discussion of the impact of her pregnancy on her contribution to the organization (lines 12–16). Clara, Peg's manager, is engaging in RP; the expressions of interest about the baby and concern for Peg's general condition are canonical (positive) face attention strategies, constructing and nurturing good workplace relationships.

However, the discussion also addresses the implications of this information for the project team's objectives. Although the content of line 12 (*you're hoping you're gonna work through*) could be simply a further expression of interest, Peg's response (lines 13, 15–16) indicates that she orients to her manager's comment as transactional (task- or goal-oriented) rather than interpersonal in intent. This is standard RP, and we have many similar examples in our data from a wide range of different workplaces.[25] Example 3.7 is taken from an interaction in a small commercial IT company.

Example 3.7

Context: Beginning of a monthly board meeting in a small commercial IT company. One board member, Samuel, will participate via a phone link to Australia.

1.	**Don**:	are we gonna give Samuel a call?
2.	**Jill**:	yep yep no he's waiting in the wings he's in Adelaide
3.	**Don**:	right /any\ problems? or +
4.	**Tes**:	/is he\ ..he er- I don't I don't know they may have read it wrongly
5.		but um er Jadon Nash and Jane were over there um e- over the weekend
6.	**Jill**:	over /where\
7.	**Tes**:	/(in)\ in Melbourne and they were (c-)
8.		and Samuel was gonna come and see them and an'
9.		they were staying in the s- the Seaforth house and they
10.		and Samuel rang and said that he had some crisis on and couldn't come
11.		and they I mean she said she thought it was ++ you know yeah
12.		and she kind of sort of frowned and sort of thought it was sort of serious
13.		but they might I mean I don't know
14.		Samuel might of /(who knows)\
15.	**Jill**:	/staying up\ the Barossa Valley somewhere I /don't know\
16.	**Tes**:	/yes [laughs]\
17.	**Jill**:	um he was off having dinner quite happily last night
18.		/when I spoke\ to him just spoke to him ten minutes ago /so\
19.	**Tes**:	/(right)\ /right\ alright no
20.	**Jill**:	( ) he didn't say anything I hope everything's /alright\ um +
21.	**Tes**:	/yeah\
22.	**Jill**:	I don't know
23.	**Tes**:	no
24.	**Don**:	do you want the computer on?

While this discussion appears at one level to be involved with personal and social topics, namely Samuel's well-being and his *crisis* (line 10), which is assessed as *sort of serious* (line 12), topics which appear unrelated to the business at hand, it can also be seen to have transactional import, since Samuel is expected to participate in the meeting which is about to start. Indeed the discussion is triggered by a question from Donald *any problems?* (line 3), which is ambiguous between social and transactional meanings; it could be an expression of interest in Samuel's welfare but may equally refer to the technology (especially since this is Donald's responsibility, as indicated later, *do you want the computer on?* (line 24)). It is also interesting that Tessa's speech is peppered with hedges and hesitations, *may, might, I mean, you know, sort of, kind of, I don't know* (lines 4–15), possibly indicating reluctance to introduce personal matters into the meeting context, or perhaps reluctance to 'tattle' on Samuel. None the less, her very ready, and possibly relieved, acceptance *right right alright no* (line 19) of Jill's reassurances in lines 17–18, suggest that she considers the information as potentially relevant to the approaching meeting and their attempts to contact Samuel.

When small-talk serves as RP, then, it achieves more than just affective, interpersonal work. While the non-work topic of an expected baby in example 3.6 undoubtedly comprises conventionally feminine talk, it also provides an entrée to explore the consequences for the organization of Peg's potential unavailability, a concern which is much less obviously stereotypically feminine. Is the manager skilfully managing the discourse for this purpose? It is impossible to know; and this kind of ambiguity is typical of authentic talk; talk is multifunctional and listeners typically deal with a range of potential meanings. Similarly, we cannot be sure whether Tessa is simply gossiping and using Samuel as a basis for small-talk, or whether she is pre-warning people that he may not be available, or that he may be a distracted or unfocused participant in their meeting.

In a similar fashion, discussions of leave and holidays frequently move very subtly from plans for how the recreational time will be spent to discussion of how the organization will cope with the person's absence, talk which clearly serves both interpersonal and transactional goals. Apparently off-topic, social talk thus functions as a means of addressing an issue of direct concern to the progress of a project, or the smooth running of a department. Such conversations are consistently located at the boundaries of workplace interaction. They typically occur at the ends of meetings, as in example 3.6, often as people are walking out of a room, and even during social breaks. In other words, these conversations usually occur 'off the record'; the transactional goal is achieved 'by the way' during a conversation which participants would consider as primarily involving social talk. They clearly fit the criteria for RP outlined above, and they illustrate the subtle ways in which off-record, apparently irrelevant workplace discourse can serve organizational goals.

To what extent does such talk instantiate gendered, and as Fletcher claims, specifically feminine, discourse? Certainly small-talk, like gossip, is strongly associated with female activities and domains, and is widely culturally coded as feminine. Earlier research on small-talk provides some support for this association of small-talk with feminine domains.[26] An interesting collection of papers edited by Justine Coupland, for example, which is devoted to small-talk, but without gender as an explicit focus, is dominated by data from stereotypically feminine contexts (e.g. hairdressing, supermarkets, travel agencies, call centres, women's health care).[27] The reasons for the association of small-talk with femininity are obvious on the basis of such research.

Our LWP analyses of the gender distribution of small-talk in meetings from a range of white-collar workplaces also support this association of small-talk with more feminine domains and relatively feminine communities of practice (defined, as described in chapter 1, by attitudinal, structural and stylistic criteria, such as their predominantly collaborative interactional style, and attention to relational aspects of interaction). Small-talk at the beginning of meetings was extended and often very personal in the most feminine workplace where we recorded, indicating that the participants regularly maintained their relationships through such talk.[28] Moreover, social talk often 'leaked' into meetings in this workplace – though, interestingly, an apparent social digression frequently turned out to have relevance for the organization's business in the longer term, demonstrating its value as RP. Certainly, it appeared that there was greater tolerance for small-talk in the more feminine white collar communities of practice that we researched.[29]

In sum, like other kinds of RP, small-talk is normatively associated with femininity. In addition, the content of much small-talk reflects stereotypically feminine interests. So, addressing superficially 'trivial' social topics or sometimes apparently irrelevant (to work) personal topics, small-talk functions to create team and establish rapport between work colleagues. It is typically accomplished off-record, as backstage, peripheral talk, addressing transactional goals in an indirect and non-threatening manner which pays attention to the addressee's face needs. In other words, small-talk is classic RP, gendered as feminine because of its functions, the interactively engaged style in which it is expressed, and even its content.

RP as a Gendered Resource in Workplace Interaction

Fletcher's analysis of RP is firmly focused on *women's* behaviour. She argues that people with relational skills, those with 'emotional intelligence', tend to *'get disappeared* from the organizational screen'.[30] The reason for this disappearing act, she argues, is that relational skills are typically associated with women, and hence devalued: 'women are relied on to be the carriers of relational responsibility in society but at the same time are devalued for taking on this role'.[31] Women, she says, are traditionally associated with background support work, the behind-the-scenes activities which make the onstage performance possible. Similarly, Fishman (1977) described women's contributions to the conversations between couples that she analysed as 'conversational shitwork', a term encompassing a range of often unnoticed, supportive moves which keep a conversation going. Fletcher argues that such backstage, low-key, support work is quintessentially women's work: 'Relational practice is not gender-neutral behaviour. It is behaviour that engages deeply held gender identities and beliefs'.[32] Eckert and McConnell-Ginet make a similar point: 'Traditional women's jobs are in the service sector, and generally involve nurturing and support roles . . . Wherever they are, women are expected more than men to remember birthdays, soothe hurt children, offer intimate understanding.'[33]

Our data demonstrates, however, that both women and men engage in RP at work. In exploring how Fletcher's concept of RP is actually instantiated in workplace verbal interaction, I have therefore emphasized not the sex of those engaged in the RP, but rather the gendered nature of that behaviour. In function and in style, and sometimes even in content, RP is normatively indexed as feminine. Fletcher's data was collected from six professional women in a predominantly male workplace, an engineering company, and consisted of observational and interview material. Her analysis supports her claim that RP is undervalued and invisible, and even 'disappeared': i.e. discounted as unimportant and irrelevant to the organization's core business. Clearly, however, she was very dependent on what she personally managed to observe, and on the reliability of people's post-hoc reports about their intentions and achievements. As noted in chapter 1, the material in our LWP database, by contrast, consists of recordings of authentic everyday interactions involving both women and men in a range of different workplaces and communities of practice, supplemented by participant observation, interviews, and in some cases focus group meetings. It therefore provides a more extensive and reliable basis for examining how people actually do RP in a wider range of work contexts. As exemplified above, our analyses demonstrate that both women and men employ RP. Furthermore, our research suggests that RP may be accomplished in a wider range of ways than has been previously considered. The next section explores the suggestion that RP may be expressed using more normatively masculine styles of interaction.

RP and Masculinity: Alternative Ways of Doing RP?

The previous sections have illustrated how the discursive strategies used to instantiate RP in the workplace may serve as gendered discourse resources for constructing a relatively feminine identity at work. While its backstage, marginal status very obviously contributes to the perception of verbal expressions of RP as feminine discourse, the styles in which RP is typically instantiated also tend to be associated with the feminine end of the masculine–feminine style continuum. However, it seems possible in principle that at least some aspects of RP could be expressed in less normatively feminine ways. In other words, despite Fletcher's focus on RP as essentially feminine discourse, it seems possible that at least some functions of RP could be expressed in more masculine discourse styles. This point can be illustrated by examining different ways of creating team. I first briefly consider evidence of more masculine ways of expressing small-talk and humour in the workplace, and then examine in a little more detail different ways of giving approval, another obvious way of creating team.

Creating Team and Small-talk

Small-talk is an obvious strategy for creating team, one of the basic functions of RP. Its content is often social or personal, and, by definition, irrelevant to the main business at hand, and it is characteristically positioned at the peripheries of more ratified legitimate business talk.[34] But if, as discussed above, small-talk is culturally coded as feminine, and is found in abundance in more feminine communities of practice, then it is interesting to ask whether, and if so how, participants in more masculine communities of practice do this kind of RP.

The material we have collected from a number of more masculine or 'masculinist' workplaces suggests this question merits further research.[35] In at least three such workplaces, we found that the topics of the pre-meeting and post-meeting talk, though unrelated to the agenda of the meeting ahead, were much more work-related than in other workplaces. In these workplaces, there was relatively little conventional small-talk focused on personal or social topics. Rather the participants used the times around the edges of the meeting to catch up on work-related topics which were typically outside the scope of the meeting's ratified business. For instance, in the six meetings of one team that we videotaped in full from before the first person entered the meeting room until after the last person left, there is scarcely a single topic that is not related to some aspect of the team's work, although none relate directly to items on the meeting agenda.

Does this talk qualify as RP? It was clearly off-record, unofficial, and backstage talk. And although it was off-topic in terms of the agenda of the current meeting, it was generally related to some other aspect of the team's work, and thus to the team's organizational goals. Hence on these two criteria it qualifies as RP. Does it also satisfy the third criterion? i.e. does this kind of talk function as a means of attending to the face needs of others? does it orientate to interpersonal aspects of interaction? It seems plausible that talk of this kind serves as a kind of social glue for the members of these teams, and can be regarded as a legitimate means of creating team. In other words, these team members fill in time by discussing topics of mutual interest which are not on the current meeting agenda. This suggests then that different communities of practice may develop different ways of doing RP. I am not referring here to differences in the distribution of particular RP strategies – such differences are inevitable – but rather to the more fundamental issue of possible differences in what the researcher 'counts' as RP in different workplaces. In other words, the gendering of RP is perhaps best considered as locatable at a variety of points along the feminine–masculine style dimension.

Creating Team and Humour

The suggestion that RP may be instantiated in masculine as well as feminine ways is also supported by our research on humour in the workplace (the focus of chapter 4). Not all workplace humour qualifies as RP, but there are many instances in our data where humour assists in the achievement of transactional as well as relational goals. Humour is quintessentially off-record in the context of workplace interaction; in other words, no matter how work-focused an utterance is, the injection or addition of a component of humour is always, strictly speaking, an extraneous element (see chapter 4 for examples). Our analyses of humour in a number of different New Zealand communities of practice suggest that there are many different ways of using humour as a positive politeness or rapport strategy, to 'create team', and that some humorous discourse strategies take a distinctly unfeminine form.

While some communities of practice, and especially those identified as overall more feminine in interactional style, tend to favour predominantly supportive and collaborative humour for doing RP, other more masculine communities of practice appear to prefer more contestive, challenging and even jocularly insulting humour for this purpose.[36] For example, as discussed in chapter 2, in a government department widely regarded as more feminine in its overall style of interaction, there was a marked orientation towards collaborative styles and processes of interaction, and this included the kind of humour which characterized the meetings in this department.[37] In this workplace, self-deprecating humour was often used as RP, in a subtle, low-key and off-record way, to re-establish good relations after the manager had been particularly directive.

In another much more masculine community of practice, where the styles of interaction were very direct, and the discussion often challenging and argumentative in style, the humour of the group was predominantly aggressive and, from my perspective (as female analyst), highly face threatening. Over 90 per cent of the humorous comments which occurred in one meeting, for instance, were sarcastic and negative jibes, apparently intended to deflate the addressee.[38] This was clearly the team's preferred interactional style, and it seems that this was their way of accomplishing one aspect of RP. The contestive humour functioned to create team – participants often competed to out-do each other and 'top' the previous witty comment – and its focus was generally closely related to their workplace objectives and goals: e.g. lambasting an individual for failing to meet their targets, ridiculing someone for overly meticulous attention to detail, accusing someone of claiming too much kudos for his work, and so on.

Similarly, in another relatively masculine community of practice, a production team within a factory, the team leader generally adopted direct, authoritarian and forceful strategies to communicate with her team as a whole, including very explicit criticism when the team failed to meet its targets. The use of humour to create team in this workplace was very different from that in more feminine workplaces: humour was more frequent and much more 'in your face', more contestive and aggressive, with a good deal of jocular abuse, good-humoured insult, and sarcastic comment.[39] Hence, in the areas of both small-talk and humour, there is some evidence that distinctively masculine styles of doing RP are possible and preferred in certain communities of practice. Exploring this point a little further, the next section considers different ways of 'giving approval' from this perspective.

Creating Team and Giving Approval

Giving approval undoubtedly contributes to creating team.[40] As Fletcher says, expressing support for others fosters *esprit de corps* and contributes to 'creating the background conditions in which group life [can] flourish'.[41] One very obvious way of giving approval is to pay a compliment. For reasons discussed below, paying compliments and giving positive feedback is a complex business in New Zealand society. Nevertheless, there is a good deal of evidence of gendered behaviour in this area:[42] and, in particular, evidence that compliments are culturally coded as predominantly feminine interactional strategies.[43] In earlier research on sex-differentiated linguistic patterns, compliments about appearance were found to be more frequent between women than between men, and, where they occurred, comments on appearance between males generally appeared 'marked', and often functioned rather as teasing than as unqualified expressions of approval. Hence the indexing of compliments as positively polite, feminine strategies is unsurprising.

This research also suggests that gender is relevant not only to the frequency and topics of compliments, but also to the styles in which they are expressed. So, in the contexts studied, women tended to use syntactically more explicit and elaborated compliments, often including intensifiers (e.g. *that's a really nice blouse*), while male ways of giving even explicit approval tended to be lower key, more often reduced to a syntactic minimum and semantically attenuated: e.g. *nice bike, good wheels*.[44] In this area, then, it is masculine styles which are relatively unobtrusive.

Against such a background, the issue of the gendering of off-record, backstage expressions of approval is not straightforward. *Any* expression of approval tends to be perceived as relatively feminine behaviour in the New Zealand context (and this may partly explain why males tend to express approval and give compliments less often). But it seems likely that how such expressions are delivered is much more relevant than their frequency in determining their gender associations. In other words the issue is again the masculine–feminine style continuum. Expressions of approval which are more elaborated tend to be perceived as more feminine, even if delivered off-record and in backstage arenas. In this chapter, I am suggesting, however, that this kind of RP can also be done in a more normatively masculine way, and, in relation to expressions of approval, it is the minimalist, low-key features which are significant in this gendering process. This is clearly an area which merits further research.

Our workplace database provides some interesting support for this argument. Example 3.8 is a paradigmatic illustration of a more feminine way of giving approval, delivered by the CEO during a strategic planning meeting of the senior management team.

Example 3.8

Context: Meeting of a group of 4 male and 4 female regional managers of a national organization. Penelope is the Chair and CEO, and she is here commenting on Hettie's performance. Hettie is a project manager who reports to Penelope.

1. **Pen:** actually I mean I I've said this before
2. but I'd like to just put it on record again h- +
3. **Mal:** mm
4. **Pen:** how extraordinarily impressed and proud we are
5. of the work you've done on this project /and\
6. **Mal:** /mm\
7. **Pen:** how I can't actually imagine anybody else [inhales]
8. certainly in my acquaintance /[laughs] who would've\
9. **Ing:** /[laughs]\
10. **Pen:** actually been able to walk in and do this
11. and I'm I have said many blessings /on the fact that we hired\
12. **Mal:** /mm mm mm\
13. **Pen:** Hettie /when we did\
14. **Het:** /thank you\
15. **Pen:** because I think we wouldn't be where we are
16. in the [name] /act\ project
17. **Mal:** /mm\
18. **Pen:** if we hadn't /[inhales] and\
19. **Het:** /thank you\
20. **Pen:** I'm terribly pleased for you that +
21. some gaps are appearing /so that you can\ actually do
22. **Het:** /[laughs]\
23. **Pen:** some other things cos /I\ know that
24. **Het:** /mm\
25. **Pen:** /[inhales]\ while you've done it very willingly
26. **Het:** /mm\
27. **Pen:** /it's\ it has been absolutely massive
28. **Het:** /mm\ mm so it feels yes it does feel wonderful
29. to be at the end of it

This is an extended, sustained and explicitly *on-record* (line 2) expression of approval and appreciation of Hettie's work for the organization. Using phrases such as *how extraordinarily impressed and proud we are* (line 4), and suggesting that no one else could have done what Hettie has achieved, Penelope pulls out all the stops in terms of acknowledging her contribution to the organization's work. This is one end of the spectrum of gendered ways of giving approval, a sustained compliment accomplished in a normatively feminine style. Similar examples can be found in the analysis of Leila's management style in the feminine community of practice discussed in earlier papers.[45] Example 3.9 is a less elaborate but equally explicit expression of approval by the Chair and CEO in a long meeting recorded in a very masculine community of practice.

Example 3.9

Context: Large meeting of a senior group of managers in a government department.

1.   **Chair:**   okay um well I support the paper the recommendations
2.   I think you've done an excellent job well done

Such comments were typically addressed by superiors to subordinates, or sometimes recorded between colleagues of equal status. However, instances such as those exemplified in 3.8 and 3.9 do not qualify as RP, since they are explicit and on-record, rather than understated and backstage.

Approval as RP takes the form of off-record, low-key and unofficial expressions of appreciation, instances of positive feedback between team members which tend to go unnoticed by those in positions of authority. Not surprisingly this kind of RP is difficult to document. However, some of the instances in our data are suggestive in terms of the issue of the gendering of RP and what counts as RP in different communities of practice. Examples of more subtle expressions of approval were typically found between equals or addressed upwards rather than downwards. Example 3.10 illustrates how the discursively difficult task of giving positive feedback to a superior was accomplished. Examples of this kind of RP in our data demonstrate great skill on the part of the subordinate, since, in New Zealand's egalitarian cultural context, it is crucially important to avoiding accusations of flattery or 'crawling'.

Example 3.10

Context: Beginning of a meeting at a large commercial organization. Jock is the Project leader and Chair and has arrived first. Benny, a business analyst, is next to arrive, and they chat as they wait for the rest of the team members to arrive.

1. **Ben**: where did you learn sort of project management type of skills
2. **Joc**: oh I never did
3. **Ben**: cos you seem really good at it
4. **Joc**: /I've just winged it\
5. **Ben**: /and awfully confident\
6. **Joc**: um I -I started in engineering and I guess that
7.   they're fairly large pro- you know they're they're quite finite bites
8.   like each [*local centre*] is a project on its own
9.   but um so you've got to you do a construction plan for it
10.   so that you know the first /thing\
11. **Ben**: /mm\
12. **Joc**: that the foundation goes in first the walls go up second (you know) . . .

In this standard position for small-talk, Benny introduces the topic of Jock's management skills and proceeds to pay a compliment *you seem really good at it and awfully confident* (lines 3, 5). In this position, before the start of a meeting, their talk is clearly off-record. Indeed it seems unlikely that, in their relatively masculine community of practice, Benny would have made these comments, especially to a male superior, once others had arrived. This is a nice example, then, of RP: an off-record, supportive comment which clearly relates to the goals of the organization. It is expressed using normatively feminine stylistic discourse features, such as intensifiers (*really, awfully*) and the epistemic verb *seem*. Appreciation, such as this, even from a subordinate, is likely to encourage Jock to continue to perform well and to maintain good management skills. Yet, by virtue of its position and off-record status, the approval has no formal or official weight.

Similar examples occur elsewhere throughout our data. In one workplace a team member who had been working on a relatively minor aspect of the organization's work for some time, expressed appreciation to the CEO for explicitly recognizing the value of this work by including reference to it in the agenda of a meeting of high-status managers. In another organization, a wry but explicitly appreciative comment, *we missed you*, from a subordinate to their manager returning from leave, served as a way of introducing a jocular complaint about the deputy who had temporarily replaced the manager. In all these cases, the expression of appreciation qualifies as RP, an indirect way of attending to workplace relationships and thus maintaining team momentum on the project. In general, too, the approval is expressed using features which could be considered relatively feminine in style.

How then might creating team through giving approval be expressed in a more masculine style at work? Interestingly, the most frequent way in which explicit approval was expressed in many of the meetings we recorded conformed to the more masculine style of compliment-giving described above: i.e. short, pithy, abbreviated, positive evaluations. We have large numbers of examples of brief comments offered at the end of a presentation or a report, for instance: *good, great, fine, well done, nice job*, and so on.[46] Such comments were produced by both women and men in giving explicit approval to other team members, and were especially frequent from managers to subordinates in reporting sessions. They were minimal, unelaborated and business-like – conventionally masculine in style. More relevant as instances of RP, however, are less explicit, off-record ways of giving approval. Can these too be accomplished in more masculine ways?

As illustrated in example 3.10, instances of off-record approval, qualifying as RP, tended, like small-talk, to occur at the peripheries or boundaries of workplace interaction. These were components of interaction which were not recorded in the minutes, or even heard by the group as a whole, and often occurred before a meeting started or after it finished. Though we do not have many examples in our data, since like other instances of RP, they tend to occur around the edges of workplace talk, masculine ways of doing RP by giving approval clearly do occur. Throwaway, laconic comments such as *nice job*, given by one colleague to another in the corridor after a presentation, for instance, or *you nailed them* following a confrontational meeting, provide examples which undoubtedly contributed to team spirit, and conform to the more masculine end of the style continuum. Characteristically low key, terse and minimal, they none the less serve the function of creating team when they occur. Again, this is clearly an area meriting further research.

Our data suggests that relatively masculine ways of giving approval, both explicit and implicit, on-record and off-record, may actually be preferred in many New Zealand workplaces. Brief, positive comments were certainly more frequent in our data than lengthy, elaborated examples such as 3.8. In terms of national ideology and the related explicit rhetoric, New Zealand is a determinedly socially egalitarian society. As I mentioned in chapter 1 (note 17), 'tall poppies' are not readily tolerated, and overt praise or on-record approval is often regarded with suspicion, especially in workplaces where more masculine discursive norms predominate, and especially when directed upwards.[47] Certainly, more effusive, on-record positive feedback tends to be restricted to relatively formal, sanctioned occasions in many workplaces. However, it is important to bear in mind that norms in this area are clearly variable, and different communities of practice develop different preferred styles of doing RP, including ways of giving positive feedback.

Conclusion

This chapter has examined Fletcher's concept of relational practice, the wide range of off-line, backstage work that people do which typically goes unrecognized and unrewarded in the workplace. A range of different ways in which people do relational practice in workplace discourse have been identified and illustrated, including ways of looking after the success of a project (preserving), looking after the professional needs of colleagues (mutual empowerment), and ways of strengthening collegiality (creating team). Illustrating how they are instantiated in interaction, I have demonstrated some of the ways in which these practices are 'disappeared' or rendered invisible in workplace discourse. It is this which transforms them into what Fletcher calls 'women's work', better described as 'feminized discourse'.

Given that RP is by definition off-record, background, relational work, which is typically discounted in the workplace, the gendered nature of the concept is an obvious issue which has been critically examined in this chapter. Fletcher points out that 'women are relied on to be the carriers of relational responsibility in society'.[48] In her conceptualization, RP is quintessentially feminine both in function and style – subtle support work, invisible and unappreciated, yet positive in its intention of fostering behaviours that will assist a team to achieve their goals. Like a great deal of stereotypical women's work (such as housework and child-care), RP is invisible and off-record relational support work. It is work which oils the social wheels, but generally goes unnoticed. The examples in this chapter have indicated how this process is accomplished – how RP often operates at the interstices of what is considered legitimate business, at the boundaries of meetings, in passing in the corridor, over lunch, and so on (making it very hard to capture on a tape-recorder, incidentally); and how it typically takes the form of off-record talk, such as small-talk which is generally not perceived as 'real' work. It is this characteristic – its off-record status – that strongly associates RP with feminine stereotypes. Like cooking, cleaning, shopping and washing, men can do it too, but the societal perception is that these are feminine activities.

This chapter has also considered, however, the possibility that manifestations of relational practice may differ in different communities of practice, questioning the absoluteness of the equation of relational practice with a feminine style of discourse. It has been suggested that the concept of RP may be too narrowly conceived, and may reflect a somewhat blinkered perspective on what 'counts' as relational work. For some communities of practice it seems possible that more masculine styles of interaction may serve as accepted and standard means of doing RP, by creating team, for example. Thus particular ways of doing small-talk, more contestive styles of humour, and very low-key and minimal ways of expressing approval can be perceived as relatively masculine ways of creating team. When one of the effects of such interactions is to further workplace objectives, and the interaction is, strictly speaking, off-record, there seems a *prima facie* case for including consideration of such interactional work as RP. The range of ways of accomplishing RP in diverse communities of practice, and their effect on workplace relationships and structures, is clearly a challenging area for further research.

In concluding this chapter, two further points deserve consideration. The first concerns the significance of strategic uses of RP. Given that one of the criteria used in defining RP relates to its function in advancing the transactional goals of the workplace, it is interesting to speculate on the potential that RP offers for strategically managing workplace talk. As illustrated in chapter 2, one characteristic of the behaviour of effective managers is their skill in integrating relational and transactional aspects of talk. Conventional RP strategies appear to offer an ideal vehicle for this purpose, especially for those who prefer low-key, less explicit methods of achieving workplace objectives. Given that indirectness is generally associated with feminine rather than

masculine patterns of interaction, this suggestion supports the interpretation of RP as a feminine means of achieving workplace goals.
However, as the discussion in the final section has suggested, it is also
possible that more masculine ways of doing RP offer different but
equally strategically effective means of achieving workplace objectives.
And, given that more feminine ways of achieving strategic objectives
often go unnoticed, or are not valued, by those in positions of power,
noting alternatives seems worthwhile for women who want to broach
the glass ceiling.[49]

A second point relates to the implications of different ways of doing
RP for levels of employee comfort at work. The suggestion that there
are differently gendered styles of doing RP provides one explanation
for the discomfort experienced by people who find that they do not
fit into a particular community of practice. Some men have reported,
for instance, that they experience discomfort with the supportive, very
personalized, and interactionally highly involved styles associated with
more feminine communities of practice. Others feel less than happy
with the contestive, challenging styles which typify some more
masculine workplaces. In her study of an Australian bank, Beck notes
that 'a considerable number of senior women managers despaired at
the ongoing masculinized culture . . . one woman referred to the Bank's
"macho" culture which had driven her to leave her post after only
eight months.'[50] Similarly, one of our participants commented that he
was so uneasy with what he experienced as the aggressive, interactional
style of his IT team that he applied to move to another team.[51] It seems
worth considering, then, how discursive strategies which appear so
alienating to some employees, may form the underpinning for or
constitute the bonds of strong working relationships between others.
In Fletcher's account, RP fosters workplace relationships through
behaviours associated with women, behaviours conventionally regarded
as polite, facilitative and feminine. The discussion in this chapter has
considered different ways of creating team, while also furthering workplace goals, ways typical of more masculine styles of interaction,
suggesting that the term RP may need to be 'de-gendered'.[52] RP may
be best regarded not as an intrinsically feminine concept, but as one
which may be expressed differently in different workplace contexts
within different communities of practice. The next chapter explores
the idea that humour may serve as a vehicle for gender identity
construction in the workplace, as well as a resource for resolving
tensions between different facets of social identity at work.

NOTES

1 This chapter draws extensively from Holmes and Marra (2004) and further extends the analysis in that paper.

2 Fletcher (1999: 2).

3 Goleman (1995).

4 Fletcher (1999: 108–9, 133). Fletcher (1999) draws on relational theory (Gilligan 1982, Miller and Stiver 1997) to develop the notion of 'relational practice'.

5 The use of the term 'face' in a technical sense derives from the work of Goffman (1974).

6 Brown and Levinson (1987: 59). For valuable discussion of the term 'rapport' as a component in an alternative model for analysing interpersonal interaction, see Spencer-Oatey (2000).

7 See Holmes and Marra (2004) for a fuller discussion of all these points.

8 Fletcher (1999: 48).

9 'Self-achieving', the fourth theme, is illustrated in chapter 6, but it is not explored further in this book, partly because it was difficult to identify instances of 'self-achieving' which qualified on all three defining criteria as instances of other-oriented RP, as opposed to instances of self-promotion.

10 Fletcher (1999: 49–55). Compare Goffman's (1967) concept of face preservation and Brown and Levinson's (1987) negative face.

11 See Holmes and Marra (2004) for a wider range of strategies and examples. See also chapter 4 on humour as mitigation, and chapter 5 on ways of avoiding conflict.

12 Holmes (2000a).

13 See also Holmes and Marra (2004).

14 See chapter 1. This claim is also extensively documented in many of the articles in Holmes and Meyerhoff (2003a).

15 The material in this section is based on and further developed from Holmes (2005a).

16 Fletcher (1999: 56). Interestingly, research in the area of organizational communication suggests that women are much less likely to have mentors than are males; see e.g. Wood (2000).

17 For discussion of mentoring behaviours, see Ashford and Cummings (1983), Bloch (1993), Williams et al. (1998), Clutterbuck (1992), Caldwell and Carter (1992), Dymock (1999), Kram (1988), Zeus and Skiffington (2002). Chapter 6 discusses how workplace narratives may instantiate this mentoring function of RP.

18 See Edmondson (1981), Schiffrin (1994), Holmes (1995) for discussion of these discourse devices.

19 See Thomas (1985) on challenging tags.

20 Bass (1998: 7), Proctor-Thomson and Parry (2001: 171).
21 See, for example, Burke and McKeen (1990), Akande (1994), Ehrich (1994), Sinclair (1998).
22 Fletcher (1999: 95).
23 Fletcher (1999: 74).
24 Holmes (2000b) explores in some detail the distribution, content and complex functions of small-talk and social talk at work. See also Coupland (2000).
25 See, for example, the conversation between a personal assistant and manager in a government organization concerning taking time off in the school holidays in Holmes (2000b: 53). Our hospital data also provides many examples of the skilful interweaving of small-talk with on-task talk in the interactions between nurses and patients. In this relationship, the small-talk functions not to 'create team' with a colleague but rather to establish good rapport with the patients, often in order to help them feel more relaxed with hospital procedures (Holmes and Major 2003). See also Macdonald (2002).
26 This section is developed from Holmes and Stubbe (2003a).
27 Coupland (2000).
28 Holmes (2000b).
29 A degree of caution is necessary here. From a methodological perspective, one can't be sure that *all* the small-talk which occurred in the relevant recording period was actually recorded by all participants. Despite reassurance on this issue, some participants may have regarded small-talk as not worth recording, and others may have edited out relevant material. So although small-talk occurred in all workplaces, comments on quantities and gender distribution must be treated with caution. The association with femininity, on the other hand, is uncontentious.
30 Fletcher (1999: 2–3), italics in original.
31 Fletcher (1999: 15). Indeed Fletcher argues that RP is not just overlooked but is actively 'disappeared' or erased because of its association with the feminine, and thus with soft rather than 'hard' business practices (1999: 3).
32 Fletcher (1999: 133).
33 Eckert and McConnell-Ginet (2003: 11).
34 This definition is discussed in detail in Holmes (2000b).
35 Baxter (2003), Harvey (1997).
36 These contrasting types of humour are illustrated in chapter 4.
37 Holmes and Stubbe (2003a: 587).
38 See Holmes and Marra (2002a, 2002b) for examples.
39 Stubbe (2000a). See also Kuiper (1991) and Kiesling (2001) for instances of this kind of 'masculine' discourse among New Zealand rugby players and US fraternity members respectively, and Bell and Major (2004) for an

analysis of the exploitation of this kind of humour in billboard advertisements for New Zealand beer.

40 See Holmes and Marra (2004a).

41 Fletcher (1999: 74). It is also worth noting that approval may serve as a strategy for *mutual empowerment*, another of Fletcher's themes, since it may encourage others in directions which could be regarded as beneficial to their careers. This is a nice illustration of the multifunctional nature of all talk, and also of the inevitable overlap between categories of RP referred to above.

42 See, for example, Herbert (1990), Holmes (1995), Johnson and Roen (1992).

43 Holmes (1988a, 1993, 1995).

44 Holmes (1988a, 1995).

45 Holmes (2000a), Holmes and Stubbe (2003a, 2003b).

46 See also chapter 2 which provides a number of examples of how Clara gives approval.

47 See Mouly and Sankara (2002), Olsson (1996), Feather (1996), Parry and Proctor (2000), Stedman (2002), Peeters (2004).

48 Fletcher (1999: 15).

49 Cf. Baxter (2003: 159ff), Kendall (2004).

50 Beck (1999: 205).

51 Cf. Trauth (2002).

52 This proposal also has interesting implications for relational theory, which assumes that the primary function of RP is to foster interpersonal relations in order to promote personal growth (e.g. Gilligan 1982, Miller and Stiver 1997). If alternative forms of RP are recognized, the answer to the question of whether they have the same transformative effects on the individual is by no means obvious.

CHAPTER FOUR

Humour in the Workplace – Not Just Men's Play

Introduction

Humour provides a rich source of insights on the complexities of social interaction, including gendered aspects of workplace discourse. Both women and men crack jokes, exchange jocular abuse, and tell funny stories at work. And the amount of humour and type of humour that occurs at work tend to vary according to a very wide range of factors. Perhaps most important is the workplace culture – the 'tone' of the particular community of practice in which people work. But, as indicated throughout this book, there are many other influences too. Our analysis of the frequency of humour in meetings between friends as opposed to business colleagues, for instance, indicated that humour was 10 times as frequent in friendship groups compared to business meetings.[1] Typically, socializing at home or in the pub, or even sharing a morning tea break, involves considerably more humour than on-task interaction at work. But humour does occur in the workplace; and while informal interactions typically generate most humour, there is evidence of a surprising amount of humour even in large formal meetings in some organizations.[2] Other factors which influence the amount and type of humour at work include the relationship between those talking; their personalities; the size of the group; the kind of interaction, speech event, or 'activity type'[3] which they are engaged in; its length; and even the particular point which has been reached in the encounter.[4] So, while gender is the focus of the discussion in this chapter, it is important to bear in mind that it is only one of a number of factors which contribute to different patterns of humour in the workplace.

On the other hand, as argued in chapter 1, gender is always there in the background. At some level, we are always aware of the sex of those we are talking to, and we bring to every interaction our familiarity with societal gender stereotypes and the gendered norms to which women and men are expected to conform. Workplace humour illustrates this well. Drawing on our extensive analyses of workplace discourse, this chapter examines three different aspects of the interaction of humour and gender in the workplace. The first section outlines the ways in which humour can be characterized as a gendered discourse resource, and characteristics of more feminine and more masculine styles of humour in the workplace are described and illustrated.[5] Then the discussion turns to ways in which women and men make use of humour in negotiating their gender identities alongside their professional identities at work, illustrating in particular how humour serves as a valuable discursive resource for integrating the conflict that some experience between power and gender identity in workplace interaction. The final section discusses how humour may act as a hard-to-contest conduit for gendered workplace behaviour, and even workplace sexism. Humour can provide an oblique means for gender to creep into workplace interaction in ways that are difficult to challenge without losing face.[6]

Gendered Humour in Interaction

Chapter 1 described and illustrated features of feminine and masculine interactional styles. Particular women and men at specific moments in specific workplace contexts draw on these gendered resources to achieve different goals. And we all draw on our familiarity with these gendered interactional resources when we interact; we exploit people's knowledge of what features index a more feminine or a more masculine way of talking, as we construct our particular social identity in any context, including our social identity at work. Humour is an important discursive resource in this process.

Explicitly articulating these gendered norms, Mercilee Jenkins claimed, in a provocative early paper on gender and humour, that 'women's humour' is cooperative, inclusive, supportive, integrated, spontaneous and self-healing, while 'men's humour' is exclusive, challenging, segmented, pre-formulated and self-aggrandizing.[7] A social psychologist, Mary Crawford, noted that the features Jenkins proposed were 'strikingly congruent' with her respondents' self-reports about the way they used humour.[8] Other researchers who have analysed humour in interaction also report that, at least in friendship groups, humour used by women tends to be more cooperative than humour used by men, in that it builds on others' humour more.[9] Context is crucial, however, and Jen Hay notes that, in particular, the composition of the audience for one's gender performance is very influential.[10] She demonstrates that different types of humour were differently distributed in single-sex as opposed to mixed-sex groups, and notes that, in her data, stereotypically gendered styles of humour appeared 'most marked in mixed groups', suggesting a contribution from 'gender stereotyping and expectations of the "appropriate" gender-specific behaviour'.[11]

Interpreting 'women's humour' as humour associated with a more feminine stance, or humour which is culturally coded as feminine, and 'men's humour' as indexing a more masculine style of humour, this research indicates that, like other aspects of interaction, styles of humour are conventionally gendered. More specifically, it appears that a co-operative style of humour is widely perceived as more feminine, while contestive and competitive humour is regarded as more masculine in style. So what exactly does it mean to use humour cooperatively as opposed to contestively?

Cooperative or Feminine Styles of Humour in the Workplace

There are at least two distinct ways in which talk might qualify for the description 'cooperative'. Firstly, the *content* may be cooperative in that the speaker supports what was said by the previous speaker; and secondly, the *style* may be cooperative, in that the participants work together harmoniously to construct the message. Both of these ways of being cooperative were identifiable in the humorous exchanges in our workplace data.

Cooperative content or supportive humour

Humour is cooperative in content when people contribute material which supports the proposition of a previous speaker. In other words, the participants cooperate in various ways to strengthen a claim, or elaborate a picture, or emphasize a point. I have described this as 'supportive' humour.[12]

In the following example (which, as is often the case, does not appear very funny to an outsider, but provided the participants with considerable amusement), Kirsty, Penelope and Scott support each other's comments about the fleeting nature of spring in the city of Wellington.

Example 4.1

Context: Meeting of a group of 4 male and 4 female regional managers of a national organization.

1.	**Kir**:	I mean when is spring and when should /[laughs]\
2.	**How**:	/[laughs]\
3.	**Pen**:	well sometimes some people think it's the first of September
4.	**Kir**:	mm
5.	**Pen**:	and some people think it's the twenty-first
6.	**Kir**:	I mean /it was\ last week here in Wellington
7.	**Pen**:	/mm\
8.	**Sco**:	er [laughs] <u>was</u>
9.	**Ral**:	/mm\
10.	**Pen**:	/mm\ I noticed

Scott and Penelope add to the humour introduced by Kirsty's comment that spring had come and gone in one week in Wellington (line 6). Scott repeats and emphasizes the past tense verb *was* (line 8), underlining the fact that spring is over, and that it was short-lived. Penelope responds with an ironic comment *I noticed* (line 10), implying that it was so short that it was easy to miss. Both Scott and Penelope thus cooperate in constructing this humorous sequence, by providing comments that are supportive of the point that Kirsten is making; their contributions are consistent with and elaborate her original proposition.

When people describe 'women's talk' as being 'supportive', they are often referring to this aspect of talk – the fact that speakers agree with, support and confirm the content of each other's contributions. Jennifer Coates, for instance, describes how participants in the women's groups she studied engaged in cooperative talk, mirroring each other's content, and affirming each other's stories by producing similar stories to support the points being made.[13] This kind of supportive talk is thus culturally coded as gendered and, in particular, as feminine.

Cooperative style or collaborative humour

Humour may also be a cooperative discursive achievement, jointly constructed by participants. When people work together to produce a humorous sequence, with each person contributing to and building on the contributions of the others, the overall effect is clearly cooperative. I have labelled this a 'collaborative' style of humour.[14] Example 4.2 provides an illustration of this style from the workplace corpus.

Example 4.2

Context: Meeting of a group of 4 male and 4 female regional managers of a national organization. There is a lot of laughter and overlapping concurrent unintelligible talk throughout this excerpt.

1. **Pen**:   the fact that we don't go to Malt [*name of a town in New Zealand*]
2. **How**:   mm
3. **Pen**:   doesn't mean that people from Malt can't
4. **Sco**:   yeah
5. **Pen**:   go somewhere to get help mm cos they were interested enough t-
6. **Ral**:   if you live in Malt you need to go somewhere /(to get help)\
7.   /[general laughter]\
8. **Sco**:   there is actually quite a big consultancy in Malt
9. **How**:   is there?
10. **Sco**:   yeah
11. **Hen**:   I was told many years ago that Malt /was the\
12. **Mal**:   /Malt\
13. **Hen**:   /heart of the\ wife swapping area for [*name of province*]
14. **Mal**:   /(Malt)\ [*pronounced with local pronunciation*]
15. **Sco**:   /isn't\ it Malt that had the highest rate of um

16. **Pen**:   /ex ex nuptial\ birth- births /ex\
17. **Sco**:   /S T oh no that's Hopeville\ /highest\ the highest
        STD rate per capita
18. **Pen**:   /Malt had th-\ the highest
19. **Sco**:   /Malt or Hopeville [laughs]\
20. **Kir**:   /did they?\
21. **Pen**:   rates of ex ex nuptial births at one point . . .
22. **Mal**:   it's the alcohol that does it
23. **How**:   [laughs] it's the alcohol
24.   [*General laughter and overlapping talk continues through-*
        out next section]
25. **Pen**:   poor old Malt
26. **Kir**:   we should be there
27. **Sco**:   we should be there
28. **Pen**:   we should be there
29.   [general laughter]

This is a section from a much longer humorous sequence. The humour revolves around the disadvantages of living in a particular small, isolated rural town. Participants work together collaboratively to develop the topic at length, making more and more outrageous claims about the horrors of life in the town, which I have here given the pseudonym Malt. Each utterance supports and further develops the proposition of the previous contributor. There is a great deal of fast and frequently overlapping speech, as well as laughter throughout. The contributions are closely integrated stylistically with one person filling in another's gaps and answering their queries. There are requests for confirmation (e.g. lines 9, 15, 20), and a great deal of repetition extending from single words and phrases, e.g. *highest* (lines 15, 17, 18), *outpost* (lines 31, 32, 34), to whole clauses, e.g. the refrain *we should be there* is repeated by several different voices at different pitches and volumes in a way which is strongly reminiscent of the different parts in a motet or madrigal (lines 26, 27, 28).

Collaborative talk has long been associated with women's discourse in the language and gender literature, as indicated in chapter 1. It is a well-attested feature of feminine interactional styles. Coates provides a detailed description of the collaborative discourse features which characterized the organization of talk in the interactions between women friends that she analysed.[15] Labelling it 'all-together-now' (ATN) talk, she illustrates how these women jointly constructed conversations, completed each other's utterances, provided encouraging feedback in the form of carefully positioned minimal responses (*mm*, *yes*), and echoed each other's comments.[16] In our workplace data, people who got on well with each other, members of close-knit teams, often made use of these strategies in constructing humorous sequences. As example 4.2 illustrates, using this feminine style of jointly constructed talk, participants smoothly link their turns to the contributions of others completing other people's clauses, paraphrasing, helpfully supplying possible words to fill the gap when a speaker is searching for a lexical item, answering queries, and contributing constructively to a shared floor.[17] (See also example 4.15 below.)

The characterization of a collaborative style as normatively feminine is reinforced by earlier research on gender and humour, especially in friendship groups.[18] Eder found girl's teasing to be mostly collaborative in style, in that the girls expanded and added to each other's teasing in a way that did not exclude others, while the boys' teasing tended to be more competitive in style.[19] There is considerable support, then, for the notion that supportively oriented, collaborative, jointly constructed humour is typically associated with more feminine styles of interaction. In other words, collaborative humour can be considered another component of more feminine discourse styles in the workplace.

 ## Contestive or Masculine Styles of Humour in the Workplace

The converse of cooperative, supportive and collaboratively constructed styles of humour is challenging, contestive and non-collaboratively constructed kinds of humour. What do such styles of humour look like?

Challenging content or contestive humour

Humour is challenging in content when people contribute material which contests or contradicts what has been said by a previous speaker. In other words, participants challenge a claim, or disagree with a point, or refute an argument put forward by a previous contributor. I have described this as 'contestive' humour.[20]

Example 4.3 is from a meeting of a group where challenging contributions to the meeting discourse occurred frequently.

Example 4.3

Context: Regular weekly meeting of an IT project team in a large commercial organization. There are 6 male participants at this meeting. Barry is the meeting chair. Callum is the minute taker. Callum has failed to update a header, leading Barry to think he's got the wrong document.

1. **Cal**: I definitely sent you the right one
2. **Bar**: [laughs]
3. **Eri**: yep Callum did fail his office management [laugh] word-processing lesson
4. **Cal**: I find it really hard being perfect at everything

In line 3, Eric makes Callum the target of a jocular insult, *Callum did fail his office management word processing lesson*. Callum responds by challenging or contesting Eric's claim with his own mock-modest claim, *I find it really hard being perfect at everything* (line 4). By asserting his overall superiority, Callum contests Eric's contribution by challenging the put-down intent of his jocular abuse.

This kind of talk, contesting the content of previous speaker's utterances, tends to be associated with more masculine ways of interacting.[21] Coates, for instance, describes how many of the men she studied, and especially the younger men, engaged in extremely competitive talk, arguing about issues such as who had drunk most, who had got the better of authority most effectively, and so on.[22] She illustrates with examples which demonstrate the use of unmitigated face-threatening acts, abusive swearing, and deflating comments in response to narratives intended to construct a heroic identity.[23] Not surprisingly, then, contestive humour is also perceived as typical of more masculine styles of interaction in the workplace, as I will discuss in more detail below.

Challenging style or non-collaborative humour

Humour can be challenging or uncooperative not only in its content, but also in the way it is expressed. In an uncooperative or less collaborative style, participants typically compete for the floor, vying with each other, for instance, to produce amusing and witty comments. Disruptive interruptions are used to challenge claims in this style, and speakers may also adopt a parrying 'one-at-a-time' (OAAT) pattern of talk.[24] Contributions often take the form of succinct quips or brief witty one-liners which are relatively loosely semantically linked, and often have a competitive edge, as illustrated in example 4.4.

Example 4.4

Context: Regular meeting of an IT project team in a large commercial organization. There are 6 male participants at this meeting. This is towards the end of the meeting and they are discussing where to go for a company dinner, and more specifically commenting on the way that Eric tends to take over the kitchen whenever they go to a restaurant.

1.	**Eri**:	I haven't I haven't done that kitchen so
2.	**Cal**:	/(yeah)\
3.	**Eri**:	/that'll\ be one for the collection
4.	**Bar**:	[laughs] you /can't you can't\ remember it
5.	**Eri**:	/( ) [laughs]\
6.	**Mar**:	lot of kitchens he doesn't remember
7.	**Bar**:	/[laughs]\
8.	**Eri**:	/[laughs]\
9.	**Cal**:	no no one else would probably want to sit with us anyway Jacob

Eric comments that the place they are proposing to go for dinner will provide him with a new kitchen to explore (lines 1, 3). Barry, Mark and Callum then each contribute comments which are semantically linked but delivered autonomously – each contribution is syntactically and prosodically independent, and the men compete to amuse each other with their comments. The contributions are independently constructed with disruptive overlapping and, unlike the collaborative sequences illustrated above, with no syntactically integrated structures.[25]

This challenging or competitive style of humour has been associated with masculine rather than feminine interactional styles by a number of researchers.[26] Hay suggests that wit and 'coolness' are traits valued

Humour

COOPERATIVE   CHALLENGING

Propositional orientation

Supportive _____ Contestive
proposition/content   proposition/content

Stylistic orientation

Collaborative _____ Non-collaborative
style   style

Figure 4.1   Cooperative vs. challenging humour: content and style

more highly by males than females.[27] Clearly, the effective use of
snappy, witty one-liners is one strategy which can contribute in
constructing a 'cool' image. And while Eder observed competitiveness
amongst girls in her study, she found that teasing humour was used
by some girls for more conventionally feminine, peace-making
functions, namely, to 'actively try to defuse jealousy and competitive
feelings'.[28] It is also worth noting that oral humour frequently has a
performance quality, and the tendency for masculine humour to be
competitive could be seen as contributing to overt qualities of display
or performance in interaction.[29] This challenging and competitive mode
of humour in interaction is generally regarded, then, as typical of a
more masculine style.

These different ways of doing humour, described here along
two major dimensions, i.e. *propositionally* cooperative (supportive) or
challenging (contestive) in semantic content, vs. *stylistically* cooperative (collaborative) or challenging (non-collaborative), provide rich
pragmatic resources which are available for the construction of gender
identity in the workplace. (See figure 4.1.)

Using Humour in the Construction of Gender
Identity at Work

Humour is a versatile discursive resource, not least for constructing
aspects of social identity. The differently gendered styles of humour
identified in the previous section provide sophisticated resources
for men and women in the construction of their social, personal and

professional identities at work. The very wide range of functions served by humour, and its inherent ambiguity and creative potential, make it a rich resource for expressing complex social meanings. In particular, humour can serve as a means of integrating and reconciling disparate and even conflicting aspects of workplace identity. In this section, I provide a range of examples to illustrate ways in which participants exploit the potential of humour to construct and integrate gender and professional identity within the context of the ongoing demands of everyday interaction in the New Zealand workplaces we researched.

The first example is a paradigmatic illustration of contestive humour from a very masculine workplace, illustrating the kind of challenging, sarcastic talk referred to in chapter 3 as endemic in this particular workplace. Indeed, as we have suggested in earlier research, this style of humour appears to function as a resource for creating team in more masculine communities of practice.[30] The relevant team (who featured in examples 4.3 and 4.4 above) was part of a large, white-collar telecommunications organization with a predominantly male staff. Team members met regularly to work on a specific IT project, though they had little face-to-face contact outside these meetings. Each member brought different expertise to bear on the task; and they shared a well-established jargon which enabled them to communicate succinctly within their areas of professional expertise.[31]

Example 4.5[32]

Context: Regular meeting of an IT project team in a large commercial organization. At this meeting there are 6 men, and a woman who is linked by telephone because she has recently had a baby and is working from home. Barry is the meeting chair.

1. **Dud**: have you read it?
2. **Bar**: I have
3. **Dud**: have you already?
4. **Bar**: [laughs]
5. **Jac**: and and Callum's read it already
6. **Bar**: [laughs]
7. **Dud**: you don't have enough work to do Barry
8. **Bar**: I read it I was up till about (   ) no /[laughs]\
9. **Jac**: /[laughs]\

10.	**Eri**:	well I was up till about midnight last night too
11.	**Cal**:	surfing right?
12.	**Eri**:	no
13.	**Bar**:	[laughs] surfing the net

This contestive and challenging exchange serves to create team and cement solidarity between members of a group who habitually inter-act in this very masculine interactional style. It also serves as a means of constructing professional and gender identity for the members of this group. The humour takes the form of almost ritualistic challenges to professional expertise and competence, a recurring theme for this team. Dudley's jocular insult (line 7) is based on the assumption that a high workload is the norm for this group. Boasting about how hard you work (lines 8, 10) is clearly acceptable in this group. Maintaining the contestive style of humour, Callum challenges Eric's claim that he worked late with the accusation that he was *surfing right?* (line 11), and Barry supports Callum *surfing the net* (line 13) when Eric denies the charge. The humour is seamlessly integrated into the normal contestive style of workplace talk for this team. There is no disjunction between their transactional style of talk and their use of humour to create team. Just as they constantly challenge each other's recommendations about the next step to take in developing their project, so they challenge each other's claims about less serious issues such as who is working hard-est. In doing so, the members of this team use a consistently masculine style of humour, a style which is characteristic of the interactions of this particular IT team in this particular community of practice.

Example 4.6 provides a similar contestive exchange between a man and a woman in another IT organization. The tone is considerably less abrasive than in example 4.5 (something which is impossible to convey in print), but the jocular teasing exchange serves similar functions in creating team, while simultaneously constructing aspects of the social identities of the participants.

Example 4.6[33]

Context: Board meeting of 2 women and 3 men in a small IT company. Jill is the company Chair. Sam is a board member. The board meeting is almost finished and the main agenda items have been covered. The participants are now discussing only minor points.

1. **Sam**: ke- keep going until there's only one person standing
2. **Jil**: [laughs] oh you've been to our board meetings before [laughs]

Though delivered in a good-humoured tone, Sam's comment could be regarded as subversive: i.e. implicitly criticizing Jill for the length of the meeting and the fact that she has not yet called it to a close. By contrast, Jill's laughter and her humorous reply though sparkily contestive in style, are supportive in content, suggesting she agrees that their meetings are lengthy. These two people get on well, and they work together in a very positive and supportive community of practice where this kind of good-humoured teasing is part of the interactional common currency.[34] In terms of identity construction, Sam's contestive and subversive humour is typical of more masculine interactional styles, while Jill's response is more complex, delivering supportive content in a contestively humorous manner. This kind of response neatly exemplifies how Jill typically manages to integrate aspects of her feminine gender identity with her more authoritative professional role as Board Chair in a male-dominated community of practice.

Example 4.7 similarly illustrates the use of humour as a strategy for integrating disparate components of social identity, but in this case Penelope, the CEO of this team (who also featured in examples 4.1 and 4.2) uses a slightly different pattern for achieving this end in her rather more feminine community of practice.

Example 4.7

Context: Meeting of a group of regional managers of a national organization. Penelope is the chair of the meeting and the CEO of the organization.

1. **Pen**: are the clients expecting you to pay /anything\?
2. **Ing**: the clients know that it /it's their\ responsibility
3. but they also know that affordability is a key
4. **Pen**: so would so you didn't answer me very directly [laughing] there did you
5. **Ing**: [laughs]

In line 4, Penelope, challenges one of her team, Ingrid, for prevaricating in response to her straightforward question *are the clients expecting to pay anything?* (line 1). Penelope's comment, *you didn't answer me very directly*, occurs in the context of a longer funding discussion, which has identified a tendency to be 'soft' on realistic charging out of services as one source of the organization's financial problems. The tone is humorous and teasing, but the comment is clearly contestive in content, and challenging in style. Thus Penelope uses a normatively masculine style in querying the content of Ingrid's response to her original question. This is a face-threatening speech act, but in this meeting, which has been very serious up to this point, Penelope's use of humour attenuates or softens her serious, critical message. Again, the apparently conflicting demands of professional and gender identity for a woman in an authoritative position are mediated through humour.

In example 4.8, Jill, the board Chair in example 4.6, makes use of a different strategy to reconcile her professional identity with her gender identity. In this exchange, she humorously adopts a maternal social role, a strategy which acceptably integrates her authoritative position with her feminine gender (a strategy discussed in chapter 2).

Example 4.8[35]

Context: Board meeting of 2 women and 3 men in a small IT company. Tessa cannot find the mouse which she needs to take the minutes on the computer, as is normal in these meetings. Don is Tessa's husband.

1.	**Tes**:	where's my mouse?
2.	**Sam**:	([laughs])
3.	**Tes**:	/(er)\
4.	**Don**:	/(no well)\ you're sitting too far away
5.		from the /receiver\
6.	**Tes**:	/oh for\ goodness sakes how am I going to be able to do this
7.	**Don**:	eh? oh well I'll do it if you want [laughs]
8.	**Tes**:	well f- just tell me from there
9.	**Don**:	no I can't do that
10.	**Jil**:	okay well while while Tessa and Donald
11.		[laughs]: have a moment [laughs] . . .
12.		um so I'll go for a quick flick through the agenda

Tessa and Donald engage in a little skirmish, with Tessa complaining about the placing of the computer (lines 1, 6) and Donald dishing out advice (lines 4–5) and offering to come and help (line 7), which Tessa irritably rejects (line 8). Jill is about to start the meeting. Instead of ignoring the skirmish, asserting her professional identity, and authoritatively taking the floor, Jill takes the opportunity to re-establish a pleasant tone and pour oil on the troubled marital waters by humorously adopting the role of 'mother' or at least 'understanding older adult' rather than 'boss'. Her humour takes a very feminine form too, in that she playfully and supportively constructs the distracting pair as lovers who need a moment's privacy.

Jill's teasing comment (lines 10–11) is an effective strategy for asserting her authority in a low-key way in the face of this diversionary spat. Using humour as an integrative discursive strategy, she manages to have her cake and eat it too. Like Clara and Ginette, discussed in chapter 2, Jill uses humour to skilfully balance the need to be authoritative with attention to workplace relationships. Jill's preferred style of humour, however, is conventionally feminine, i.e. low-key and gentle (like her management style), rather than contestive and 'in your face'. By adopting a socially acceptable feminine (in this case 'maternal') style of doing authority, she effectively finesses the stylistic conflict which faces women in positions of authority.

In a very much more feminine community of practice, Leila frequently makes use of the same strategy, as illustrated in example 4.9. She humorously plays the role of mother to offset the more decisive and authoritative managerial stance required to get things done at other points in the meeting.

Example 4.9[36]

Context: Regular team meeting of 6 women in a government organization. The team is discussing the best use of resources to address some staffing problems.

1.   *[laughter throughout this section]*
2. **Lei**: Emma you are part of the solution in that I think that
           ( )
3. **Em**: I only want to be part of the problem
4. **XF**: really

5. **Lei:** [laughs] [in fun growly tone]: don't you dare be part of the problem
6. I'll keep on giving you vitamin C, bananas [laughs], chocolate fish [laughs]
7. I gave I gave um I you know everyone had chocolate fish last week
8. but Emma had more chocolate fish than anybody
9. the only thing was she had holes in her teeth /[laughs]\
10. **Em:** /I couldn't eat them\
11. **Lei:** she couldn't eat them [laughs]

In this excerpt, Emma establishes the humorous key by contesting Leila's statement that she is *part of the solution* (line 2) to the staffing problem, joking that she only wants *to be part of the problem* (line 3). Leila then playfully threatens to feed Emma with various goodies (line 6), points out that Emma had *more chocolate fish than anybody* (line 8) when they were handed out the previous week, and then reveals information about the holes in Emma's teeth (line 9).[37] The exchange concludes with a supportive comment from Emma, *I couldn't eat them* (line 10), which is echoed by Leila, *she couldn't eat them* (line 11). Listening to the recording confirms that despite the teasingly contestive content of lines 3 and 5, this is extremely collaborative, harmonious all-together-now talk. This good-humoured exchange, characterized by laughter and a joking tone, clearly reinforces the supportive team culture of this close-knit and feminine community of practice, but it also constructs Leila in a nurturing, motherly role.[38] Like Jill, Leila here uses the maternal option to reconcile authority and gender identity.

Humour is thus a useful strategy for constructing complex aspects of workplace identity, and especially for integrating the competing demands of power and politeness in the workplace, as well as the different aspects of professional and gender identity.[39] Chapter 2 described the different ways in which Clara, in a white-collar commercial organization, and Ginette, in a blue-collar factory context, balanced the often conflicting demands of power and gender.[40] In both cases, humour proved a crucial discursive resource in facilitating effective management, a pattern which was evident throughout our dataset. Leaders like these often choose to 'do power' authoritatively, issue orders peremptorily, and summarize action points succinctly, while also adopting a sparky, witty, and contestive style of humour – a style consistent with a predominantly masculine style of management.[41] Others, like Jill in example 4.8, Leila in example 4.9, and Smithy in example 2.19, more often take a different route, using humour expressed in a low-key and conventionally feminine style to defuse tension and consolidate relationships.

Clearly humour is used in a wide variety of ways at work, including, as argued in the previous section, ways that may be perceived as gendered in approach and style. In this section, I have illustrated how people exploit the potential that humour offers for constructing different kinds of gender identity in the workplace, and especially for harmoniously integrating the construction of particular kinds of gender identity with aspects of professional identity at different points in workplace interaction. Moreover, while more research is clearly needed, I have indicated in this section how humour may offer, for people in management positions in particular, one means of reconciling the potentially conflicting requirements of one's workplace or professional identity with one's preferred personal style of interaction.

Humour a Subversive Channel for Reinforcing Gender Stereotypes[42]

Humour sometimes acts as a channel for more explicitly gendered discourse at work, a discourse which may act to reinforce stereotypes of women's and men's interests and behaviours, or which, more subversively, may subtly undermine the rights of women to be treated as equals in the workplace.[43]

I have suggested that gender is always potentially relevant in interaction; in other words gender should always be considered in attempting to interpret the social meanings conveyed in talk, even if participants are not always conscious of its influence on their behaviour. In general, it seems likely that awareness of the relevance of gender in interaction moves in and out of participants' consciousness. Sometimes people are very aware of gender as an issue in workplace talk; at other times gender creeps into workplace discourse more subtly. On occasion, then, participants' gender identities are explicitly invoked or become the focus of humorous exchanges; at times gender emerges as an overt topic or issue in humorous interaction; at other times, gender emerges less blatantly as a focus of humorous discussion. Some examples will illustrate these points.

Gender stereotypes as a source of workplace humour

In example 4.10 the participants perform or construct a stereotypical feminine identity, reflecting and reinforcing patterns associated with female behaviour in New Zealand society more widely. The exchange draws on the shared experience and attitudes of three professional women who work for a government ministry, expressing their awareness of the fact that on any particular working day they might not be dressed appropriately to 'meet the Minister'.

Example 4.10[44]

Context: Three professional women at morning tea break in a government ministry discussing the problems which arise when someone is unexpectedly summoned to see the Minister.

1.	**Eve**:	I think we need a ministry suit just hanging up in the cupboard
2.		/[laughs]\
3.	**Lei**:	/you can just\ imagine the problems with the length /[laughs]\
4.	**Eve**:	/it would have\ it would have to have an elastic waist so
5.		/that we [laughs]\ could just be yeah
6.	**Lei**:	/[laughs] yes that's right [laughs]\
7.	**Eve**:	bunched in for some and [laughs] let it out
8.	**Lei**:	/laughs\
9.	**Eve**:	/out for others\
10.	**Les**:	and the jacket would have to be /long to cover all the bulges\
11.	**Lei**:	/no I'm quite taken with this\
12.	**Les**:	/so\
13.	**Eve**:	/[laughs]\
14.	**Lei**:	/now that\ that is very nice

The three colleagues construct a humorous fantasy sequence, an imaginary scenario describing an all-purpose suit which could be used by anyone unexpectedly summoned to see the Minister. These women are 'doing collegiality' in a very feminine collaborative style, jointly constructing a humorous sequence for mutual amusement. This is supportive discourse since the three women clearly agree with each other in terms of the overall idea and content of the excerpt. In addition to positive feedback explicitly endorsing the ideas proffered, such as *yeah* (line 5), *yes that's right* (line 6), *I'm quite taken with this* (line 11), *that's very nice* (line 14), the content of each suggestion supportively adds to, expands and elaborates the initial concept (lines 3, 4, 7, 10). The collaborative style is equally gendered with neat and cooperative latching of utterances between contributors: e.g. Eve's *let it out for others* (line 9) is picked up and expanded by Leila with *and the jacket would have to be long to cover all the bulges* (line 10).

This is most obviously gendered discourse, however, in that it is concerned with clothes and appearance – topics stereotypically associated with women. While one could conceive of men discussing the idea of an 'all-purpose Ministry suit', the specific requirements detailed, and the use of lexical terms such as *bunched in* (line 7), to describe the skirt, and *bulges* (line 10) to refer to body shape, identify this is as distinctly feminine collaborative humour.[45]

Example 4.11, by contrast, illustrates humorous discourse which is decidedly masculine in style and content. In this exchange, a group of men from a large commercial organization who are working together on an IT project, tease one of their team for voluntarily 'communicative' behaviour – behaviour which the others clearly regard as unmanly or feminine. The underlying assumption which provides the basis for the humour is that IT guys don't actually *talk* to clients.

Example 4.11

Context: Regular weekly meeting of an IT project team in a large commercial organization. There are 6 male participants at this meeting. Barry is the meeting chair. Callum is the minute taker. Callum's colleagues pretend to be horrified that he has actually talked face-to-face with clients.

1. **Bar**: but we can we can kill this
2. **Mar**: /well yep\

3. **Bar:**   /particular action\ point
4. **Mar:**   you can kill this particular action point
5. **Bar:**   and you /guys\
6. **Cal:**   /are\ you sure +++
7.   I took the opportunity of talking with some of the users
8. **Bar:**   what, again? [laughs] /[laughs]\
9. **Mar:**   /not again what are you doing talking to them\
10. **Bar:**   [laughs]: go on /Callum come on\
11. **XM:**   /[laughs]\

Barry and Marco suggest a particular proposed action be *killed*, i.e. dropped (lines 1–4), a stereotypically masculine metaphor. Callum protests, pointing out that the proposed action emerged from his discussions with users (lines 6–7). Barry and Marco then proceed to make fun of Callum's complaint, ridiculing the notion that he should actually talk, i.e. verbally communicate face-to-face, with clients (lines 8–10). They use a classic, competitive, OAAT style, each contribution attempting to 'top the previous speaker's contribution' in the humorous section (lines 8–10). (The verbal contributions overlap laughter, not other people's contributions.) The humour in this example is thus paradigmatic, masculine humour: it is contestive or challenging in its focus; it involves a competitive, minimally collaborative floor; and its content assumes, and implicitly reinforces, masculine conceptions of what count as acceptable communicative strategies for men at work. In such cases, the humour is predicated on underlying assumptions about gendered norms of interaction and shared understandings about what constitutes appropriately gendered discourse.

Example 4.12 provides a further brief instance of the exploitation of gender stereotypes as a source of workplace humour.

Example 4.12

Context: Meeting of members of a project team in a multinational white-collar commercial organization. Smithy, the project manager, is in the chair. There are 7 women and 7 men present. Two of the women comment on a colleague.

1. **Cla:**   he wants to get through month end first
2.   he's [smiling voice]: he can't multi-task:

3.   [Females laugh]
4. **Peg**: it's a bloke thing
5.   [general laughter]
6. **Cla**: [laughs]: yeah yeah:

Clara makes a disparaging, teasing comment on the limitations of a specific colleague in relation to managing complex work demands: *he can't multi-task* (line 2). The humorous effect is achieved not only by her tone, which is arch and teasing, but also by the group's knowledge that women have been promoted as 'multi-taskers' in the media recently. Peg's supportive humour, *it's a bloke thing* (line 4), makes the gender orientation of Clara's point explicit, broadening the scope of her remark to men in general. The humour constructs and emphasizes female solidarity, while simultaneously subverting wider societal values which, especially in large commercial organizations, tend to value male skills more highly than female, as discussed in earlier chapters.

These examples thus exploit and reinforce society-wide gender stereotypes, and humour serves as a legitimizing strategy, allowing people to make comments and express ideas that might be less acceptable if not packaged using a socially acceptable, humorous key. This point is even more apparent when sexual behaviour itself becomes a topic of workplace discourse.

Humour as a conduit for sex as a topic and sexist discourse at work

Sex in a variety of guises was a frequent source of workplace humour, and, not surprisingly, any reference to sex tended to thrust participants into adopting overtly gendered positions in the ensuing discourse. Hence, when the topic of sex surfaced in workplace talk, humour typically provided a conduit for even more explicitly gendered discourse.

Example 4.13 is from a small meeting in a government department where the participants, 2 women and 2 men, are discussing a strategy for managing the next phase of their work on performance schemes. In the opening lines (1–5), the women discuss the positioning of a chart on the wall. Gradually the relationship between the height of the chart and the length of the women's skirts becomes the focus of jointly constructed humour involving all the participants.

Example 4.13

Context: Towards the end of a meeting of 2 men and 2 women discussing performance schemes. The chair and most senior person is a woman, Selene.

1.	**Sel**:	it's also going on the wall I've decided
2.	**Wen**:	is it no
3.	**Sel**:	yes it's going on the wall <u>there</u> up high in the middle
4.	**Wen**:	up high so /people\ have to write like this
5.	**Sel**:	/yes\ up high so I don't have to lean down
6.	**Wen**:	/oh\
7.	**Sel**:	/and expose my\ underwear when I write on it
8.	**Wen**:	oh
9.	**Sel**:	which [laughs] I feel like in all the other ones [laughs] you're all
10.		cos you're always doing the same sort of ducking down
11.		and holding your skirt /kneeling on the floor\
12.	**Wen**:	/I guess I am\
13.	**Sel**:	so it's going up high /in the middle\
14.	**Wen**:	/either that or I wear\
15.	**Jon**:	/you're gonna\
16.	**Wen**:	a longer skirt /[laughs]\
17.	**Jon**:	take away his pleasures from work
18.		[*general laughter throughout lines 19–21*]
19.	**Don**:	we hadn't noticed
20.	**Don**:	never
21.	**Sel**:	no

The most senior woman, Selene, introduces the sexual element by a reference to exposing her underwear (line 7), and the two women then develop the point with a description of the problems of bending down in a short skirt (lines 10–12). Wendy makes the point even more explicit, *either that or I wear a longer skirt* (lines 14, 16), at which point one of the men, Jon, finally responds, and plays the part he has clearly been set up for. Jon extracts extra humour by suggesting it is the other male, Don, whose *pleasures* at work will be removed, rather than his own (line 17), if the chart is positioned high rather than low.

Gender is clearly a salient dimension in this jointly constructed humorous excerpt. In response to the introduction of a sexual component into the workplace talk, the participants adopt stereotypically gendered identities; the women identify as sexual objects and the men perform their expected role as titillated audience. Wendy supports Selene's contention that unless the board is placed high on the wall they will expose their underwear (line 12) and elaborates it (lines 14, 16). The women's contributions are classically feminine in style – supportive and agreeing in content, and collaborative ATN talk stylistically, with each contribution expanding on the previous woman's suggestion, using mirroring syntactic structures and exact repetitions: e.g. *up high in the middle* (lines 3, 13), *up high so people have to write like this* (line 4), *up high so I don't have to lean down* (line 5).

The men's contestive contributions (lines 15, 17, 19, 20) are delivered in a more typically masculine, competitive discourse style, at first overlapping Wendy with a protest (line 15), and then in standard OAAT style, as brief, quippy comments. This exchange thus illustrates once again how humour can provide a means for participants to enact gendered identities in their discourse style, as well as in the explicit content of their workplace talk.

A sexual or sexualized topic clearly encourages participants to adopt stereotypically gendered positions. Example 4.14 is an excerpt from a high-energy exchange during a meeting of a project team in a private commercial organization. A sexualized comment (line 7) about the number of men included in a photo of the organization's call centre seeds a humorous exchange which develops into a fantasy sequence around the idea of the call centre as a brothel.

Example 4.14

Context: Weekly reporting meeting of members of a project team in a multinational white-collar commercial organization. Smithy is the chair. There are 4 women and 4 men present.

1. **Cla:** well there's a there's a um a photo . . . an icon or a pic- picture
2.   that's going to come up at (the) business review meeting tomorrow
3.   when I talk about the fact that we've (. . .) all the jobs

4.	**Peg**:	yep
5.	**Cla**:	and there are too many men in the picture
6.		like there are about equal numbers of men and women
7.		I was going to say I think that the testosterone level has been overstated
8.		in this photo in this picture but I don't know if I can actually say that . . .
9.		[laughter]
10.	**Rob**:	what's the point you were trying to get to
11.		there's too many men in
12.	**Dai**:	/in the photo\
13.	**Cla**:	/(there's four)\ in the picture
14.		/+ and there are not many men in\ the call centre
15.	**Smi**:	/cos there's only\ one man in the call centre
16.	**Cla**:	the picture overstates the number of men in the call centre
17.	**Rob**:	oh okay
18.	**Smi**:	/there's one\ gigolo and one pimp and the rest of them are
19.	**Cla**:	/[laughs]\ call girls
20.	**Smi**:	call girls
21.	**Peg**:	[laughs]
22.	**Mar**:	and you'll need some more /chunky gold jewellery\
23.	**Peg**:	/there's always a complete [*name of organization*] service\ though isn't it
24.		when you think about it [laughs] /[laughs]\
25.	**Cla**:	/and maybe a moustache\
26.	**Mar**:	yeah and a shirt that unbuttons (to the waist)
27.	**Cla**:	a shiny shiny shirt
28.	**Rob**:	what's Ange then /the top moll or something\ . . .
29.	**Peg**:	[laughs] yeah she's the madam [laughs]
30.	**Smi**:	madam Ange
31.		[general laughter]
32.	**Cla**:	moving right along

In this humorous fantasy, again it is the women who make the running. Clara, the manager introduces the topic of the desirability of gender realism in the visual representation of the call centre (lines 5–6), which is, not surprisingly, predominantly staffed by women.[46] The official photo, however, presents the centre as staffed by equal numbers of women and men, and is thus a misrepresentation. At line 7, Clara proposes a humorous way of dealing with the issue by referring to *the testosterone level* rather than the number of men in the photo i.e. she introduces a blatantly sexual element into the talk. This is picked up by Smithy, the deputy manager, at line 18, *there's one gigolo and one pimp and the rest of them are*, and Clara wittily completes his clause with *call girls* (line 19). Thus the discussion of a gender issue quickly develops into a humorous fantasy around the concept of the call centre as a brothel, an association which is not too far-fetched given the existence of telephone sex workers.[47]

Though Smithy introduces the brothel concept, it was seeded by Clara (line 7), and it is the women (Marlene, Peg and Clara) who pick up the idea and develop it, elaborating particularly on the clothes and ornaments required to maintain the picture being painted. So Marlene introduces the idea of appropriate dress for the pimp, namely *chunky gold jewellery* (line 22) and *a shirt that unbuttons to the waist* (line 26), and Clara joins in with further supportive contributions *and maybe a moustache* (line 25), and more precisely, *a shiny shiny shirt* (line 27), elaborating Marlene's mention of a shirt. Clara's contributions are stylistically collaboratively constructed to mesh neatly with Marlene's.

Although this humour sequence is clearly a joint construction with all members of the team making a contribution, the different kinds of contributions again divide along gender lines. So at one point a contestive sub-theme develops, with the women focusing on elaborating the characteristics of the *pimp* (line 18), while the men focus on the role of the senior women in the call centre as *the top moll* (line 28), or *the madam* (line 29). Rob competes with Marlene and Clara for the floor as he develops the theme of Ange as *the top moll* in opposition to their focus on the *pimp*. Peg and Smithy finally bring the team back together, collaborating with their echoing, repeated structures agreeing on Ange as *the madam* (lines 29–30). Sex and gender intertwine interestingly in this example, as in example 4.13, in that sexually based humour provides a vehicle for gendered discourse patterns in workplace interaction.

Humour may also serve as a camouflage for workplace sexism. When sexism infiltrates workplace interaction using a humorous key, it is much more difficult to contest. When humour exploits sexist stereotypes in subtle and oblique ways, it is not easy to challenge without losing face or attracting pejorative labels such as a 'wet blanket', 'killjoy' or 'misery-guts'. Subversive comments expressed in an ironic or sarcastic tone are much harder to deal with than 'straight' criticisms, since they automatically put the recipient or target on the back foot.[48] Thus, especially between participants of different status, humour can be a double-edged sword in workplace interaction.

The final example illustrates this point by demonstrating how gender may creep into workplace talk in rather more subtle ways. And whereas in examples 4.13 and 4.14 it was the women who were responsible for introducing the topic which led to a focus on gender identities, in this example it is the men who introduce gender as an issue. Example 4.15 is an exchange from a meeting in a male-dominated, traditional, and rather conservative workplace. In this example, the women use humour to contest and challenge stereotypical gender-based assumptions, and especially assumptions about the way women and men should behave at work.

Example 4.15[49]

Context: Regular meeting of senior team of 9 men and 9 women in government department.

1.	Jak:	he's also very popular locally as well
2.		cos he actually looks after his workforce he's /kept them\
3.	Stu:	/oh right\
4.	Jak:	he's kept them on payroll while there's been no stuff
5.		going through the factory he's he employs far more people than
6.		than [*company name*] across the ro- er
7.	Stu:	no
8.	Jak:	across the way he's he's got a quite high profile
9.		and he's considered to be + /you know a bloody\
10.	Con:	/a good chap\
11.	Stu:	/a good guy\
12.	Jak:	good bloke
13.	Stu:	a good guy /oh okay\
14.	Jak:	/and the\ Minister thinks so as well so you know
15.		/an- and\ he's quite an honourable guy
16.	Wen:	/( )\

17. **Con:** [quietly]: mm:
18. **Jak:** he's a sort of a handshake and I trust you type guy
19. so you know + when you've got another good bloke
20. talking to another good bloke then you've got a
21. [general laughter]
22. **Stu:** they didn't go to the same school /did they\
23. **Jak:** /us good\ blokes have gotta stick together
24. [*general laughter, buzz of sceptical noises and comments including 'oh right' from more than one woman*]
25. **Wen:** /bloody good bloke\
26. /[general laughter]\
27. **Jef:** bet he doesn't employ many women workers
28. [general laughter]
29. **XM:** no
30. **Con:** (oh) I probably wouldn't want the job /either\
31. **Jak:** /it\ depends on your definition of /good bloke\
32. /[general laughter]\ (. . .)
33. **Jak:** /yeah no a good good\ bloke
34. /[general laughter]\

The pervasiveness of 'the old boys' network' gradually becomes the focus of the humour in this example: i.e. gender issues slowly emerge as the focus of attention as the women's contributions to the humour indicate their unwillingness to accept the values implicit in the picture of how the business world works, as constructed largely by the men at the meeting.

The excerpt begins with the development of a collaboratively shared floor between two of the men, Jake and Stu (lines 1–9). Connie makes a supportive contribution with the phrase *a good chap* (line 10), indicating she 'gets' the picture being constructed. Her contribution is practically simultaneous with Stu's synonymous *a good guy* (line 11), and Jake's *a bloody good bloke* (line 12). This is maximally cohesive, collaborative and supportive discourse, with all three clearly on the same wavelength and developing a single shared floor.

Jake then proceeds to develop the concept of *a good bloke* (lines 15, 18–20), which elicits laughter. The issue of gender becomes gradually foregrounded, allowing Stu an opportunity for further humour with an implicit reference to the influence of the old boys' network, *they didn't go to the same school did they* (line 22). Jake picks this up with an overlapping turn, *us good blokes have gotta stick together* (line 23), an explicitly gendered development of the humorous comment. This comment elicits a swell of reaction: there is laughter and 'knowing' noises such as *aaah* from the men, together with protesting comments such as *oh right*, and sceptical noises *nah* from the women. Wendy can be heard (line 25) contributing a contestive and sarcastic echo *bloody good bloke*.

The sex boundaries are now explicit and Jeff joins in (line 27) with a taunt to the women *bet he doesn't employ many women workers*, to which Connie responds challengingly *I probably wouldn't want the job either* (line 30). The humour is sustained with Jake's ambiguous comment *it depends on your definition of good bloke* (line 31), which elicits another gale of laughter, suggesting that gender is still to the fore of the agenda here. The comment emphasizes the indications that the women and men at the meeting have recognized in the course of the exchange that they have rather different views about at least some of the characteristics of *a good bloke*.

The men in this interaction thus construct a stereotypically positive masculine identity *the good bloke* – good blokes are, it is suggested, reliable, collegial and loyal. The humour revolves around male claims about the strength and pervasiveness of the old boy's network, and the suggestion that its foundations are laid at school. The women contest these claims, signalling scepticism and lack of agreement with the men's positive construction of *the good bloke*. This is gendered humour: the propositional content is explicitly concerned with gender, and exploits established gender stereotypes.

By contrast, the discourse patterns evident in this example challenge stereotypical gendered discourse norms. The women adopt normatively masculine pragmatic strategies, both in propositional orientation and in style, to contest the men's assertions. As Jake's humour becomes more explicitly 'gendered' and sexist in its focus, the women's contributions to the exchange become correspondingly more contestive (lines 25, 30). This is an interesting instance of women in the workplace challenging the gendered content of male humour using strategies which also challenge normative gender patterns. These women adopt a contestive, normatively masculine orientation to the previous propositions, rather than the supportive orientation stereotypically associated with women in interaction. As the gender issue emerges, the contributions also become much less cohesive and collaboratively integrated. Individuals provide their own syntactically complete and pragmatically challenging contributions. The floor becomes a competitive site, an OAAT floor, with both women and men making independent contributions (lines 25–31).

These examples give some indication of how humour can serve as a resource for making gender issues salient in meetings, and the range of ways in which participants respond. So, while the earlier sections of this chapter illustrated how gendered discourse patterns may be instantiated through a supportive or contestive propositional orientation, or in a more or less collaborative style of doing humour in workplace interaction, this section has demonstrated that, in addition, gender roles and stereotypically gender-appropriate behaviour can be (or emerge as) an overt focus of humour.

Conclusion

In this chapter I have explored and illustrated some of the varied ways in which gender and humour interrelate in workplace interaction, illustrating how humour provides a flexible resource for constructing gender identity at work. The discussion in this chapter has demonstrated how supportive humour, which builds on and expands previous humorous propositions, and humour which is expressed in a collaborative style, provide resources for constructing a normatively feminine gender identity. By contrast, statements which humorously contest the previous speaker's proposition, or which are expressed in a humorous but non-collaborative style, enact a conventionally masculine gender identity. Thus, in its propositional orientation (supportive vs. contestive) as well as in discursive style (more or less collaborative), humour may serve as a useful resource for indexing a relatively masculine or relatively feminine gender identity at particular points in workplace interaction in specific contexts within different communities of practice.

The analysis of workplace humour not only illustrates how people use humour to construct aspects of gender identity, but also how humour may serve as a resource for integrating different aspects of a person's social identity at work. The conventionally feminine role of background support person and peacemaker, for instance, is evident in many workplace exchanges where humour is used as a resource for damage control, for easing tensions and smoothing ruffled feathers. Humour can assist in mending fractured or fragile relationships, help things run more smoothly, and nurture good workplace relationships, i.e. serve as a strategy for accomplishing aspects of relational practice (see chapter 3). The examples in this chapter have illustrated how humour serves as a valuable resource in constructing this more feminine stance at work. Not only do we see Leila cementing and nurturing workplace relationships (example 4.9), we also find Selene and Clara (examples 4.13, 4.14) playing a typically feminine role in 'seeding' humorous exchanges, or 'keying' the humorous modality.[50] And there are also many examples in our data where men use humour in this normatively feminine style to defuse tensions after a confrontational exchange between team members.[51] Conversely, example 4.15 provides evidence that women may reject the stereotypical supportive discourse role, constructing in the process a more critical and challenging conventionally masculine identity. Hence, subtly, through aspects of style, and more overtly, through gendered content, humour provides a conduit for both women and men to negotiate complex aspects of gender identity, enacting and reinforcing masculine and feminine interactional norms, constructing, at times, a stereotypical gender identity, while challenging and undermining those norms on other occasions.

Gender is an underlying, pervasive influence not only on how we perform our social identity but also on how we perceive the behaviour of others – we view people through social spectacles and gender is one very important and unavoidable component of the lens. Spontaneous, collaborative humour provides an excellent illustration of the way participants in workplace interaction use discourse to construct different aspects of their social identity, including their gender identity, in their everyday interactions with fellow workers or colleagues. For leaders who are women, in particular, humour is a valuable resource for integrating the competing demands of their professional identity and their gender identity. The analysis of workplace humour can also provide an indication of how people perceive the gender identities of those they work with, and how people contribute to or contest the construction of those identities. Finally, the discussion in this chapter has also illustrated how humour may provide a hard-to-contest conduit for sexism or sexist discourse at work. In other words, humour has negative as well as positive potential, and raises serious problems of contestation for those wishing to challenge subtle and not so subtle sexist assumptions in workplace interaction. In the next chapter I turn to the issue of workplace conflict and examine the contribution of gendered norms in the analysis of ways of contesting the assertions of others.

NOTES

1 Marra and Holmes (1999).
2 See Holmes, Marra and Burns (2001), Hay (1994, 1995).
3 Levinson (1979: 368).
4 See Marra (2003) on this last point in particular.
5 See also Holmes and Marra (2002a, 2002b).
6 Hopper and Le Baron (1998: 61) talk of gender 'creeping into' discourse.
7 Jenkins (1985).
8 Crawford (1989: 161). See also Crawford and Gressley (1991), Crawford (1995).
9 See, for example, Ervin-Tripp and Lampert (1992), Lampert (1996).
10 Hay (2002: 32).
11 Hay (2002: 32, 28).
12 Holmes (2005d).
13 Coates (1996: 117ff).
14 Holmes (2005d).
15 Coates (1996).
16 Coates (1989: 120).
17 Edelsky (1981).
18 Jenkins (1985), Hay (1995).
19 Eder (1993).
20 Holmes (2005d). See also Plester (2003) for examples of this style of humour in Auckland IT organizations.
21 See, for example, Coates (1997, 2003), Cameron (1997), Edley and Wetherell (1997).
22 Coates (2003: 56ff).
23 See also Daly et al. (2004) for similar examples from our workplace data set.
24 Coates (1989: 120).
25 See Holmes (2005d) for further examples.
26 See Jenkins (1985), Ervin-Tripp and Lampert (1992), Hay (1994).
27 Hay (1995).
28 Eder (1993: 29).
29 Kotthoff (1999, forthcoming), Jenkins (1985), Hay (2002).
30 Holmes and Marra (2004).
31 Trauth (2002) suggests that this is typical of many IT professionals and describes IT as a very masculine profession.
32 This example has been used in previous publications, but it is analysed here from a somewhat different perspective.

33 This example is also analysed in Holmes and Schnurr (2005).
34 See Schnurr (forthcoming) for further discussion of humour in this community of practice.
35 This example is from Holmes and Schnurr (2005).
36 This example is discussed more extensively in Holmes and Stubbe (2003a).
37 Chocolate fish are chocolate-covered, fish-shaped marshmallow bars, which constitute a well-established currency as prizes and rewards in New Zealand workplaces.
38 See Holmes and Marra (2002a), Holmes and Schnurr (2005), Holmes and Stubbe (2003a), for further discussion of the ways in which analysis of the distribution and type of humour may be used to characterize different workplace cultures and communities of practice.
39 See Holmes and Stubbe (2003), ch. 6.
40 See also the discussion of the opening example in Holmes and Stubbe (2003b: 1) which involves Clara, and the examination of Ginette's skilful use of humour in Holmes and Stubbe (2003b: 126–130).
41 See Holmes (2000c), Holmes, Marra and Burns (2001), Holmes and Stubbe (2003b) for further examples.
42 This section draws on Holmes (2005d).
43 Holmes (2005c), McRae (2004).
44 This example is from Holmes and Stubbe (2003b: ch. 6). It is re-used here because it illustrates the point so succinctly.
45 Cf. Kotthoff (2000).
46 See Cameron (2000) on the discourse implications of this.
47 Hall (1995, 2003) discusses how these workers use discourse to construct appropriate gender identities.
48 For further discussion and exemplification, see Holmes and Marra (2002c).
49 The example and discussion draw on Holmes (2005c).
50 Kotthoff (1999: 126–7).
51 See, for example, Smithy's contribution in example 2.17.

CHAPTER FIVE

Contest, Challenge and Complaint – Gendered Discourse?

Introduction

This chapter considers the relevance of gendered discourse norms in managing disagreement, conflict and problematic encounters in the workplace. When people disagree, complain or refuse to cooperate, they have a wide range of discourse strategies at their disposal for indicating their position. In relaxed and informal contexts, between intimates and close friends, differences of opinion and refusals of requests are often expressed quite directly, and without much hedging. In the workplace, however, things are more complex. Although a good deal of workplace communication proceeds relatively smoothly, there are inevitably occasions when participants engage in interactions which entail challenges to the views expressed by others, expressions of dissatisfaction, refusals, and varying degrees of conflict and disagreement. While some cultures and communities of practice engage in contestive talk in certain contexts with relish,[1] there are many New Zealand workplaces where managing these more contentious aspects of interaction presents participants with a challenge. This chapter explores a range of responses to this challenge, and examines, in particular, the relevance of sex stereotypes and gendered interactional norms in managing negatively affective talk at work.

The term 'negatively affective talk' is used here to refer to talk which involves some degree of face threat or even face attack.[2] At one end of the spectrum, this may involve a disagreement expressed in a relatively mild way, as illustrated in example 5.1.

Example 5.1

Context: Regular team meeting of 6 women in a government organization. The team is discussing possible roles for Kerry, who was expected to be leaving but has indicated she wants her contract extended.

1. **Lei**: so it could be another month
2. **Ker**: mm
3. **Lei**: that could help us out quite a lot actually
4. **Lis**: yep so you'll be like you won't be based in the library
5. you'll be around
6. **Lei**: /well we don't know yet\
7. **Ker**: /I'm not sure\
8. **Lei**: we haven't had that conversation yet Lisa [laughs]

Leila checks out that Kerry could be available for another month of work for the department (line 1), and when Kerry confirms this (line 2), notes that this could be helpful in resolving a problem the team is addressing. Lisa infers from Leila's comment that Kerry will be more generally available during this month for a wider range of work than the library work on which she had been previously deployed: *so you'll be like you won't be based in the library you'll be around* (lines 4–5). At this point Leila disagrees; she challenges Lisa's assumption by saying *well we don't know yet we haven't had that conversation yet Lisa* (lines 6, 8). In other words, Leila indicates that she and Kerry still need to negotiate the terms of her contract extension, including what she will be doing during the next month. This is a very politely expressed disagreement, perhaps because the issue is a sensitive one (we know from ethnographic data and other recorded interactions that the issue of how exactly Kerry is to be deployed is not uncontentious), but perhaps also because on many criteria this is a very feminine community of practice. Leila uses indirect strategies to indicate that Lisa's assumption is not necessarily correct, and she softens her disagreement with laughter and the use of Lisa's name, a common positive politeness strategy in such situations.

On the other hand, contentious talk may involve ways of speaking that are very face threatening, including verbal abuse and insult, as illustrated in example 5.2.

Example 5.2

Context: Two factory production team members. Alex in the office is speaking to Bert on the production line over the intercom system.

1. **Ale**: yeah Bert bro check our pallet downstairs for us please
   bro+
2. **Ber**: no I fucking won't
3.   do it yourself you tight bastard

This looks like a direct and unmitigated refusal, intensified by the use of swear words and terms of insult. It can serve here to represent a normatively masculine style of refusal, a stark contrast to the more polite feminine style of disagreement illustrated by example 5.1.

In fact, as indicated throughout this book, context is crucial in interpreting social meaning, including the force of such a refusal. The precise strength of utterances cannot be assessed out of context. The norms of each community of practice, as well as factors such as tone of voice and volume, are relevant in assessing what counts as an insult and what indicates solidarity in any context. Hence, an interpretation of the degree of negative affect or potential offence of such talk requires careful analysis of the context in which it was produced, as well as consideration of the wider workplace culture and community of practice to which the participants belong. Swear words and conventional terms of abuse serve a very wide range of functions; intentional insult is only one of these, and a relatively rare one in practice.[3] Furthermore, as in previous chapters, it is important to note that although my focus is gendered discourse, many other considerations impinge on the way people handle conflict talk. Workplace participants select strategies which take account of a range of contextual factors, such as the setting and formality of the interaction,[4] the power relations and the relative status of those involved,[5] and the social distance between participants,[6] as well as the kind of community of practice to which they belong,[7] and the wider cultural context.[8]

It must also be recognized that the expression and exploration of different views may be an explicit objective of a meeting; conflict is not undesirable *per se*, but may in fact serve as a productive way of making progress towards transactional or organizational objectives. The articulation of reservations can encourage a deeper exploration of issues and may lead to better understandings, and more creative solutions to problems.[9] There is no necessary implication, then, in this exploration of gendered ways of handling negatively affective speech acts, that conflict should be avoided at all costs. Rather, the focus of interest is the range of discourse strategies used by participants in different workplace contexts to manage negatively affective talk at work, as well as the relevance of gender in the negotiation of such talk. In particular, the discussion will demonstrate that people draw on a wide range of both feminine and masculine discursive resources to manage conflict in the workplace.

I first discuss in broad terms the potential relevance of gender as a social variable in conflict talk at work, before focusing on disagreements and refusals, to illustrate in more detail how gendered discourse may infiltrate particular areas of workplace interaction.

Conflict Talk and Gender[10]

There is a substantial body of research indicating that the 'preference for agreement' which has been identified as a structural feature of conversation by discourse analysts, is also a functional reality in many middle-class professional contexts, including white-collar workplaces.[11] In such contexts, people generally try to avoid explicitly disagreeing with or contradicting others, and they use a range of strategies to minimize the negative impact of direct refusals.[12] Mitigation, negotiation and indirectness are common devices for maintaining good relations and 'saving face' in situations where participants encounter potential conflicts of interest.[13] They are also, of course, strategies which are associated with more feminine approaches to managing conflict, and when used extensively in a workplace they can contribute to the construction of a gendered (feminine) community of practice.[14]

On the other hand, the current business communication literature tends to focus on the positive aspects of conflict, suggesting that the most effective way to deal with workplace conflict is often to adopt a proactive approach, countering arguments and actively suggesting alternatives to a dispreferred line of action.[15] Moreover, as discussed in chapter 2, the models in many books on leadership present a charismatic, authoritarian and even autocratic style of management as characteristic of the hero managers they describe.[16] As Parry puts it, '[t]here is nothing passive about leadership'.[17] Evidence from our extensive workplace corpus also supports the view that there are occasions when people do need to say and do things which threaten the face of other participants. Indeed, speakers with enough power or status may decide that it is not necessary or desirable to avoid directly refusing a request, or expressing disagreement 'bald on record'.[18] Nevertheless, the use of such direct strategies to manage conflict or express disagreement is more common in some workplaces than others, and these strategies typically contribute to the construction of more masculine communities of practice.

Thus, the management of conflict in the workplace may bring differently gendered discourse norms into play in different contexts or at different points in an interaction. The pressure to reach a desirable outcome from a task-oriented or transactional perspective may result in more direct, authoritarian and normatively masculine ways of handling conflict, while the need to pay attention to collegial relationships, and to other people's face needs (standard relational practice), tends to encourage more feminine strategies. In examining the range of ways in which people balance these competing demands in different communities of practice, it is useful to organize them along a continuum from more conventionally feminine strategies which take account of relational factors and individuals' face needs, to more stereotypically masculine strategies focusing more directly on transactional goals and organizational objectives.[19] In the next section, I illustrate this continuum in relation to different ways of disagreeing in workplace interaction, drawing largely on data from meetings in white-collar professional contexts.

Disagreement and Gendered Discourse[20]

There are many ways of dealing with workplace disagreement. Three strategies identified in the meetings in our workplace corpus will serve to illustrate different points along a continuum of gendered discourse in this respect: (1) conflict avoidance, (2) negotiation, (3) resolution by fiat. The discussion will demonstrate that this gender continuum is inevitably something of a macro-level simplification; matters are considerably more complex when we examine exactly how the three macro-strategies are instantiated in workplace talk. It is none the less a useful heuristic device for organizing the discussion.

Conflict Avoidance

At the extreme, the simplest way of dealing with a potential conflict is to avoid it: i.e. 'don't do the Face Threatening Act', in Brown and Levinson's terms.[21] Colleagues are often well aware of each other's views, and it is possible in some contexts to avoid confronting issues that are known to be contentious. While something which remains unsaid is obviously difficult to pinpoint, our analyses of the strategies used to manage meetings identified a number of instances where effective chairs minimized the potential for explicit conflict by avoiding discussion of a specific issue. Using an avoidance strategy is widely regarded as a stereotypically feminine response to conflict; sex stereotypes suggest women tend to steer clear of overt conflict and divert discussion if they anticipate problems. But conflict avoidance may be strategic; effective management entails making decisions about, for instance, the most appropriate time and the most relevant group to discuss a contentious issue.

Our data provides a number of examples of effective male and female managers making decisions about which issues to confront and which to put on hold or divert for later discussion. One simple technique for dealing with a contentious issue which has the potential to divert discussion from more central or important issues is simply to stick firmly to the agenda. Phrases such as *to get back to the agenda, moving forward,* and *just moving on* regularly occur in meetings as explicit discourse markers of this tactic. And, interestingly, when the meeting chair was someone other than the manager, it was noticeable that the manager would on occasion 'move the meeting along' by overtly indicating that it was time to proceed to the next agenda item. In this situation, one manager simply said firmly and clearly *next*; another regularly used the phrase *moving right along*. These short intrusions on the rights of the meeting chair were always strategic moves to get the meeting back on track, but on occasion they also served to divert discussion from contentious areas which the manager judged irrelevant to the primary objectives of the meeting. They provided a way of avoiding problematic and, possibly in the manager's view, unproductive debate.

Such examples suggest that while *avoidance* might appear a relatively feminine strategy at the macro-level, its instantiation may be very masculine in style. Intrusions on the rights of the chair to run the meeting, and short pithy phrases such as *next item*, certainly do not conform to a feminine stereotype. As always, the discursive reality is complex. Example 5.3 illustrates this point more fully. The excerpt involves a team manager from a government organization actively controlling the discussion in order to more effectively manage a potential area of conflict and disagreement.

Example 5.3

Context: Meeting of 5 women and 3 men in a government organization. The team is discussing a number of training programmes. Len is the team leader and the chair of the meeting.

1.	**Bel**:	that's the way they came out
2.	**Aid**:	yep
3.	**Len**:	yeah yeah okay
4.	**Cli**:	one that I am surprised at is [institution] engineering
5.	**Len**:	hang on can we can we stay in the do this block first
6.	**Cli**:	oh okay you want to /do service first\
7.	**Len**:	/all right\
8.		do service first otherwise we'll
9.	**Cli**:	okay
10.	**Len**:	we'll we'll dart a bit
11.		I just want to try and [clears throat] deal with the a
12.		do the scores make sense with people's perceptions
13.		or if there's a difference big difference in the scores
14.		that we've got some comment that covers that big difference
15.		so um + we've done that one

Len, the meeting chair, here directs the attention of the group to a general issue which he wants to obtain agreement about before they embark on the discussion of specific cases, i.e. the issue of the relative alignment of perceptions and evaluation, and especially the problems that arise when different teams assign evaluations. He suggests that when the scores assigned don't *make sense with people's perceptions* (line 12), then the team should provide *some comment that covers that big difference* (line 14). By explicitly discussing this issue first, and in the abstract rather than in relation to a specific case, Len adopts a strategy which has the potential to avoid the recurrence of a very problematic issue, and a possible source of recurring friction throughout the meeting.

Len's macro-strategy of conflict avoidance is instantiated in this example with relationally oriented discourse, indicating sensitivity to people's face needs. He expresses his wish to deal with the general issue, rather than move to a discussion of a specific case, with a friendly colloquial phrase, *hang on*, and a proposal which uses the inclusive pronoun *we* and the colloquial verb *do* (line 5). He then provides a reason for his request, again using informal language, *we'll dart a bit*, and ends his explanation in the same tone, *so um + we've done that one* (line 15). Using this informal style, Len effectively diverts Clive's move to a more specific level of discussion (line 4), and provides good reason for dealing with the general issue first, thus defusing a potentially face-threatening situation.

A contrasting style of achieving the same end is illustrated in example 5.4. Dudley, the overall project leader (but not the meeting chair), redirects his team back to the central criteria which should be guiding their decisions about training, at a point where they are digressing to consider what he apparently perceives as peripheral issues which have the potential for generating conflicting (and, we deduce, in his judgement, irrelevant) views.

Example 5.4

Context: Regular weekly meeting of an IT project team in a large commercial organization. There are 6 male participants at this meeting. Barry is the meeting chair. (The word 'gizmo' has been substituted for a term which could reveal the identity of the team.)

1.	**Eri:**	yeah no no I meant that as soon as people
2.		like we're getting questions now people know that [gizmo] is coming up
3.		so what does this mean oh I'd like to know the profile of people
4.		who carry these things
5.	**Dud:**	(oh you'd like to)
6.	**Eri:**	as you get those questions that's what drives the
7.	**Bar:**	mm

8. **Dud**: you you need to drive the training from a from your objectives

9.   of what are you going to use the the the [gizmo] data for

10. **Bar**: yep

11. **Dud**: and and what are your objectives that you want to achieve with that

12. **Bar**: mm

13. **Dud**: and base your training around those objectives

14.   because I think isn't the reality is at the moment . . .

15.   and really it's a bit of sort of touchy feely stuff at the moment

Dudley here intervenes in a discussion between three project team members who are beginning to express disparate views about what they should be doing next, and especially about whose views they should be seeking. He first reminds the team of the relevant criteria for their specific project from the organization's perspective: *you need to drive the training from a from your objectives of what are you going to use the the the [gizmo] data for* (lines 8–9). By contrast with Len, Dudley begins by using *you* rather than *we*, and his contribution is a direct and challenging question designed to stop people in their tracks. He goes on to elaborate his reasons, but his style is confrontational rather than consultative, and he ends with a very critical and dismissive comment on the team's position, *it's a bit of sort of touchy feely stuff at the moment* (line 15). Dudley's strategy of drawing attention to the high-level organizational objectives here very effectively pulls the plug on what he apparently regards as a potentially unproductive argument about irrelevant detail (such as what sort of people use the gizmo being discussed and what they use them for). At one level Dudley's strategy is similar to Len's in that he re-directs the discussion to issues he considers relevant, but in the context of this team of competitive IT experts, a very different community of practice from Len's government department, Dudley adopts a rather aggressive and masculine discursive style.[22]

Hence, the stereotypically feminine macro-strategy of conflict avoidance may be accomplished using a range of styles, including a relatively masculine discourse style. In another meeting where a group of IT experts began discussing an issue which was contentious, the chair gave a clear direction, stating firmly *okay well you guys need to talk about it tomorrow not not now.* In a similar situation in a different meeting, the chair again indicated that a disagreement was to be discussed in another forum, saying *you guys have got to sort that out*; and in yet another meeting where a conflict arose, the chair said quite explicitly *shall we deal with that out- outside of this outside of this meeting.* In each case the message is very clear, and the potentially contentious issue is diverted for discussion elsewhere than in the current meeting. Overt disagreement in the formal context of a large group meeting is thus avoided. However, the style of these statements is increasingly consultative, with the third example using the inclusive *we*, and signals of tentativeness, as opposed to the directive *you* pronoun and the firm modals of obligation *need to* and *have got to.* These examples further illustrate that the conventionally feminine strategy of conflict avoidance may be expressed in a variety of ways, and that the construction of disagreement is a dynamic matter. Strategies used at the micro-level to avoid conflict vary markedly in the extent to which they draw on normatively feminine discourse resources. This is illustrated even more clearly in relation to the next strategy.

Negotiation: Working Through Conflict

A second strategy for dealing with conflict and disagreement is to acknowledge the contentious issues, and 'manage' rather than avoid or divert them. This approach generally involves negotiating consensus among participants, a stereotypically feminine strategy, often cited in the management literature as one of the advantages of increasing the number of women in the workforce.[23] Again it is useful to examine how this is actually accomplished.

Our database provides many examples of groups in different communities of practice negotiating their way through areas of disagreement and conflict to group consensus.[24] These examples are typically lengthy, complex and very context-dependent discussions which are difficult for outsiders to fully understand. Succinct summary of such complex talk is a challenge, but I have selected one instance to illustrate some of the complexities of the process of managing disagreement through negotiation. Example 5.5 (featuring the same group as in example 5.3) is taken from an organization where there is a strong consensus culture. In this excerpt the manager skilfully leads the discussion from a position where different participants are clearly at odds with one another to a consensus conclusion that is consistent with the organization's transactional objectives.[25] His facilitative skills could be characterized as normatively feminine, including the ways in which he pays attention to relational aspects of the interaction. In the leadership literature, such skills are labelled 'transformational' (see chapter 2).

The group is discussing the wide range of evaluations assigned by different evaluators to the various training programmes for which the department is responsible. At the start of this section of the discussion, one participant, Belinda, identifies an evaluation which she considers surprising, and then goes on to signal that she disagrees with the 'A' rating assigned to the designated programme. In the extensive discussion which follows, the manager, Len, leads the group through to a conclusion which ratifies the 'A' rating on grounds of trainee performance, while noting that there are questions to be answered concerning the management of the programme. He achieves this by directing the team's attention to the central criterion which he considers relevant, i.e. evidence of subsequent success in higher education by those who have taken the course. The discussion extends over some time – just the key stages are provided below to illustrate the complexity of the discourse strategies used to manage the areas of contention.

Following her expression of surprise at the high rating of the programme under consideration, Belinda is asked to comment. She notes that the programme has *occupancy* problems (line 1): i.e., it does not have enough enrolments to justify the amount of space being used or the level of allocation of resources.

Example 5.5a

Context: Meeting of 5 women and 3 men in a government organization. The team is discussing a number of training programmes. Len is the team leader and the chair of the meeting. (A couple of words have been deleted to protect the identity of the participants.)

1. **Bel**: having heaps of problems with occupancy and stuff
2. **Len**: is that A A rating that says for those who actually do the course

3.   do quite well in it
4. **Bel**: I don't /know [*name*] did the performance rating\
5. **Sio**: /[drawls]: oh: yeah yeah\ probably
6. **Len**: would that be a way of describing it
7. **Sio**: yep
8. **Iri**: I think that's being generous
9.   [laughter]

In response to Belinda's comment, Len asks a question which directs attention to the trainees' performance as a basis for the evaluation (line 2). Note that he phrases his point as a query rather than a challenge (a clear contrast to Dudley's approach in example 5.4), although he effectively presents an alternative interpretation of the data. He takes the same approach in line 6, again asking if this is a possible interpretation, rather than asserting this view as the correct interpretation. The use of the modal *would* indicates that this is a suggestion, a hypothesis for consideration.

Example 5.5b

10. **Sio**: what all the all the /present ( ) go through the course\
11. **Bel**: /don't know what ( )\
12. **Sio**: go on to further training I mean
13.   and they get really good high outcomes
14.   but you're obviously your occupancy's low
15.   and the percentage for the last few weeks has been 68
           per cent
16. **Cli**: yeah I think that was probably based on
17.   it's on the processes

Responding to Len's query, Sioban acknowledges that all those who complete the course *go on to further training* (line 12) and *they get really good high outcomes* (line 13), but then the discussion moves back to focus on processes, with a number of participants contributing information about the ways in which the evaluation process was unsatisfactory. There is then further discussion about the unsatisfactory nature of the course's evaluation processes, but Val also acknowledges that those who take the course are happy with it (lines 20–3 below). Len's contribution during this discussion is simply *mm*.

Example 5.5c

18. **Bel**: what did [X] say to you when he talked about it?
19. **Val**: um that just a little bit about the ( ) processes at that
20.   and what they're where they get to
21.   the um the trainees who finish the course
22.   or the trainees who who actually go through it
23.   are full of praise for it and that kind of thing
24. **Len**: mm
25. **Val**: um but

At this point Len raises the issue of the programme's outcomes once again, and this time it is phrased not as a question but as an assertion followed by a tag question, inviting confirmation *but the trainees do get quite high high outcomes don't they* (line 28).

Example 5.5d

26. **Len**: /but but um\
27. **Val**: /( )\ yeah
28. **Len**: but the trainees do get quite high high outcomes don't they?
29. **Sio**: off?
30. **Len**: off that course
31. **Sio**: yeah they all go on to further /training\
32. **Val**: /mm\
33. **Len**: onto /college\
34. **Sio**: /being full time\ yeah /( ) full time\
35. **Len**: /( ) yeah\
36. **Bel**: yeah
37. **Sio**: one-year certificate course
38. **Iri**: mm what happens after that one?
39. **Sio**: well then they shoot off to uni um /college
40.   finish that and come out\ with their
41. **Len**: /college and come out with a diploma\
42. **Sio**: come out with their diploma and shoot off to all the ( )
43. **Cli**: so it's really an occupancy thing
44. **Sio**: yeah
45. **Iri**: oh no

46. **Len:** the ( ) it's more a whole course management
47. /thing I\ think /it is\
48. **Bel:** /yeah\ I was just going to /say that it's\ probably not a
49. shall I /make a note\
50. **Cli:** /oh okay\
51. **Len:** occupancy is an indication

The discussion continues to address other issues relating to this programme, but Len has achieved his main objective by this point: he has obtained explicit agreement that the course is achieving desirable outcomes, and that occupancy is a secondary consideration. The remainder of the discussion ratifies the decision to focus on the course management issue. Len makes relatively few interventions in this discussion, but all are strategic and effective in facilitating agreement on an issue that promised initially to be a contentious and very problematic one.

Len's discursive style is decidedly feminine compared to those of other managers in our database. He makes suggestions, phrases his contributions in a tentative rather than a challenging form (e.g. lines 2, 6), and makes effective use of attenuating devices such as tag questions (line 28) and pragmatic particles such as *I think* (line 47). So while the contentious issue is explicitly identified, the progress to consensus is characterized by a facilitative and non-confrontational style. Thus negotiation, a stereotypically feminine strategy for managing disagreement, is here expressed in a normatively feminine, consensus-seeking and facilitative discourse style.

Negotiation may also be undertaken in a more stereotypically masculine, confrontational style, though when this occurs, it is perhaps more commonly characterized as argument than negotiation.[26] In such cases, a resolution is often achieved through the overt exercise of authority and power.

Resolution by Fiat: Imposing a Decision

While avoidance and negotiation are typically considered more feminine ways of managing conflict, direct confrontation is generally considered a more masculine strategy. Thus when they disagree, people may simply assert their point of view, and if they have enough status or authority they may succeed in getting their position accepted. Typically, it is the powerful players in a workplace interaction, the managers or team leaders, who are likely to express disagreement or opposition overtly.[27] Those in positions of power can ignore, discount and over-ride the views of others, and insist that what they say goes.

In practice, however, such behaviour is not common. While people argued fiercely and disagreed 'bald on record' on relatively trivial issues or minor matters of factual accuracy such as what date a meeting had been held or how much something cost, there were very few instances of a direct confrontational approach over more substantial and serious issues. Clara's veto (example 2.17, chapter 2 above) is one of the clearest instances of the use of a direct and confrontational strategy in a situation of disagreement. Clara simply over-rides the opposition of her team members using the very effective strategy of an explicit, unambiguous and repeated statement, *no screendumps*. She indicates clearly that she is not prepared to negotiate, and nor is she willing to discuss the matter further. Her decision is final. This stereotypically masculine strategy exemplifies the most confrontational resolution of a contentious issue in our extensive data base.

A second, less extreme example involves the same leader. In example 5.6, the team are discussing the form of the initial greeting on the organization's answerphone. Clara's response on this issue is again uncompromising.

Example 5.6

Context: Meeting of members of a project team in a multinational white-collar commercial organization. Smith is chairing. Clara is section leader. There are 4 women and 4 men present at this meeting.

1.	**Smi**:	we were going to have a vote on
2.		it's 'welcome' or is it 'kia ora'
3.	**Cla**:	oh it's 'welcome'
4.	**Smi**:	you sure
5.	**Cla**:	yes
6.	**Peg**:	you phone up and say whatever they /want to out-side business hours\
7.	**Vit**:	/laugh\
8.	**Peg**:	but in business hours it's 'welcome'

Clara firmly asserts her decision *it's welcome* (line 3), albeit with an introductory prefatory *oh* which serves not as a hedge, but rather to acknowledge that she realizes this is unexpected information for the hearers.[28] The team accepts the decision, although the wry, humorous comment from Peg (lines 6, 8) functions to release the tension generated by Clara's direct and explicit challenge to Smithy's proposal that the issue be decided democratically by a vote (line 1). As noted in chapter 2, the exploitation of such normatively masculine discourse resources for managing conflict serves some women in senior leadership positions very well.

A third example, discussed in detail elsewhere,[29] is very similar. A member of an IT team, Eric, disagrees with a decision of the group, saying explicitly *no don't do that*, and when they argue with him, he simply repeats his position, *don't do it*. The decision relates to Eric's area of expertise within the project, and he makes it clear that he will not take responsibility for a decision with which he is unhappy. Eric's 'expert power'[30] provides him with the platform for his explicit and repeated expression of disagreement. He finally requests in an only semi-facetious manner that they record his disagreement, but then ends with a humorous understated comment, referring to himself in the third person, asking them to write *Eric does not think this is a good idea*. So, again, a section of very confrontational interaction is followed by wry humour in an attempt to defuse the tension it creates.

Example 5.7 provides a final illustration of a very direct and stereotypically masculine style of handling disagreement. It is taken from a documentary film, *Getting to Our Place*, which comprises edited but authentic footage of the meetings and discussions which led to the establishment of the New Zealand National Museum, named 'Te Papa', (translated as 'Our Place').[31] The excerpt is taken from a small meeting preparing for a formal full board meeting. The participants, the board chairman Sir Ron Trotter and Cliff Whiting, the Māori museum CEO, can be identified, since the excerpt is in the public domain.

The excerpt relates to a central issue for the Board, namely, how the museum would represent and reflect the relationship between the two major cultural groups in New Zealand, the indigenous Māori[32] people, and the Pākehā settlers. The museum was to include within it a marae, a traditional Māori meeting house and surrounding area for speech-making, for which Cliff Whiting was responsible. Most traditional New Zealand marae are built by and for Māori people, and located in particular tribal areas, though there are also some urban marae which are non-tribal. The museum marae was unusual in that it was clearly visible and public. At the beginning of the excerpt, Sir Ron Trotter is just finishing a statement of how he sees the museum marae as being a place where Pākehā as well as Māori people will feel comfortable.[33]

Example 5.7

Context: Meeting of a small group to prepare for a full board meeting of the New Zealand National Museum Planning Committee. (*Tangatawhenua* = 'indigenous people', 'people of the land'. *Pakeha* (as opposed to Pākehā) indicates an Anglicized pronunciation of this word.)

1.	**Ron:**	but comfortable and warm and + part of the place ++
2.		for any Pakeha who er ++ part of the ( ) that we talked about
3.		in the concept of we're trying to + develop
4.	**Cli:**	there are two main fields that have to be explored
5.		and er + the one that is most important is it's customary role in the first
6.		place because marae comes (on) and comes from + the tangatawhenua
7.		who are Māori ++ /to change it\
8.	**Ron:**	/but it's not just\ for Maori
9.	**Cli:**	/no\
10.	**Ron:**	you you <u>must</u> get that if it is a Maori institution and nothing more
11.		<u>this</u> marae has failed + and they <u>must</u> get that idea
12.	**Cli:**	/(how)\
13.	**Ron:**	because
14.	**Cli:**	/( )\
15.	**Ron:**	/[shouts]:we are bicultural + bicultural (talks about two):
16.		and if it is going to be\ totally Maori ++ and all +
17.		driven by Maori protocols and without regard for the life
18.		museum is a is a Pakeha concept I will not +

There is much that could be said about this excerpt. I use it here to illustrate just one point – the way that Sir Ron Trotter, the Chair, registers his disagreement with Cliff Whiting.[34] When the Chair finishes speaking at line 3, Cliff Whiting begins to explore the complexities of trying to adapt a fundamentally Māori concept to a bicultural perspective. He signals clearly in his opening statement that he has at least two points to make *two main fields that have to be explored* (line 4). However, as soon as he mentions the Māori people, and especially uses the Māori word for the indigenous people *tangatawhenua* (line 6), Sir Ron Trotter aggressively interrupts him. He does so with a statement that is phrased as a disagreement, *but it's not just for Maori* (line 8), although in fact Cliff Whiting has not asserted that the marae is just for Māori, and indeed he responds with an agreeing *no* which is ignored as the Chair speaks loudly and assertively over the top of his contribution. Sir Ron Trotter twice uses an aggressive modal *must* which is very strongly stressed to emphasize his point. Moreover, he switches from *you you must get that* (line 10), a very aggressive directive addressed specifically to Cliff Whiting, to *they must get that idea* (line 11), referring to the Māori people more generally, positioning them as 'other', and clearly distancing himself from this group. Implying Cliff Whiting represents all Māori, or even that he has a responsibility to convey this message to all Māori, is obviously insulting, and the Chair is behaving here in a culturally very insensitive way. He goes on to raise the volume of his voice to drown out Cliff Whiting's words with an assertion about his view of the issue, and an assertion that he will not tolerate the museum marae being *all driven by Maori protocols* (lines 16–17).

Leaving aside the complexities of the content of this exchange, the excerpt provides a clear example of a very autocratic and authoritarian way of disagreeing. Sir Ron Trotter uses a disruptive interruption strategy, bolstered by strongly stressed words and high volume to register his disagreement and silence the person he disagrees with, illustrating stereotypically masculine discourse behaviour.

As mentioned above, this confrontational and autocratic style of handling disagreement is exceedingly rare in the day-to-day meetings of the white-collar professionals whom we recorded in New Zealand workplaces. More negotiative, consultative and normatively feminine responses to conflict situations are much more common. In a very detailed examination of 10 different meetings, for example, involving over 12 hours of talking time, we identified only 15 instances of overtly articulated disagreement, and less than a handful of those instances could be characterized as serious disagreements expressed in an overtly confrontational way.[35] People manage conflict in complex and variegated ways.[36] At all levels of responsibility colleagues make use of a range of strategies, including normatively gendered discourse resources, to respond to different kinds of potential workplace conflict. Direct confrontation is not common. The next section illustrates this point in relation to another negatively affective speech act, refusal.

Refusals

Previous research on refusals emphasizes the importance of contextual factors, such as the kind of relationship which obtains between the participants, as well as the nature of the request, in determining the appropriate way of expressing refusals.[37] Most of this research has, however, involved self-report data or Discourse Completion Tasks which elicit a very different kind of data from that produced in authentic face-to-face interaction.[38] And there is scarcely any research on differently gendered ways of refusing.[39]

In fact, despite the factory example, 5.2 above, clear-cut and explicit examples of the way people manage to refuse requests in the workplace are not very frequent, especially in white-collar professional contexts. While there are trivial examples of refusals of offers of food, drink or a cigarette, which elicit simply a brief *no thanks*, sometimes with a reason, people are skilled at avoiding explicitly refusing serious, legitimate requests in the workplace, and they use a range of discursive means to avoid going on record with a refusal. Direct refusals do occur (see examples 5.9 and 5.10 below), but the following example is much more characteristic of the way people respond to a request which they don't want to comply with. In example 5.8, Bea uses conventionally feminine negotiating strategies to avoid directly refusing her manager's suggestion about what she, Bea, should do to address their problem.

Example 5.8[40]

Context: Senior manager and policy analyst in a government department discussing strategy for dealing with a problem.

1. **Ros**: is there anyone else we can talk to?
2. **Bea**: Tim Halligan
3. **Ros**: talk to him couldn't we couldn't you?
4. **Bea**: [laughs] [drawls]: oh: I suppose
5. **Ros**: I thought we had an okay relationship with
6. **Bea**: I've been fairly grumpy about stuff
7. **Ros**: about this study oh some of their criticisms of our our work
8. **Bea**: oh no I've been really [laughs] criticizing an article of theirs [laughs]
9. **Ros**: of theirs well they were quite critical of ours
10. remember their review their external review was a bit
11. **Bea**: [drawls]: ah: yeah but that was because he thought it was too narrow
12. **Ros**: yeah
13. **Bea**: and I we renamed it so that it wasn't you know
14. **Ros**: it was more reflective of what it was about
15. **Bea**: we were at w- yeah mm
16. **Ros**: well we haven't received any criticisms of ours that it's not
17. analytically sound
18. **Bea**: no
19. **Ros**: so okay
20. **Bea**: rightio I'll ring him then

Ros, the manager, first suggests that *we* could talk to Tim Halligan (lines 1, 3), but then shifts to explicitly suggesting Bea take on this task: *couldn't we couldn't you?* (line 3). Her tag question invites agreement, and Bea does technically agree, though with a hedged response *I suppose* (line 4), following a laugh and articulated in a drawled manner, clearly indicating reluctance. Ros's response indicates that she has registered Bea's wish to avoid doing what has been suggested and is puzzled as to the possible reason: *I thought we had an okay relationship with* (line 5). Bea then indicates the reason for her reluctance: she has been critical of Tim's section's work (lines 6, 8). Ros counters by pointing out that Tim's section had also been critical of work that her section has produced (lines 9–10). Bea responds by suggesting the criticism was specific and, she implies, minor (line 11, *he thought it was too narrow*) and easily rectified (lines 13–15, *we renamed it so it was . . . more reflective of what it was about*). Ros then checks that no more serious criticisms have been raised (line 16), and when Bea replies *no*, she indicates that this implies there is no barrier to contacting him. Bea capitulates, and in line 20 she finally agrees to do what Ros has asked: *rightio I'll ring him then*.

This is a typical example of the way people negotiate their way through potential conflict in the relatively feminine community of practice to which Ros and Bea belong. At no point does Bea directly refuse to do what Ros is asking, and nor does Ros insist explicitly that her directive be followed. Rather Ros elicits and systematically addresses Bea's concerns, and then concludes *so okay* (line 19), allowing Bea to offer to comply with her request. The strategies adopted are facilitative and collaborative, i.e. normatively feminine.

Example 5.9 illustrates again the complexities of authentic workplace talk. This refusal occurs in a professional, and again relatively feminine, community of practice, and it involves a comparatively junior person who is refusing in advance a task she anticipates will be assigned to her. At first sight, the excerpt seems to provide a simple, explicit and single utterance refusal, *I'm not doing it* (line 2); in fact, however, the complete refusal sequence is relatively extended and negotiated over many turns. [The refusing utterances are in bold.]

Example 5.9

Context: Meeting in a government organization to evaluate training programmes. Turning to a specific proposal, the team leader, Len, decides a verbal presentation is required in order to deal with it fairly.

1. **Len**: um + and we would need to do a verbal for this one
2. **Bel**: **I'm not doing it**
3. **All**: [laughter]
4. **Sio**: [laughs] [laughs] (bags not /yeah)\
5. **Bel**: **/seriously\ /seriously**
6. **Len**: /+ that's a\ separate question [laughs] that's a separate question
7. but + as a general principle /+ last year we established\
8. **Bel**: **/[laughs] I don't think (it'd) be appropriate for me to do it**

9. **Len**: that any existing provider that we were in danger of dropping
10. we did a verbal with + to ensure that they had had every opportunity . . .
11. **XF**: mm
12. **Aid**: mm
13. **Val**: /I think Iris needs to do it\
14. **Bel**: **/but it wouldn't be appropriate for me to do it\ would it**
15. **Len**: eh?
16. **Bel**: **it wouldn't be appropriate for me to do it /would it**
17. **Len**: /it may\ well be appropriate for you to do it Belinda
18. [general laughter]
19. **XF**: [laughs] /(oh no)\
20. **Bel**: **/I don't think it is I can't\ I can't you know [voc] I'd be biased**
21. **XF**: yeah
22. **Len**: I think we did a verbal for them last year actually
23. **Bel**: /(no they weren't in anything)\
24. **Len**: /no they weren't in\ the mix
25. **Bel**: **I'm definitely /biased Len [laughs]**
26. **Len**: /alright so they need to be they need to be\verbalized
27. **Sio**: good way of getting there [laughs]
28. **Len**: we may be we may be quite keen on your bias
29. **Val**: oh no
30. **Bel**: **use Clive [laughs] (   ) no I've had enough**
31. **Len**: alright

Belinda's initial refusing utterance actually anticipates the allocation of the task to her, and it is expressed very baldly and succinctly *I'm not doing it* (line 2). Similarly her concluding statement is equally direct, addressing her manager Len with an imperative *use Clive* (line 31), albeit mitigated with a laugh, and then followed by another clear statement of refusal *no I've had enough* (line 30). This is very confrontational and normatively masculine discourse.

However, scrutiny of example 5.9 indicates that these book-ending, challenging statements in fact enclose a very extended negotiation, in which Belinda provides a number of reasons why she should not be expected to undertake the verbal presentation (see bold lines in transcript: i.e. lines 5, 8, 14, 16, 20, 25, 30). In this central section, then, the style in which Belinda elaborates her refusal is stereotypically feminine in many respects: e.g. the use of repetition (e.g. lines 14, 16, 20, 25), intensification (*definitely*), and of a positive politeness marker in the form of her manager's name, *I'm definitely biased Len* (line 26). Hence, although the specific utterances which comprise the core of the refusal are concise, and apparently confrontational, in fact this refusal involves a complex negotiation process, and makes use of a range of face saving politeness strategies.[41]

This pattern proved remarkably robust. Refusals often appeared very direct between people who knew each other well, and who worked together regularly, even when they were directed to someone of higher status and power. But, attention to the surrounding discourse usually identified ameliorating strategies, sometimes involving collaborative humour as in example 5.9, which modified the superficially confrontational refusal. Previous research on refusals suggests that refusers generally make use of elaborate politeness strategies to mitigate the face threat of the refusal.[42] But in our workplace data, the amelioration was often achieved not so much by hedges and mitigators within the refusing speech act, but rather by the use of cognitively oriented strategies such as arguments, reasons and alternative suggestions which addressed the transactional imperatives of the organization. So (apart from one use of his name) Belinda does not address Len's face needs. Rather she raises issues of appropriateness and bias, and suggests another more suitable person (in her view) to do the job, strategies that address the requirements and responsibilities of the organization to complete the job. The personal face threat which her refusal constitutes to her manager takes a background position, and is dealt with rather by the team as a whole, who defuse it with their laughter and collaborative jocular responses.

The complexities of the gendering of workplace talk are well illustrated in this example. Belinda's core refusal utterance is direct and unmitigated, and stereotypically masculine, but the fact that it is just one component of an extended sequence accomplishing the refusal provides a different perspective. The embedding of the utterance in the extensive negotiation, and the contributions of others in the surrounding discourse, considerably attenuate the apparent directness of the refusal. And the strategies used for attenuation combine feminine stylistic discourse features (repetition and intensification) with argumentation addressing the transactional objectives of the organization from Belinda, together with collaborative teasing humour from her colleagues. Gendered discourse is a resource available for exploitation in a variety of complex and intersecting ways, as this example illustrates.

Example 5.10 is taken from a different professional context, a hospital ward. A young doctor asks a senior and older nurse to get him a piece of equipment, and she refuses quite bluntly, telling him to go and get it himself.

Example 5.10

Context: Doctor to nurse in the nurse's station of a hospital ward. There is another nurse present who is eating her lunch.

1.	**Doc:**	[softly]: there's another um: + thing that I would like to ask for
2.	**Nur:**	what's that
3.	**Doc:**	somewhere in delivery suite or at ward 11
4.		er there are those plastic er red containers for ++ for blood tests
5.		I need I need beside the the line there's a plastic end for this . . .
6.		[*some discussion between all three of what exactly is needed and where one*
7.		*might be*]
8.	**Doc:**	yeah so er we + could you just could we maybe have one
9.		from from er ward eleven oh this stuff er +
10.	**Nur:**	well you go down to ward eleven and get it
11.		cos I don't want to have to

The doctor begins with a tentative and softly expressed pre-request, which includes a hesitation and a pause, *there's another um + thing that I would like to ask for* (line 1), and goes on to express his request with a number of hedges, hesitations and repetitions, finally switching from a relatively direct *could you* to a much less direct structure *could we maybe have one* (line 8). This is canonical feminine discourse. The nurse, when she works out what the doctor wants, uses no such mitigating strategies; rather she tells him very bluntly to go and get it himself:

you go down to ward eleven and get it cos I don't want to have to (lines 10–11). This is particularly bald on record, direct, and normatively masculine discourse. The exchange challenges not only stereotypical expectations of the ways in which women and men talk, but also those regarding status, since one might expect a nurse to express a refusal more circumspectly to a doctor. Once again, the crucial factors appear to be contextual, including the norms of the relevant community of practice, and the relative medical experience of the two participants. The relative status of doctors and nurses as perceived by the wider society is quite evidently irrelevant here. More relevant is the nurse's age, seniority and extensive experience, compared to the relative inexperience of the young intern.

The importance of contextual factors in accounting for the different ways in which people accomplish refusals at work is equally apparent in data from a very masculine and blue-collar community of practice, a factory production team. Example 5.2 above, repeated here for convenience as example 5.11, clearly illustrates normatively masculine workplace talk. Despite Alex's use of explicit positive politeness devices (*bro* and *please*), Bert is not willing to be cooperative. It is difficult to imagine a more confrontational refusal.

Example 5.11

Context: Two factory production team members. Alex in the office is speaking to Bert on the production line over the intercom system.

1. **Alex**: yeah Bert bro check our pallet downstairs for us please bro+
2. **Bert**: no I fucking won't
3.   do it yourself you tight bastard

In this community of practice, expressions of refusal between close workmates were consistently direct and confrontational, and frequently intensified by the use of swear words which functioned as solidarity markers in the team's talk.[43] This is certainly not standard polite refusal behaviour, nor the kind of behaviour reported in previous studies of refusals.[44]

Team membership was a crucial factor in accounting for the ways in which workmates refused each other's requests in this community of practice. Example 5.12 illustrates how Ginette, the team coordinator, refuses a request from one of her team members to go and collect a piece of equipment that he needs.[45]

Example 5.12

Context: Ginette is the team manager of a factory production team, and Russell is a packer in her team on the factory floor.

1. **Russ:**   can you get me one please [in Samoan] :fa'amolemole: ['please']
2. **Gin:**   you get one
3. **Russ:**   ah you're not doing anything
4. **Gin:**   you go and get one
5. **Russ:**   fuck it +++ fuck you go get your fucking legs out here (fatters)
6. **Gin:**   why didn't you get one before I talked to you about that yesterday
7. **Russ:**   because we're busy + I got to get all that out of the way

Given the close relationship that we know exists between these team members, and their normal very 'in-your-face' style of interacting with each other illustrated in example 5.11, Russell's initial request *can you get me one please fa'amolemole'* (line 1) can be interpreted as tongue-in-cheek conventional politeness – a send-up rather than a genuinely respectful request (cf. *pretty please*). Team members simply do not talk to each other in this conventionally polite way. This interpretation is confirmed by what follows. Ginette's reply is not only a refusal, it is a bald-on-record, direct refusal with no mitigating features, *you get one* (line 2).

The exchange continues in this direct, confrontational style, with Russell's explicit and provocative challenge to Ginette's refusal *you're not doing anything* (line 3). Ginette then repeats her bald refusal *you go and get one* (line 4), to which Russell responds with a group of expletives, *fuck it fuck you go get your fucking legs out here* (line 5). Ginette's response to the string of expletives gives no indication that she is surprised or offended by them. Rather, she adopts a more feminine and even maternal discourse, issuing a 'motherly' reprimand, *why didn't you get one before I talked to you about that yesterday* (line 6), i.e. implying 'you have got yourself into this situation, serves you right, why should I help'.

Outside her workplace team, however, Ginette expresses refusals more circumspectly, drawing on a more conventionally polite discourse. In example 5.13, Ginette refuses not a fellow team member, but a status equal who works across the factory in a quality assurance role. Here Ginette's refusal is much closer in style to the feminine negotiation of Bea and Ros (example 5.8) than to the more masculine style she adopted in interaction with Russell.

Example 5.13

Context: Ginette, the team manager of a factory production team, talking to Francie, the quality assurance checker, who is not a team member.

1.	**Fra**:	do you have an NCR[46] for that (box) over there?
2.	**Gin**:	yeah I've I'm waiting for a number + +
3.		I need to see Vicky about the NCR thing
4.		I haven't got a number for it yet
5.	**Fra**:	oh how would you get it
6.	**Gin**:	when I get to see Vicky +++
7.	**Fra**:	oh how's about you just give it to me now +
8.		take a copy of that + so I can compare it
9.		and I'll take the number then +++
10.	**Gin**:	(where are they) + do you want it right now
11.	**Fra**:	if it's possible [laughs]
12.	**Gin**:	it's just I've left a + I've got um Jennifer's working +
13.		going through it as well
14.	**Fra**:	oh okay is it possible tomorrow then?
15.	**Gin**:	I'll get it to you tomorrow morning yeah

Francie's initial request is direct and clear: *do you have an NCR for that box over there?* (line 1). Ginette does not have the required number and has to refuse Francie's request. Her refusal is conventionally polite and extended. She prefaces it with a polite conventional agreement marker, *yeah*, and then elaborates in the form of a full explanation, *I've I'm waiting for a number I need to see Vicky about the NCR thing I haven't got a number for it yet* (lines 2–4).

Francie does not simply accept this refusal to comply with her request. She follows up with three further distinct attempts to elicit what she wants: *oh how would you get it* (line 5), and then *oh how's about you just give it to me now* . . . (lines 7–9), and finally *okay is it possible tomorrow then?* (line 14). The pauses (marked +) following Francie's requests indicate Ginette's reluctance to respond. Ginette's request for clarification *do you want it right now* (line 10) buys her time before she provides another explanation (lines 12–13) for why she cannot give Francie the NCR right now. Finally they negotiate a compromise (lines 14–15), and the transaction is satisfactorily brought to completion.

The careful negotiation evident in this exchange illustrates Ginette doing normative femininity: i.e. being conventionally respectful of Francie's face needs. While pursuing their transactional goals (Francie to see the relevant NCR, and Ginette to ensure her team's paperwork is in order before it is checked by Francie), the two women skilfully avoid confrontation and direct disagreement. By contrast with her much more direct style when refusing Russell (example 5.12), in her interaction with Francie Ginette uses a range of negative politeness strategies to convey her refusal in an acceptable way: avoidance strategies (lines 2–4, 10, 12–13), pauses (lines 2, 9), hesitations (line 12), syntactic false starts (lines 2, 12), explanations (lines 12–13), and hedges (line 12). In other words, Ginette here adopts classically feminine politeness strategies.

Hence, in this community of practice, refusals are often expressed very directly and explicitly, in a conventionally masculine way, between members of the production team, but in a much more circumspect and more feminine style when non-team members are involved. Between team members people use concise and apparently confrontational strategies, without elaboration or mitigation, and frequently intensified by the use of expletives. Refusals to people outside the team tend to be longer and more indirect, and strong expletives simply do not feature. Team membership, rather than gender, is a crucial factor in determining how such speech acts are constructed, negotiated and interpreted. But the resources that are exploited are conventionally gendered as I have indicated.

Conclusion

Like other aspects of workplace interaction, managing workplace conflict effectively and appropriately involves taking account of a range of socio-linguistic factors. In this chapter, I have focused in particular on the importance of the kind of community of practice in which people are operating. The examples have illustrated the complex relationship between different ways of managing conflict, and different workplace social relationships. Even within the same organization or company, speaking to close colleagues and team mates often involves a very different kind of discourse than speaking to someone from a different section of the workplace. Gendered discourse norms for managing conflict are thus a valuable resource for employees.

This point is nicely illustrated in a final example, which involves a misunderstanding. Neil is a consultant who has been brought in to assist the management of a commercial company to deal with a complex HR issue. At this stage he is still feeling his way, and example 5.14 illustrates the strategies he uses when he finds he must refuse an invitation to a staff meeting where he would meet members of the rest of the organization.

Example 5.14

Context: Formal meeting of five men and one woman, the senior management team in a medium-sized commercial IT organization.

1.	**Sha**:	I think it's important you do go to the staff meeting
2.		and get introduced
3.	**Nei**:	yeah . . .
4.		er I can't do it today unfortunately I've
5.		I've already booked in some time with someone else this afternoon
6.		but the next one I can come along to yeah
7.	**Sha**:	we'll think about it
8.	**Nei**:	pardon
9.	**Sha**:	we'll think about it
10.	**Nei**:	/[laughs uncertainly]\
11.	**Sha**:	/we don't take kindly to\ being rejected
12.	**Nei**:	oh I'm sorry I've got a yeah got a meeting this afternoon
13.		which I can't get out of
14.		if I'd have know I would've changed it yeah
15.	**Sha**:	what is our formal position on Neil (5)

Because he is likely to be around for a while, Shaun makes the point that it is important that Neil be introduced to the wider staff of the organization (lines 1–2). The easiest and usual way to accomplish this is for him to attend the monthly staff meeting which is to occur that day. Shaun initiates the humour with his semi-serious question. Neil states that he is not free to attend, *er I can't do it today unfortunately* (line 4), and immediately provides a reason, *I've already booked in some time with someone else this afternoon* (line 5), followed by an offer of reparation, all standard components of a polite apology.[47] At this point Shaun adopts the masculinist, joshing discourse which characterizes this community of practice and teases Neil with a comment, *we'll think about it* (line 8), suggesting that Neil can't simply assume it is OK to come along to the next meeting. Neil laughs uncertainly, and Shaun maintains the tease, *we don't take kindly to being rejected* (line 11). Neil takes him seriously and responds with an elaboration of his excuse (lines 12–14). Shaun then asks an ambiguous question which could be interpreted as critical of Neil's behaviour, *what is our formal position on Neil* (line 15). It seems likely, in the context of the wider discourse, that Shaun is asking about what the staff will be told about Neil's role in the organization, but in the context of Neil's misunderstanding of his teasing, it is also possible to see it as a veiled threat.

Neil is here being introduced to the distinctively masculine interactional style of this senior management team, a very close-knit community of practice.[48] This style is characterized by extensive competitive teasing, a style which serves as a means of creating team, or constructing solidarity between members of the community of practice. Getting integrated into the team involves learning to handle this style and learning to respond appropriately and energetically to the critical comments, teases and jocular insults which are consistently being thrown at all team members. In this excerpt, it is clear that Neil does not recognize what is going on. His responses are redolent with appeasement, stereotypically feminine, and overly conventionally polite in the context of this very masculine community of practice. Eventually, our data shows, he learned to match his discourse style to this distinctive community of practice, and to switch rapidly between serious transactional talk and contestive 'joshing'. The issue of choosing an appropriate way of refusing an invitation thus nicely illustrates the extent to which discourse is implicated in the construction of differently gendered communities of practice.

The analysis in this chapter has also demonstrated that managing workplace conflict is a complex process which can rarely be captured in a single speech act or a single utterance. The process of expressing disagreement or refusal often involves extended negotiation over several speaker turns. Indeed, a complex contentious issue is often worked through dynamically, sometimes throughout a long meeting, and in some cases over several meetings. Any account of workplace conflict must therefore consider the wide range of relevant factors which come into play as participants actively construct disagreement and work their way through conflictual situations at work. This chapter has demonstrated how gendered discourse norms can serve as valuable resources in managing this process.

It is interesting to reflect on the implications of this analysis for women in the workforce, an issue explored further in chapter 7. A good deal of research in the area of organizational communication identifies negotiation as a characteristic of more feminine workplace cultures. Moreover, feminist theorists have suggested that the increasing numbers of women in the workplace will have the effect of changing the dominant masculine patterns of conflict resolution observable in many workplaces.[49] Commenting on American patterns of workplace interaction and ways of managing conflict, for example, Berryman-Fink says, 'for the most part, workplace organizations operate on masculine assumptions and approaches to life and women are expected to adjust to this male model if they are to be successful in the workplace'.[50] She draws attention to feminist research indicating that as 'organizations adopt collaborative and participative styles, they move toward feminine organizational styles, though gender issues inherent in organizational cultures are rarely perceived'.[51] The analysis in this chapter has suggested that women do not have a monopoly on relationally sensitive, conventionally polite or normatively feminine strategies for managing conflict. Both women and men in our data draw on normatively masculine and normatively feminine conflict management strategies as they judge appropriate to the specific contexts in which disagreements arise, and to the communities of practice in which they operate. The likely effects of more women in more senior positions in more workplaces on acceptable styles of managing disagreements are thus by no means easy to predict.

Finally, it is worth critically considering the fact that this chapter has categorized disagreements and refusals as negatively affective aspects of workplace talk. This categorization could be considered, at a deeper level, to reinforce a gendered assumption about acceptable ways of interacting. As noted in chapter 1, the language and gender literature suggests that masculine interactional styles are characterized by competition, contestation and challenge, while cooperation, smooth talk and facilitative interaction index more feminine styles. Fletcher's discussion of relational practice is predicated on the assumption that conflict avoidance is not only feminine but also desirable in an organization, an assumption discussed further in chapter 7. 'Preserving', for instance, involves taking steps to make sure the project is not held up by misunderstandings or disputes. It entails damage control, mitigating potentially threatening behaviour, minimizing conflict, and negotiating consensus.[52] And in Fletcher's view this is paradigmatic women's work. The analysis in this chapter has revealed that, as in other areas of interaction, the gender lines are anything but clear-cut in relation to ways of managing conflict. Effective employees, female and male, draw extensively on discursive resources indexed both as masculine and feminine to achieve their transactional and relational objectives in different workplace contexts. And the ability to draw on differently gendered discourse norms for managing conflict must surely be regarded as advantageous in most communities of practice.

The next chapter examines the role of workplace stories, a topic which serves to draw together many of the threads explored in earlier chapters. Narrative provides a rich resource for workplace identity construction, a means of accomplishing all aspects of relational practice, and a way of contributing to the development of one's community of practice.

NOTES

1 See e.g. articles in Grimshaw (1990) and Yaeger-Dror (2002).
2 Austin (1990).
3 See Daly et al. (2004) for a discussion of forms of the swear word *fuck* as a solidarity marker.
4 See e.g. Jacobs (2002), Clayman (2002), Heritage (2002).
5 See e.g. Yaeger-Dror (2002), Holmes and Stubbe (2003b).
6 See e.g. Morand (1996a, 1996b, 2000).
7 See e.g. Eckert and McConnell-Ginet (2003), Wenger (1998).
8 See e.g. Kangasharju (2002), Kaufmann (2002), Kakavá (2002).
9 See Fisher and Ellis (1990), Willing (1992), Putnam (1992), Tjosvold, Dann and Wong (1992), Holmes and Stubbe (2001).

10 The discussion in this section draws on and integrates material from Holmes and Stubbe (2001), and Holmes and Marra (2005b).

11 See e.g. Pomerantz (1978, 1984), Edmondson (1981), Wootton (1981), Levinson (1983), Brown and Levinson (1987), Sacks (1987), Houtkoop (1987), and Bublitz (1988). For a discussion of the formal meaning of 'preference for agreement' in conversation analysis, see Schegloff, Jefferson and Sacks (1977: 362), Levinson (1983), Sacks (1987).

12 See e.g. Taylor and Cameron (1987: 114).

13 See e.g. Boden (1994), Firth (1995), Stalpers (1995).

14 See Holmes and Stubbe (2003a), Thimm et al. (2003), Baxter (2003).

15 See e.g. Darling and Walker (2001), Heaney (2001), Knippen and Green (1999).

16 See e.g. Proctor-Thomson and Parry (2001), Jackson and Parry (2001).

17 Parry (2001: 4).

18 Brown and Levinson (1987: 60). See Holmes (1987), Stubbe (1991), Vine (2001) for further discussion and examples.

19 For a related but somewhat different perspective, see Blake and Mouton (1978), who propose five styles of conflict management: avoiding, accommodating, competing, confronting, and compromising. This analytical approach to our data is illustrated in Holmes and Stubbe (2001).

20 This section is based on Holmes and Marra (2005b), where the continuum is more extensively discussed. The discussion here develops this research by exploring gender considerations.

21 Brown and Levinson (1987: 69).

22 See also Trauth (2002).

23 See e.g. Berryman-Fink (1997), Wood (2000), Harris (2002).

24 See Holmes and Stubbe (2003b), Marra (2003).

25 The same group feature in example 5.3.

26 See McRae (2004) for discussion of this issue.

27 See Locher (2004), Holmes and Stubbe (2003b).

28 See Heritage (1998).

29 Holmes and Stubbe (2001).

30 Thomas (1995: 127), Spencer-Oatey (1992).

31 The directors gave us permission to view the extensive unedited reels of film they shot of the many planning meetings which preceded the opening of Te Papa.

32 I use the macron to indicate long vowels in writing Māori words as advocated by the Māori Language Commission. In the transcript the variation between Maori and Māori indicates a Māori pronunciation as opposed to an Anglicized pronunciation.

33 Pākehā is a Māori word used widely in New Zealand to refer to people of European (mainly British) descent.

34 While this is an authentic interaction, it should be remembered that this is a de-contextualized excerpt from a commercial film; the confrontational features may thus be subtly exaggerated for dramatic effect.

35 See McRae (2004) for a detailed socio-linguistic and pragmatic analysis of 199 disagreements collected in 35 hours of recorded data in 11 different organizations.

36 More recent research in business and communication studies also emphasizes this point, identifying a range of strategies available for managing conflict. See e.g. Brewer, Mitchell and Weber (2002), Morris, Williams, Leung and Larrick (1998).

37 See e.g. Takahashi and Beebe (1987), Beebe, Takahashi and Uliss-Weltz (1990), Beebe and Cummings (1996), Sasaki (1998), Gass and Houck (1999).

38 See Turnbull (2001), Morrison and Holmes (2003) for detailed discussion of this point.

39 Folkes (1982) comments that turning down a date is a situation more familiar to female than male respondents, and Besson, Roloff, and Paulson (1998) subsequently confined their DCT study using such a scenario to women. But there is no research of which I am aware on the interaction of gender and refusals in authentic face-to-face interaction. But see Morrison (forthcoming).

40 This example and the discussion is taken from Holmes, Burns et al. (2003).

41 See also Houck and Gass (1996: 49), Gass and Houck (1999: 2–3), Chen, Ye and Zhang (1995).

42 See e.g. Besson, Roloff and Paulson (1998), Gass and Houck (1999).

43 Daly et al. (2004).

44 See e.g. Kline and Floyd (1990), Besson, Roloff and Paulson (1998), Gass and Houck (1999), Saeki and O'Keefe (1994), Wootton (1981), Takahashi and Beebe (1987), Turnbull (2001).

45 This section is taken from Daly et al. (2004), with some minor modifications.

46 An NCR is a Non-Conformance Report, or a sheet filled out when a product is not up to standard.

47 Cohen and Olshtain (1981), Holmes (1990).

48 See Schnurr (forthcoming) for a full description of this community of practice.

49 See e.g. Astin and Leland (1991), Johnson (1993), Carr-Ruffino (1993), Karsten (1994), Berryman-Fink (1997). Note that these theorists are assuming that the presence of more women will increase the use of feminine styles of interaction in the workplace.

50 Berryman-Fink (1997: 266).

51 Ibid.

52 Fletcher (1999: 49–55).

CHAPTER SIX

Women and Men Telling Stories at Work

Introduction

Narrative is a powerful means of constructing a complex social identity, including gender identity. A number of researchers have demonstrated that women and men tend to tell rather different kinds of stories: women's stories, for example, focus more on people and relationships, while men prefer to talk about activities and adventures.[1] Such narratives have usually been collected in domestic or informal contexts, and often in interviews; the workplace is not an obvious context for collecting stories.[2] But our Wellington Language in Workplace (LWP) Project database provides evidence that people do tell stories at work, and their stories serve a wide range of functions. Most relevantly in the context of this book, narrative is a useful resource for accomplishing and integrating sometimes disparate aspects of one's professional and gender identity.

Workplace stories also provide a means of constructing the professional identities of others as effective or inadequate, competent or incompetent team members. They provide a legitimate and acceptable, but unofficial and off-record, outlet for dissatisfaction, jealousy or irritation in the workplace. Moreover, like humour and conflict management, narrative can be analysed as a means of enacting particular aspects of the gendered concept, relational practice, including 'self-achieving' and 'mutual empowering'.[3] Narratives offer a means of constructing particular kinds of communities of practice and workplace relationships, collegial or competitive, self-promoting or other-oriented, supportive or aggressive, and culturally coded as relatively masculine or feminine. Through their narratives, groups (often jointly) construct themselves as a productive team, or a competitive squad, as a 'family business', or a streamlined organization.[4] Conversely, narrative also provides a subtle means of contesting or subverting the prevailing organizational ethos or workplace culture, through stories which present an alternative reality. This chapter focuses on narrative as a discursive resource for individuals in the workplace, a resource which can be used to construct different kinds of workplace identity, and especially gender identity, while also dynamically creating and sometimes contesting the dominant ethos of differently gendered communities of practice.

Integrating Professional and Gender Identity at Work[5]

Workplace narratives are typically multi-functional; they contribute to identity construction at work, while simultaneously serving other functions as well. They contribute to the construction of 'the professional self',[6] and also to the construction of 'the gendered self', though the precise way this is achieved tends to differ in different workplace cultures or communities of practice. Judith Baxter's study of a dotcom company, for example, uncovered 'a pervasive discourse of *masculinisation* . . . a set of ways of making sense of the world and inscribing its discursive processes which harness[ed] stereotypical constructs of masculinity, such as hierarchy, order, structure, dominance, competitiveness, rivalry, aggression and goal-oriented action'.[7] Our study of Leila, a manager in a small government department, illustrated a much more normatively feminized discourse, where status was de-emphasized, egalitarian and democratic practices prevailed, and cooperation and open communication were valued.[8] Narrative can make an important contribution to such gendered discourse. Moreover, the particular emphases of different stories tend to reflect the varied interactional practices in which they are embedded, and from which they emerge.[9] Again, gender is one important component in this mix.

Doing Masculinity Through Stories at Work

I begin by considering workplace narratives where professional identity and gender identity line up relatively neatly for men, but not so comfortably for some women, namely hero-manager stories of successes, and stories of effective authoritative behaviour at work, stories which emphasize the professionalism and competence of the narrator, sometimes at the expense of other characters in the story. Our database includes a number of narratives which tell stories of success, often in the form of a stereotypically masculine narrative of contest, where the hero overcomes great odds to succeed.[10]

Example 6.1 is a brief excerpt from an interview in which the narrator, Victor, tells the story of the beginnings and growth of the company of which he is the Managing Director. This is a classic company myth story, part of the 'historical legacy' of the company contributing to the 'authorized company ethos'.[11] Moreover, since it does important identity work for Victor, it could also be regarded as an example of 'self-achieving', a type of relational practice.[12]

Example 6.1

Context: Interview with the Managing Director of a relatively large and steadily growing IT company.

1.	**Vic:**	we went away and in our discussions said
2.		actually there's an opportunity for someone else to go and do that
3.		and why shouldn't it be us? +
4.		so we spent a few months devoting most weekends
5.		to planning of whether it was feasible
6.		or how we should do it, what we could do
7.		and then decided it was worthwhile
8.		and in the meantime during that period of planning er
9.		we'd been saving frantically
10.		so that come the day when we stepped out
11.		er we didn't need to take anything out of the company
12.		for a period of time + . . .
13.	**Int:**	and so right at the beginning it was just the two of you?
14.	**Vic:**	mhm + sort of just the two of us
15.		er our wives had been involved in the planning +
16.		and er they were very very much instrumental in setting the thing up
17.	**Int:**	so um + so in a sense it was like a family business?

18. /+++ as\ it grew in the initial stages
19. **Vic:** /yes very much a family business\ for several years
20. **Int:** yep
21. **Vic:** and um + it would have been about ++ probably five years in
22. + when we + realized that + we would either have to +
23. er + get things organized to perpetuate a family / firm\
24. **Int:** /mm\
25. **Vic:** or we would have to consciously change to something new +
26. and we made the decision to change
27. because we couldn't see the family firm side of things in consulting
28. growing any big any further than we'd taken it
29. and we were keen to carry on that growth path
30. so that meant we needed to migrate to a a proper corporate structure

There is much one could comment on here,[13] but I focus on the elements which contribute to the construction of Victor's professional and gender identity. Victor presents himself and his business partner(s) as people with vision; they were the ones who saw an opportunity to develop a new company: *why shouldn't it be us* (line 3). He then describes the careful planning that they undertook to work out whether their vision was feasible (lines 4–8), and the saving they undertook to provide the safety net they would need to launch onto the market (lines 9–12). Their proactive role is evident in the repeated use of the agentive *we* (lines 1, 4, 6, 9, 10, 11). Until this point it is unclear who the referentially ambiguous pronoun *we* refers to throughout Victor's account, though the preceding discourse has suggested that *we* comprises him and his male business partner, the company's Board Chair, as the interviewer's question indicates, *and so right at the beginning it was just the two of you?* (line 13).

Interestingly at this point, Victor first provides a hedged confirmation *sort of just the two of us* (line 14), and then acknowledges that their wives had also contributed, *our wives had been involved in the planning and er they were very very much instrumental in setting the thing up* (lines 15–16). The interviewer asks, *so in a sense it was like a family business?*

(line 17). After briefly acknowledging this, Victor moves on to an account of further developments where he and his male business partner again take front stage, *we made the decision to change* (line 26), *we were keen to carry on that growth path* (line 29). As Victor presents it, then, and despite the elicited acknowledgement (lines 15–16), there is a strong impression that the women have been largely erased from this story. Moreover, the prevailing discourse here is 'masculinized' discourse in Baxter's terms, *we needed to migrate to a a proper corporate structure* (line 30). Victor thus presents a hero story in which he and his partner established what has now become a very successful IT company through their careful planning, hard work (involving *most weekends*, line 4), willingness to save hard, and also to do without any financial reward initially – *we didn't need to take anything out of the company for a period of time* (lines 11–12). Thus, despite the slight wheel-wobble generated by the interviewer's query, this can be considered a typical masculine narrative of contest, where the heroes succeed despite formidable hurdles.

My second example of a relatively masculine workplace story is told by Ginette, the factory production team manager referred to in earlier chapters. The factory is a hierarchical organization with clearly demarcated professional roles for staff at different levels. Ginette was universally recognized within the factory as outstandingly good at her job, a recognition well supported by our detailed ethnographic observations.[14] Ginette's authority as team leader was unquestioningly accepted by her team. She was a straight-talking and authoritative manager who provided direct criticism when the team failed to meet its targets or made errors. She did not suffer fools gladly, nor tolerate slack work, or lateness, and her humour often had an incisive and merciless edge.[15] In other words, many aspects of the interactional style of this factory manager could be described as normatively masculine, a style which was a good fit with her male-dominated, blue-collar community of practice.[16] In the following workplace narrative, Ginette constructs her identity as a tough and demanding team manager.

Example 6.2

Context: Ginette, the manager of a factory production team, is working in the scales area of the packing line and talking to other members of the team who are within hearing.

1. **Gin**: yesterday + afternoon Christian and I were standing at the end
2. by the elevator over there talking
3. and David was coming round with the vacuum by the two-kilo elevator +
4. and just along the wall there on the ( )
5. there's a trail of powder just went right along +
6. we were standing away talking
7. and David had the hose and had that long thing connected t-
8. hosing um vacuuming by the two-K-G elevator +
9. and then he went over to clean that trail of powder + along side the wall +
10. what he did h- he disconnected the hose off + off the end piece
11. and then he walked over
12. and he swept [voc] + the trail [laughs]: of powder up with that:
13. **Hel**: how stupid
14. **Gin**: [laughs]: with that metal bit:
15. **Hel**: yeah
16. **Gin**: when he finished that he connected the hose back on
17. and then he vacuumed it up +
18. the pile of powder that he'd swept up with just (the end)
19. me and Christian were just cracking up laughing
20. and (he turns to me) (   ) said + this is very [laughs]: embarrassing:
21. **Hel**: [laughs]
22. **Gin**: I thought what a dick + you know
23. all he had to do was go along with this thing /and suck it all up\
24. **Hel**: /(   )\ and suck it up + it's actually easier + (   ) for that one +
25. **Gin**: [said to someone in distance]: that's a nice one: eh
26. (6)
27. **Gin**: dumb eh?

Ginette's story exposes a third (absent) team member, David, to ridicule for stupid behaviour. The story is told with little embellishment. Ginette first establishes the context in which she observed David vacuuming the floor (lines 1–3). Then she describes how David first manually brushed up a trail of powder with one of the vacuum cleaner attachments, before then using the vacuum cleaner to suck up the pile he had made (lines 4–12). The story is a simple one, and its most obvious point is to provide amusement at David's expense. But, if we examine the narrative style more closely, it is clear that this story also does identity work. Ginette presents herself as a tough manager, drawing on gendered discourse resources to achieve this.

This is a concisely presented narrative; the 'complicating action' is sparely described (lines 9–18), with no wasted words.[17] There is not a single attenuating hedge, no mitigating devices, and no unnecessary descriptive adjectives. By contrast, the evaluation is more fully elaborated. The ridiculousness of David's behaviour is emphasized by three different devices: firstly, we are told that it evoked paroxysms of laughter from those watching: *me and Christian were just cracking up laughing* (line 19). Secondly, Ginette indicates explicitly how simple the alternative sensible behaviour was: *all he had to do was go along with this thing and suck it all up* (line 23); and Helen signals she has taken the point by using an echoic phrase *suck it up* (line 24), and a confirmatory evaluation, *it's actually easier* (line 24). Thirdly, and most tellingly, Ginette provides two no-punches-pulled explicit evaluations of David's behaviour, *I thought what a dick you know* (line 22), emphasized in the coda, *stupid eh* (line 27). The accompanying addressee-oriented pragmatic particles *you know* and *eh* are solidarity markers, indicating her confidence that she and others share the negative evaluation (as clearly signalled by Helen in lines 13, 24).

Ginette's story has a number of features that could be considered normatively masculine. It focuses on arguably the weakest team member and exposes his stupid behaviour for others' entertainment.[18] It constructs Ginette as a tough task-master. Here, as in other contexts, Ginette indicates that she does not readily tolerate mistakes, especially those which could damage the team's record or adversely affect their productivity. She presents herself as someone who expects high levels of performance from team members. Her direct, unelaborated and relatively masculine narrative style, with no hedging, no mitigating devices, and no spare adjectives is an interesting discoursal instantiation of her direct, authoritative managerial style.[19]

Ginette's style of narration and narrative theme is consistent with and contributes to the construction of the relatively masculine community of practice in which she works, and the competitive and hierarchical workplace culture of the factory. The factory culture reflects the factory's goals, and the means by which they are achieved – namely material outputs and heavy machinery. Ginette's focused and normatively masculine style – even in her workplace anecdotes – is an interesting verbal instantiation of this culture.

I turn now to an example of the construction of a masculinist hero narrative by the protagonist's colleagues rather than by the hero himself, illustrating how others can contribute to the construction of a person's professional identity at work. The participants in example 6.3 draw on a relatively masculine discursive style to emphasize professional and stereotypically masculine aspects of workplace behaviour. The excerpt is taken from the interactions of a high-performing and highly qualified computer development project team in a white-collar commercial organization. It is a very brief story about Eric's success in making a presentation at a conference, told by a colleague in a style that suggests envy and reluctant admiration. Eric is presented as hero, but the style of presentation is in tune with the competitive and somewhat verbally aggressive interactional style which is typical of this particular community of practice.

Example 6.3

Context: Regular weekly meeting of an IT project team in a large commercial organization. There are 6 male participants present in the meeting room and one female who has telephone contact. Barry is the meeting chair.

1.	**Bar:**	I don't think it's an issue anymore /is it\?
2.	**Eric:**	/nah\
3.	**Bar:**	cos you've got their attention /now\
4.	**Eri:**	/yep\
5.	**Bar:**	[laughs] /[laughs]\
6.	**Eri:**	/yep\
7.	**Cal:**	what did you do? +
8.	**Bar:**	he got a standing ovation
9.	**All:**	/[laughter]\
10.	**Dud:**	/(oh is that right?)\
11.	**Cal:**	that's why he got their attention

12. **Bar:** and now he's developed a whole project around it
13. **All:** /[laughter]\
14. **Jas:** /yeah\
15. **Mar:** (could need) more staff
16. **Bar:** talk about empire-building [laughs]

This elliptical story about Eric's successful presentation, *he got a standing ovation* (line 8), draws on a good deal of in-group, contextual information shared by the team about what Eric was presenting, to whom, and why. The team members are IT experts; they share a great deal of professional knowledge, values and attitudes. We have extensive evidence that this is a very competitive community of practice; as described in chapter 4, they engage in cut-throat, sarcastic humour, for example, and in challenging arguments at almost every point throughout their discussions.[20] Here we see a narrative told by Barry about Eric in a style which suggests grudging admiration. Rather than producing a coherent and fluid story, Barry offers a series of short, pithy contributions which present the story in a complex reverse order. He first presents the implications of the story – the coda – using a tag question which could be seen as inviting Eric to tell the tale, *I don't think it's an issue anymore is it?* (line 1). Only Eric could know at this point that the reason that there is no longer an issue requires an account of his successful conference presentation. Barry's follow-up, however, establishes that there is a story to be told, *cos you've got their attention now* (line 3); he is here referring to the attention of the wider audience that Eric's presentation had been so successful with, but the potential relevance to their current context adds another layer of meaning. This is all presented in a provocative, teasing style, goading Eric to tell the tale, but he resists, laconically contributing only agreement signals, *yep* (lines 4, 6). Finally Callum follows up Barry's oblique invitation with a direct question to Eric, *what did you do?* (line 7).

When Eric, perhaps subversively, does not respond, Barry provides the main action of the story *he got a standing ovation* (line 8), a simple clause with the minimal amount of information needed for this team to get the point. He subsequently adds two evaluative comment clauses, each of which encode an envious and possibly censorious perspective, *and now he's developed a whole project around it* (line 12), and *talk about empire-building* (line 16). The contributions of others confirm Barry's interpretation of Eric's ambitious motives, *that's why he got their attention* (line 11) and *(could need) more staff* (line 15). Like Ginette's narrative,

Barry's wastes no words; it is told sparely and minimally. By exploiting the team's shared knowledge, Barry is able to keep his complimentary narrative to the bare bones, an approach which is very compatible with this team's preferred interactional style, as well as with a normatively masculine style (as described in chapter 3). Hence the overtly competitive and predominantly masculine interactional style which characterizes this community of practice is exemplified even in this brief, jointly constructed narrative exchange.

Stories thus provide useful resources for the construction of gender identity. Each of these three narratives illustrates the construction of a masculine, success-oriented, professional identity, using a conventionally masculine discursive style. It is also worth noting the occasional cracks in the constructions – real life does not always measure up to myth. None the less, such stories contribute to the creation and maintenance of relatively masculine work contexts and communities of practice. When men tell such stories, their professional identities and their gender identities are in alignment. For women like Ginette, there is a potential conflict between the two. As mentioned in chapter 2, Ginette resolves this in her role as leader by combining the stance of tartar or battle-axe with that of 'good joker', and she makes extensive use of humour as an attenuating device.[21] Narrative provides another strategy for resolving the classic double bind facing women in management positions.[22]

Doing Femininity Through Stories at Work

Narrative can equally provide a resource for performing a relatively feminine gender identity and contributing to the creation of a relatively feminine community of practice.

One theme which emerged from our analysis was the use of workplace narratives to attenuate the enactment of authority and leadership. Some managers used stories to play down their skills and abilities, and to present themselves, albeit often facetiously, as incompetent, naive, or even ludicrous (though, interestingly, usually also as successful in achieving their goals). This was a noticeable, though often subtly expressed, component of the stories told by some of the women in our database, and especially the senior women in more feminine communities of practice where explicit manifestations of authority were not always well-received. In such contexts, narratives represented another means of managing the potential conflict between an authoritative and professional identity on the one hand and a feminine gender identity on the other.[23]

In example 6.4, Marlene describes how in a professional, multinational, white-collar organization she found herself in an embarrassing position responding to a caller on the phone.

Example 6.4

Context: Meeting of 6 women and 5 men, members of a project team in a multinational white-collar commercial organization. The meeting is chaired by Clara, a senior manager, since the usual chairperson is absent.

1.	**Mar:**	I got a phone call from someone
2.		who thought that I was Renee
3.	**Cla:**	[drawls]: oh:
4.	**Mar:**	and at first I didn't realize
5.		cos they just sort of asked kind of general questions
6.		and then by the time I realized
7.		sort of as I was just about to get off the phone
8.		that they thought I was Renee
9.		I thought this is going to be too embarrassing
10.		for this person now
11.	**Cla:**	[drawls]: oh yes yes:
12.	**Mar:**	I quickly rushed off and told [laughs]: Renee: . . .

In this humorous anecdote, which is explicitly concerned with issues of professional identity, Marlene recounts a uncomfortable experience in which her identity was mistakenly construed by a caller as that of her colleague Renee. The story is encapsulated in the first 2 lines, the 'abstract'; the remaining 10 lines provide an elaboration of the narrative, indicating Marlene's attitude to the event described, and some insights into her management of her workplace identity. Rather than asserting her identity, Marlene allows the caller to continue to assume she is Renee, even after the mistake has become evident to Marlene.

There are a number of pragmatic signals of embarrassment and discomfort, indicating that Marlene is self-aware and conscious of threats to her own face needs. In addition to the overt disclaimer *and at first I didn't realize* (line 4), there is also a distinctive prosody in the form of high rising intonation contours, and a number of features indexing a feminine gender identity such as attenuating hedges and mitigators, *sort of, kind of, just* (lines 5, 7), which indicate that Marlene is less than comfortable with the situation. A further stereotypically feminine aspect of this narrative is the way that Marlene presents herself as a person who is sensitive and responsive to the opinions and feelings of others. She indicates, for example, that she does not wish to embarrass the caller, *I thought this is going to be too embarrassing for this person now* (lines 9–10), and she is similarly concerned to inform Renee at once of what has happened, *I quickly rushed off and told Renee* (line 12), suggesting she does not want to be badly thought of, or to be misjudged as having impersonated Renee. Moreover, her disclaimer, *I didn't realize* (line 4), also signals concern that her addressee should be aware that she did not deliberately mislead the caller. None the less, it is noteworthy that Marlene reports that she succeeded in handling the call, thus demonstrating that she could do Renee's job convincingly (as well as her own).[24]

In this brief anecdote, then, Marlene presents a rather ambiguous identity. On the one hand, she was involved in an embarrassing and somewhat ludicrous situation; on the other she managed it successfully, demonstrating sensitivity to her audience. In the telling, she makes use of a range of strategies to construct a discursively feminine identity – consciously polite, caring, and responsive to the needs and feelings of others – within her male-dominated, commercially-oriented professional community of practice.

In a different and identifiably feminine community of practice, Leila, a senior manager, tells a story which is entirely consistent with her workplace culture. She recounts how she found the 'flying filers', a team of outside experts who come in and file backlogged materials for any organization.[25] Her story serves to introduce a solution to a workplace problem facing Leila's team.

Example 6.5

Context: Regular team meeting of 6 women in a government organization. The team is discussing the best use of resources to address some staffing problems.

1. **Lei:** mm /[voc]\ didn't you hear my little story
2. **Em:** /oh\
3. **Lei:** about coming back from somewhere and seeing this little dirty
4. **Em:** I haven't actually seen it ( )
5. **Lei:** v van I saw this little dirty v van
6. and on the back it had flying filing squad +
7. /and I was trying to drive\ round to [laughs]: see who it was
8. **XF:** /I think I have seen them\
9. **Lei:** and I was cos: they didn't have their phone number
10. on the back only on the /side of the van\
11. **Zoe:** /yeah that's there's\ a lot that do that
12. **Em:** (for)
13. **Lei:** mhm no well they were in front of me [laughs]: you see:
14. **Lei:** /so just at our corner\ you know like
15. **Ker:** /flying filing squad\
16. **Lei:** just at the point they were going up Brooklyn hill
17. and I was proceeding up Aro [laughs]: Street: or into Willis
18. and I was trying to sort of edge round
19. and I was [laughs]: stretching this way in the /car: [laughs]\
20. /[general laughter]\
21. **Lei:** /I was a wee\ bit like ( ) [laughs]
22. **Em:** /(they must have) thought you were a maniac\
23. **Lei:** you must have been away the day that I told this
24. **XF:** [laughs] /[laughs]\
25. **Lei:** /that I'd found\ these funny people

The most overt point of Leila's story is that she managed with some difficulty to identify the name and telephone number of a firm that offered a potential solution to a problem the team was facing – relating to keeping records and getting their filing up-to-date. One could see this workplace anecdote, then, as Leila constructing her professional identity as a competent manager with her wits about her, finding a solution to an on-going problem faced by her team.

The manner in which Leila tells the story, however, has much in common with Marlene's narrative style. In recounting what happened,

Leila constructs a stereotypically self-deprecating feminine identity, casting herself as a bit of a clown to amuse her colleagues, perhaps. Note, for instance, her tongue-in-cheek use of a phrase associated with police accounts in court, *I was proceeding up Aro Street* (line 17), where her accompanying laughter suggests she is aware of the formal echoes invoked by using such a structure in this informal story. She then repeats the syntactic pattern twice more, *I was trying . . . I was stretching* (lines 18–19), painting an absurd and amusing picture of herself leaning out to see the side of the van. Emma's laughing comment, *they must have thought you were a maniac* (line 22), picks up exactly Leila's tone, and provides an appropriate response to the slightly ridiculous self-image that Leila has presented.

A range of linguistic devices personalize and feminize the story. Leila describes her account of how she found the firm as *my little story* (line 1), using the personalizing possessive pronoun *my* rather than an article such as 'a', a diminutive *little*, and choosing the friendly lexical item *story*, rather than a more objective word such as 'account' or 'description'. She uses a number of addressee-oriented, pragmatic particles, such as *you see, you know*, appealing to the audience's understanding; and attenuating phrases such as *sort of* (line 18), and *a wee bit like* (line 21), indexical features of a feminine speech style, as noted in chapter 1. Colloquial adjective choices also contribute to this overall effect: e.g. *this little dirty van* (lines 3, 5) *these funny people* (line 25).

In many aspects of the way she managed her department and ran meetings, Leila was a firm and capable manager, but, at the same time, the self-deprecating self-presentation illustrated in this narrative was by no means unusual, and was often particularly evident following occasions when she had needed to assert her authority and emphasize her professional identity and responsibilities. Again, however, it is worth noting that it is finally a story of success, since she solved a long-standing problem.[26]

Even in more social contexts within the workplace, such as the tea-room, many of the stories Leila tells have a distinctively self-deprecating style, constructing her as a victim exploited by others or portraying her in a slightly ludicrous light. In one story she describes how she was manoeuvred into providing board and lodging for an unwelcome acquaintance; another narrative describes how she was unexpectedly summoned to see the Prime Minister when she was dressed in an inappropriately casual style.

Example 6.6

Context: Tea break in a government organization. Three women are chatting together.

1.	**Lei**:	once I had to go over and see the Prime Minister
2.		you were there I think
3.		about the suffrage stuff
4.		it was very last-minute one afternoon
5.		the <u>Prime</u> Minister called me over and all I had on was my cream linen
6.		trousers and like a white shirt or something it was re-
7.		I was really casually dressed on this particular day
8.		so Veronica found me I mean a really non-my-colour <u>green</u> jacket
9.		[laughs]: /you should have seen me\
10.	**Lis**:	/oh I know I've never seen you wear\
11.	**Lei**:	I went over to see the prime minister in it
12.	**Lis**:	I know I've never /seen you wear green before\
13.	**Lei**:	/[laughs]: and I sat there with sort of:\ this) [laughs]

Leila again emphasizes the ludic elements of her story, presenting herself as a slightly comic figure, firstly in being inappropriately casually dressed, and then in having to wear a jacket in a colour that did not suit her and made her feel slightly ridiculous. Again, she makes use of a number of conventionally feminine linguistic features, including strong stress on intensifiers, e.g. *I was really casually dressed on this particular day* (line 7), and hedges and addressee-oriented phrases (e.g. *you were there I think* (line 2), *I mean a really non-my-colour green jacket [laughs] you should have seen me* (lines 8–9).

This is a very feminine story in its content, its point and its style of presentation. Moreover, it contributes to the construction of a much more feminine identity for this senior woman, who in other contexts behaved at times in more normatively masculine ways. However, overall, such stories are consistent with the dominant features of Leila's personal leadership style, which was consultative and emphasized negotiation, and which paid careful attention to the face needs of others. They are also a good fit with the wider community of practice within which this team operated, and which at the time of our study was very consensus-oriented, democratic and feminine in style at all levels.[27]

In this egalitarian workplace, then, Leila, the capable and efficient manager of the policy team, uses workplace anecdotes, even in business meetings, to add complexity to the professional image she presents. This use of narrative as a means of managing contradictory aspects of self-presentation has been noted by others.[28] Analysing the lecture-room narratives of two (male) professors, Dyer and Keller-Cohen draw a parallel with the narratives told by Jewish mothers analysed by Schiffrin, noting that in both cases,

> the narrators are figures of authority attempting to construct selves both by displaying their authority and at the same time downplaying it, because of the democratic nature of the society they live in. Such dilemmatic discourse may therefore characterize the construction of self in a situation where the speaker is in a position of authority in the narrative, but is cautious about how this should be presented.[29]

Clearly this is not just a gender issue, nor an issue confined to women, though the problems raised by the inherent conflict between doing power and doing collegiality are particularly salient for senior women in a masculinist society.[30] Attenuating one's authority by telling stories which emphasize more feminine characteristics is one available strategy here. Olsson, for instance, notes that the often humorous and covertly subversive narratives she collected from professional women 'make up a distinctively female paradigm'; these women 'acknowledge their womanhood and the issues of gender in their careers' while also privileging 'the discourse of femininity'.[31] Leila's self-deprecating anecdotes similarly attenuate the authority of her managerial position; her self-mockery has the effect of 'democratizing' as well as feminizing the more managerial discourse of the surrounding text.

In the first example in this book (1.1), Jill, the Chair of the Board of a male-dominated IT company, used a similar strategy, though in a very self-aware and rather ironic fashion. Jill's embryonic story of her visit to the company's computer expert drew attention to her technical ignorance and lack of computer know-how; she described herself as a *technical klutz*, a stereotypically female role. Furthermore, in telling her story she made copious use of linguistic features indexing a feminine style, such as hedges and intensifiers, thus constructing, overall, a very feminine identity within her predominantly masculine community of practice. Our data provides evidence that Jill is a confident, competent and professional chair of the company board. Together with the sardonic tone of her narration, this supports an ironic and subversive reading of her construction of an ultra-feminine identity in this story. In other words, while Leila's self-deprecating narrative fits well into her feminine, democratic community of practice, Jill's story rather challenges the predominantly masculinist norms of her IT community of practice, asserting her feminine identity in an unapologetic manner. By refusing to treat IT incompetence as a serious matter, she implicitly raises questions about the validity of a position which disparages women who are technically inexperienced. Like the American adolescent girls Eder researched, Jill here parodies 'traditional norms about feminine behaviour',[32] and, as a demonstrably intelligent woman and competent manager, implicitly contests or troubles them, thus transforming their role as unquestioned and unquestionable reference points.[33]

These narratives are stereotypically feminine both in their themes and in their self-deprecating and other-oriented style of construction – and the addressees respond sympathetically and constructively, a point discussed further below. They illustrate one means of managing the conflict between professional and gender identity for women in the workplace. These capable and competent women tell stories which subvert their professionalism; they present themselves as imperfect and vulnerable, and even as people who make fools of themselves at times. In this way, workplace narratives contribute to the development of a particular gendered style of interaction, a style which is consistent with the observations of a number of researchers that women 'often create and display their authority in ways that downplay rather than emphasize it'.[34] Problematically, as Kendall notes, this may be mistakenly perceived as evidence of incompetence or insecurity by those with different expectations of how people 'do leadership'.[35]

It is not only women, however, who use this self-deprecating feminine strategy in their workplace narratives. It is available to both men and women who want to reduce status differences or emphasize the fact that they are fallible human beings. Example 6.7 is what I have labelled a 'working story', a workplace narrative which is more obviously oriented to workplace business than to relational goals.[36] This story is Gerry's response to a comment from a trainee, Henry, who has expressed frustration that he was not able to complete a set task on time and to his own standards.

Example 6.7

Context: Session in a training programme run by Gerry, an experienced member of a professional IT commercial organization, for 3 female and 3 male young, new graduates who have recently joined the organization. 'C-plus-plus' is a computer programming language.

1.	**Hen**:	I just realized that (we only had) so much time
2.		I didn't really want to be here all night
3.		. . . that kind of frustrated me
4.		cos I don't really like sacrificing my own quality /standard\
5.	**Ger**:	/yep\
6.	**Hen**:	of my work /so\
7.	**Ger**:	/I\ can totally understand that
8.		I've worked on projects um when I was at [*company name*]
9.		the er my project manager thought I was a C-plus-plus guru
10.		she shipped me up to Auckland to work on this project with this guy
11.		doing um inventory reporting . . . [*describes what he had to do*] . . .
12.		he wanted me to use his C-plus-plus framework
13.		and er I had something like a week or two to finish this off
14.		it was quite a lot of work and I got to the end of the two weeks
15.		and the money ran out for them to pay for me
16.		and I just felt really bad cos I failed, I hadn't done a good job
17.		um it got to the last couple of days and I said to this guy
18.		look this is just crazy what you're doing you're doing this in C-plus-plus
19.		I said I could have (sorted) things out using X scripting
20.		and the database loader in half a day
21.		I mean he wanted sort of 20 different files to be loaded

22.   I could have done one in half a day um and I hadn't
         finished
23.   he had to get some other guy to come in and finish
         off my work
24.   so I felt stink
25.   you know I'm under pressure I'm supposed to be
         this expert
26.   and I'm not I'm walking away I'm failing . . .
27.   so exactly what you've found . . .
28.   you'll (all) hand in quality of work that you're not
         happy with ++
29.   so um be prepared for a little bit of failure and learn
         from it

Gerry's story is designed to encourage the young graduates he is
mentoring not to give up when the going is tough. The example is one
of many he uses during their training programme to illustrate a point,
personalize the material being discussed, and maintain interest in what
he is telling them about the company's ways of doing things. Contrary
to the stereotypical 'narrator as hero' stories, this narrative presents
Gerry as a failure who did not achieve his goals, *cos I failed I hadn't
done a good job* (line 16), *I'm supposed to be this expert and I'm not I'm
walking away I'm failing* (lines 25–6). He does not romanticize the
account but rather emphasizes his dissatisfaction with his own
performance, repeatedly using the agentive pronoun *I*, and very
colloquial expressions *and I just felt really bad* (line 16), *so I felt stink*
(line 24). He clearly intends his mentees to learn from such experiences, *so um be prepared for a little bit of failure and learn from it* (line 29).
And in order to make this useful pedagogical point he presents
himself as someone who was naive and inexperienced at an earlier
point in his career.

   In addition to the self-deprecating content, Gerry uses a number of
stylistic features which index more feminine ways of speaking: e.g.
hedges (*something like, quite a lot, just, I mean, a little bit*), intensifiers
(*totally, really, just*), and addressee-oriented pragmatic particles (*you
know*). So, while the story's location in time, as well as his role as
mentor, provide some degree of distancing from the failure described,
this is none the less a story which adopts a relatively self-deprecating,
somewhat rueful, and normatively feminine stance and style of
presentation to make its point.

Gerry's story could also be regarded as providing an alternative to the culture of success that predominates in the male-dominated and masculinist workplace in which he is operating. Others in this workplace tend to tell hero stories with successes rather than failures as their point. It is interesting that in his role as mentor, inducting new recruits into the company's ways of doing things, Gerry is prepared to present a different and more realistic perspective on the potential outcomes of problem-solving in this community of practice. His story is classic relational practice, doing both 'mutual empowering' and 'creating team', themes identified in chapter 3. These functions of workplace narrative are further illustrated in the next section, which addresses more directly the issue of how narrative may contribute to differently gendered ways of doing relational practice, and thus to the construction of more or less masculine and feminine communities of practice.

 ## Constructing Workplace Relationships in Gendered Ways

Workplace narratives provide gendered resources not only in terms of constructing professional, heroic and normatively masculine identities, as opposed to amateur, self-deprecating and normatively feminine social identities, but also in terms of how they accomplish relational work in different communities of practice, and contribute to the gendering of the workplace. Many workplace narratives serve as ways of doing relational practice, qualifying on all three criteria discussed in chapter 3. They are concerned with interpersonal relations, and with face maintenance and attention. They are oriented to a greater or lesser extent to furthering transactional workplace goals. And, like workplace humour, narratives are, strictly speaking, redundant: excising a narrative may leave the discourse impoverished, but the excision does not usually remove a component crucial to the workplace business.

Example 6.8 illustrates how narrative lines up with small-talk and gossip as a strategy for creating team, an important aspect of relational practice. Narrative is easily integrated into the dynamic process of constructing good relationships between team members in an organization. In a workplace which was in many ways normatively masculine (e.g. corporate, male-dominated, hierarchical, status-oriented, with authoritarian decision-making), narrating stories about out-of-work activities was part of the pre-meeting ritual at the beginning of each week for the team featuring in example 6.9.

Example 6.8

Context: Meeting of regular project team of 7 men and 5 women in a multinational white-collar commercial organization. Smithy is in the chair.

1. **Smi**: but we should I guess start in the traditional manner
2.   and have Neville give us a tale of his weekend
3. **Nev**: oh there's no tales to tell mind you last night
4. **All**: [laugh]

Smithy here parodies the formal role of meeting chair by opening the meeting with an invitation to Neville to contribute not a report, as might be expected in this business meeting, but *a tale of his weekend* (line 2). His use of the phrase *in the traditional manner* (line 1) signals that this is part of a regular routine for this team, or community of practice, one way in which they have established their belongingness as a group. Smithy's invitation clearly expresses approval of Neville's contribution to the team's spirit and rapport, and Neville himself sustains the good-humoured key by first declaring he has no tale to tell (line 3), but then, without taking breath, immediately signalling with the discourse marker *mind you* that he does in fact have a contribution to make. This is classic gendered (feminine) relational talk. Like small-talk and humour, narratives can contribute to constructing good workplace relations.

The beginning of a meeting is an obvious site for talk which contributes to the cementing and nurturing of good workplace relationships. The following story, collected from the same team, was similarly positioned, and it illustrates that the *style* of narrative construction can also make a contribution in this respect.

Example 6.9

Context: Meeting of regular project team of 7 men and 5 women in a multinational white-collar commercial organization. They are discussing a TV programme of the Golden Globe film awards.

1. **Nev:** actually did you see that um that actress from um [tut] Chicago
2. Hope was in the toilet when she /got her\ award
3. **Mar:** /mm\
4. **Nev:** shit that was funny see that?
5. **Smi:** no
6. **Mar:** she missed it so /Robin Williams got up for her\
7. **XM:** /([*says something indicating amazement*])\
8. **Mar:** /yes he did\
9. **Nev:** /the whole crowd\ was going /where is she\
10. **Mar:** /yeah her husband\ went up
11. and then Robin Williams /went up and pretended to be like\
12. **Nev:** /(and then Robin Williams got up)\
13. **Mar:** this Spanish waiter going [in Spanish]: eh eh (blah) Signorita Leate
14. [Spanish accent]: your (award) is waiting: [laughs]:
15. like this into the podium he was being really funny:
16. **Nev:** shit that was a laugh ( ) /( )\
17. **Smi:** /did they\ did they have the camera in the toilet
18. just to catch her /the facial expression\
19. **Peg:** yes they /did\
20. **Set:** /ironic\
21. **All:** [*laugh and talk at once*]

This relatively self-contained excerpt from a long, humorous interchange is paradigmatic social talk, stereotypically feminine gossip about movie stars, which is licensed by the (male) meeting chair, Smithy (see, for instance lines 17–18), and contributed to by almost all those present. Moreover, while it is initiated by Neville (lines 1–2), it develops as a very collaborative and cooperative joint construction, a typically feminine style of narration.[37] Marlene picks up Neville's introduction and completes the 'abstract' at line 6, *she missed it so Robin Williams got up for her.*[38] The two then contribute alternately through lines 9–16, at which point Smithy asks a humorous question, to which Peg and Seth respond. The contributions of Marlene and Neville nicely complement each other at some points and polyphonically overlap at others: for example, they both produce exactly the same words *and then Robin Williams went up*, at almost exactly the same time (lines 11–12). It is always clear, however, that they are 'in tune' with each other and working together to present the story in an amusing way. This is underlined by Neville's appreciative comment *shit that was a laugh* (line 16), following Marlene's skilful imitation of Robin William's rendition of a Spaniard (lines 13–14). This anecdote is pure entertainment; it serves a relational function in strengthening the social ties between members of this cohesive project team. No team member is the butt of the humour and the participants provide good evidence through their polyphonic contributions that they are on the same wave-length. In its functions, its content and its style of expression, then, this narrative contributes to the feminization of a workplace that is predominantly masculine in its style of doing business.

Narratives, like humour, can also help de-toxify the atmosphere when things have been tough. Leila's story above (example 6.5), for instance, was strategically positioned in the meeting, serving to release tension and enhance team cohesion, and reduce attention to the status differences and power imbalances that authoritative behaviour inevitably highlights. Similarly, example 6.10, which occurs towards the end of a meeting in which Eric has been held up as a heroic model (see example 6.3 above), serves to neutralize the threat to team cohesion which such behaviour represents. Here we re-encounter Eric in a very different role, constructed as 'clown' or 'jester', rather than 'hero'. The team members are discussing plans to have dinner together at a restaurant, a social event arranged by their organization. In order to understand this exchange, the reader needs to remember (from example 4.4) that Eric has a reputation for invading the restaurant kitchen and 'helping' the chef on these occasions.

Example 6.10

Context: Regular weekly meeting of an IT project team in a large commercial organization. There are 6 male participants at this meeting. Barry is the Chair. The example is preceded by a discussion of the seating plan for a company dinner to be held in the near future.

Preamble:
i. **Jac:** I wanted to get er maybe your opinion
ii. we can do open seating or we can do assigned as far as dinner

iii.		do we want to do er assigned or do we want to do open?
iv.	**Eri:**	how are you going to assign it? . . .
v.	**Bar:**	we'll just make it open won't /we\
vi.	**Eri:**	/yeah\
vii.	**Jac:**	(great) /that's easier\
viii.	**Cal:**	/(you'll but)\

Narrative:

1.	**Cal:**	you'll be off to the kitchen pretty quickly though /won't you?\
2.	**Eri:**	/yeah I\ know yeah
3.	**Bar:**	cooking
4.	**Eri:**	after that third bottle of wine I'll be in there /( )\
5.	**Bar:**	/[laughs]\ [laughs]: making dinner: [laughs]
6.	**Eri:**	/I haven't\ I haven't done that kitchen so /that'll\ be one
7.	**Cal:**	/yeah\
8.	**Eri:**	for the collection
9.	**Bar:**	[laughs] [laughs] you /can't you can't\remember it:
10.	**Eri:**	/( ) [laughs]\
11.	**Mar:**	there's a lot of kitchens he doesn't remember

Eric is here constructed as a 'performer' who, on social occasions, enacts a routine familiar to his team mates or co-participants, adopting a role he clearly relishes, namely 'playing the fool'.[39] The social identity constructed through this account of Eric's drunken assaults on restaurant kitchens is certainly very different from his professional identity (team expert on particular aspects of the company's computing programs). The narrative thus rather neatly combines elements of maverick hero with incompetent drunken jester. It adds complexity to and elaborates Eric's role as an individual within the team, and contributes to team cohesion by 'cutting him down to size', and emphasizing that he is 'one of the boys'.[40]

This story also performs important relational work through the style of its telling. It is a jointly constructed story told by the team members in a typically masculine, competitive and contestive interactional style. It is not just Eric's story – it has become part of the shared history of this competitive team as reflected in their contributions. The narrative is introduced by Callum (line 1), and elaborated both by Barry (lines 3, 5, 9) and Eric (lines 4, 6, 8), with a final jibing contribution from Marco (line 11). There are conventionally feminine cooperative elements in the way the story is introduced, including Barry's use of a facilitative tag question, *won't you?* (line 1); and his completion of Eric's clause *I'll be in there* with the phrase *making dinner* (line 5). However, the style of delivery and the particular 'humorous key'[41] which is developed by all four contributors is competitive and contestive in the more usual masculine style of this team's interactions. So the jibes at Eric which are initiated by Callum's comment, *you'll be off to the kitchen pretty quickly though* (line 1), are sustained by Barry, *you can't remember it* (line 9), and Marco, *there's a lot of kitchens he doesn't remember* (line 11). These strategies are consistent with other ways in which members of this particular team do relational practice – through contestive and competitive humorous repartee (see chapter 3). The narrative's status as a jointly constructed, familiar and often re-run tale thus serves the function of actively constructing this group as a team, and strengthening team solidarity: it creates team in this very masculine community of practice both through its content and its manner of construction.

As mentioned, this characterization of Eric as a drunken joker who misbehaves in restaurants on company social occasions, is interestingly positioned at the end of a meeting in which he has overtly demonstrated his expertise, and where his outstanding performance has been explicitly referred to. The restaurant anecdote could thus be regarded as counteracting a very much more authoritative professional identity which could potentially threaten the team's cohesion by emphasizing Eric's identity as a 'good joker', and a well-integrated member of this masculine community of practice.

My final example brings together many of the points made in earlier examples, and also demonstrates how narratives may serve other aspects of relational practice, including the themes of mutual empowering, preserving and self achieving, within a relatively feminine community of practice. Example 6.11 comprises excerpts from a long 'working story' recounted in a meeting of senior managers of a national organization (here given the pseudonym Scope). We have met the participants before in chapters 3 and 4. In example 6.11, two team members, Hettie, the main narrator, and Penelope, the CEO of the organization and chair of this meeting, describe how they were badly treated by members of an external organization (with the pseudonym Ration) who invited them to a meeting which turned out to be a confrontational set-up. The recounting of this narrative does complex identity work for both participants. Both use the story to construct aspects of their professional and their gender identities, skilfully presenting themselves in a positive light (despite the fact that this is an account of a humiliating put-down), while also paying attention to each other's face needs and those of other team members. I focus here on just the components of relevance to this discussion.[42]

The narrative is prefaced by an explicit speech of appreciation from the chair, Penelope, for Hettie's work on a specific project (discussed in chapter 3 as example 3.8). Hettie responds by saying how proud she feels of what their organization achieves, and she uses this as a jumping-off point for her narrative about how she and Penelope were invited to a meeting and then 'told off' by the CEO of the organization who had invited them. Hettie's point appears to be that she defended Scope when it was under attack ('preserving'), but she manages en route to do a good deal of complex identity work ('self-achieving') as well as other-oriented relational work ('creating team' and 'mutual empowering').

Example 6.11a

Context: Meeting of a group of 4 male and 4 female regional managers of a national organization. Penelope is the Chair and CEO.

1.	**Het**:	um Penelope and I were at a meeting
2.		with another big national organization just recently
3.		and + [tut] in the course of that I was talking a little bit about it
4.		and I felt you know really proud to say +
5.		this organization felt that they should have had a very great input
6.		into the development of our programmes
7.		that they should have delivered our training for us and whatever
8.		that they knew a lot about this and mm yeah yeah and they
9.	**Pen**:	explicit it was Ration we had a horrible [laughs]: meeting: [laughs]

Hettie opens the story in an explicitly professional way, discreetly not naming the organization she is complaining about, and expressing positive and loyal feelings towards her own organization. She also constructs her personal identity as a woman of strong feelings, articulate and always ready to back up her claims with detailed evidence. Penelope similarly integrates two different aspects of identity construction at the opening of the story. Firstly she 'does power' and constructs an authoritative, professional identity by giving Hettie permission to name the objectionable organization. On the other hand, she provides an evaluative frame, *we had a horrible meeting*, and thus contributes to the story which will follow, a story which portrays her (and Hettie) in a rather unflattering light as the objects of criticism and victims of bullying behaviour. In this role, she presents herself and Hettie as a pair of colleagues and equals, collaboratively handling adversity with courage and dignity. And Penelope's contributions throughout the subsequent story can be interpreted as maintaining these two different aspects of identity construction – a professional, authoritative, powerful (more masculine) identity and a collegial, other-oriented (more feminine) identity. On the one hand, she attempts to 'manage' the narrative as Hettie recounts it, exerting her authority; on the other hand, she identifies with Hettie's feelings of outrage and presents herself as a sympathetic co-participant in the narrative.

Example 6.11b illustrates further how Hettie balances two contrasting aspects of identity construction, one more authoritative, professional and masculine ('self-achieving'), the other more other-oriented, relational and feminine ('mutual empowering'). She is describing the behaviour of the chief executive of Ration. The excerpt opens with a reference to a psychological instrument, *the duluthe power and control wheel* (line 12).

Example 6.11b

10.	Het:	and and um + fulfilled at /least three or four segments\
11.	Pen:	/[sighs]\
12.	Het:	on the (duluthe) power and control wheel
13.		/things like blaming\
14.		[*loud general laughter*]
15.	Kir:	/sounding very much like it\
16.	Het:	[raises voice]: blaming manipulation intimidation I'm
17.		sure she would've actually: e- /emotional\ abuse

18. **Mal**: /( )\
19. **Het**: um /sh- she would definitely have moved on to\
20. **Pen**: /[*laughs with gusto appreciatively*]\
21. **Het**: o- she definitely wanted isolation that's another one on it
22. she wanted to isolate us + and um when I come to think
23. [*laughter, comments*]
24. **Het**: of it probably the only one that she didn't do was um physical abuse
25. and I'm sure she would've if she thought she could've got away with it

Hettie here skilfully and amusingly analyses the behaviour of the chief executive in terms her colleagues appreciate (lines 10–16). She introduces the analysis in a cool, professional tone (lines 10, 12, 13), and gains support from a colleague, Kirsty, for her analysis (line 15). The language is sophisticated and technical, and the grammar becomes increasingly complex as she moves into hypotheticals (lines 22–5). In response to the laughter she evokes, Hettie extends the analysis to an obvious hypothetical exaggeration (lines 19–25), which serves to elicit more mirth from her colleagues, including Penelope, whose laughter is clearly appreciative. This short excerpt represents a pattern observable throughout the story, where Hettie begins describing something in an objective, professional, normatively masculine manner, and then moves on to a more emotionally involved, stereotypically feminine interpretation of what was going on.[43]

Penelope's identity construction work in this narrative is equally complex and somewhat similar in its core components. We have extensive evidence from our ethnographic data, as well as recordings of her management of other meetings, that her general management style is a consummate mix of feminine and masculine characteristics. Penelope is positive, supportive and appreciative, as is evident from her explicit praise for Hettie's work; but she is also a firm and authoritative manager, who skilfully keeps people to the point and maintains a focus on her organizational objectives. So, while she expresses admiration for Hettie's work for the organization, she also needs to keep her on track and constrain the length of her contributions to the discussion. Moreover, from Penelope's standpoint, the story is somewhat ambivalent in terms of its overall message. Hettie's story of the attack, and how she (Hettie) responded, provides Hettie with several opportunities to construct herself as a strong, articulate advocate of Scope, and to elicit further appreciative comments from Penelope. Hettie emerges from her story as a hero. Penelope, however, has good reason to keep the story short, firstly because the meeting has strict time constraints, and secondly because the image of her, as a CEO, being roundly scolded by the Ration CEO (who, as Hettie relates, *basically told us off like chi- as if we were children*) does not contribute to the kind of professional identity that Penelope fosters in her leadership behaviour in general.

Penelope's response is to construct an authoritative identity by framing Hettie's working story as a moral tale from which they can all learn. After allowing Hettie to develop the story at some length, Penelope contributes an evaluative meta-comment which frames the encounter and indicates how it should be perceived *and they saw it as a confrontation . . . they'd set up a confrontation*. The restatement here identifies the Ration group as explicitly agentive in manipulating the situation to ensure an unpleasant encounter between the two organizations. She intervenes again at a later point to provide a further evaluative and interpretive comment for the benefit of the rest of the team.

Example 6.11c

26.	**Pen**:	I think I mean basically this attack came from one person in the room
27.		not from the group really /and many I would think
28.		many of the others the others colluded\+
29.	**Ing**:	/( )\
30.	**Het**:	/(yes set her up for it)\
31.	**Pen**:	but many of them would have been sitting there feeling quite embarrassed
32.		and + that kind of bullying behaviour of /course
33.		is very difficult to challenge when it's your leader that's doing it\
34.		/[*others murmur agreement*]\

Penelope here takes the floor firmly, and talks over the top of Hettie and Ingrid (lines 26–30), using pauses, low volume and a serious tone of voice, to effectively keep people's attention. She identifies the attack with the chief executive, and then provides an analysis of the position of those who might not have agreed: e.g. *and that kind of bullying behaviour of course is very difficult to challenge when it's your leader that's doing it* (lines 32–3). Again the evaluative perspective contributes to a construction of Penelope as an authoritative analyst, standing above the petty game-playing of the scene that Hettie is describing. Together with the serious tone, the pragmatic particle *of course* (line 32) does sterling service here in constructing this stance, since it asserts a proposition as common knowledge among those addressed. *Of course* often occurs in formal contexts as a negative politeness device, skilfully asserting as common knowledge information which may not in fact be known to all, and thus, paradoxically, subtly asserting superior knowledge.[44]

After a good deal more good-humoured collaboration, Penelope finally takes over Hettie's story, at which point she adopts again the authoritative, distancing tone she has used at strategic points throughout, bringing the story to a close with a very overt statement of the 'moral':

Example 6.11d

35. **Pen**: I mean that's of course what happens when people abuse you
36. that's what you do feel angry and and uncooperative
37. and all of the things that we were feeling

Again, the use of the distancing, negative-politeness pragmatic particle *of course* (line 35) asserts the moral of the story as common knowledge among such a group of sophisticated people.

It is interesting to note that, despite her obvious desire to limit the length of the story, Penelope does not undermine Hettie. She supports her and constructs her as a competent, dignified professional throughout the story. Moreover, Penelope does not disavow any aspect of Hettie's story, and indeed she overtly identifies with her reactions, using *we* frequently to describe how they responded to the treatment they received. This collegial and supportive attitude is the other important component of Penelope's workplace identity. It is very apparent in her initial praise of Hettie; it is apparent in her appreciative, hearty laughter, and in the collaborative section where she emphasizes that they were on the same wave-length, despite the fact that she has clearly found the story personally somewhat discomfiting as well as overly discursive and lengthy.

This brief analysis suggests something of the remarkable variation and dynamism evident throughout this elaborate narrative in the negotiation of both participants' identity construction as competent professional, yet passionate individuals, and responsive team members. These apparently contradictory elements are skilfully integrated, and the narrators move between different aspects with ease. They are constantly responsive to the demands of the discourse context, and to the reactions of other team members, as well as each other.

It is also apparent from questions, comments and feedback from team members throughout the story that this workplace narrative provides useful information to the other team members about the dynamics of the relationship between Scope and Ration. And finally, as a story which is fundamentally about relationships – albeit professional relationships – the narrative contributes to the construction of this community of practice as a relatively feminine one.

In this section I have explored the ways in which people make use of gendered discursive resources to achieve an integrated workplace identity, exploiting feminine and masculine stances as appropriate in pursuit of both relational and transactional goals. While workplace narratives contribute to the construction of a particular kind of personal and social identity, they are often concurrently doing transactional and relational work. They typically contribute to creating team, and may also exemplify mutual empowerment (as in example 6.7), both aspects of relational practice. The final complex narrative also exemplified the accomplishment of the relational themes of self-achieving and mutual empowering through narrative. The narratives in this section have thus illustrated some of the complexities of identity construction in the workplace, as well as the function of narratives in developing and maintaining often gendered social relationships at work, and their potential contribution to the construction of relatively masculine and feminine communities of practice.

Conclusion

Workplace communication provides many different means for constructing and negotiating social identities in the workplace, including gender identities, and workplace narratives are one such discursive resource. This chapter has illustrated how workplace narratives may contribute to constructing gendered aspects of social identity, and also to the discursive interactional norms which distinguish differently gendered communities of practice. The narratives in the first and second sections focused on stories which to a large extent could be characterized as normatively masculine ('narrator as hero') and stereotypically feminine ('narrator as embarrassed or incompetent'), though it was evident, as others have found, that authentic narratives rarely fit neatly into such categories.[45] Pursuing this further, the third section illustrated that the social identities constructed in many workplace stories are often complex, ambiguous and multi-faceted.

Workplace narratives also serve as ways of doing relational practice. And as indicated in chapter 3, they offer a range of different resources for accomplishing this, including differently gendered styles of interaction. Typically positioned at the margins of 'official business' or serious transactional talk at work, workplace anecdotes serve as useful discursive resources for negotiating the public–private interface, acting as the conduit between people's private lives and their professional identities. As illustrated by a number of examples in this chapter, for some women, workplace anecdotes can contribute to dealing with the professional–feminine double bind, providing a means of reconciling potentially conflicting aspects of social identity, and serving as effective vehicles for reconciling the varied and often competing demands of different aspects of their professional roles at work.

In sum, I have suggested that narratives in the workplace may contribute to the construction of complex personal, professional and gender identities for workplace participants, allowing them to emphasize particular facets of their social identities and different dimensions of social meaning – professional status, team solidarity, authority responsibilities, gender category, group affiliations, distinctive workplace culture, and so on. They provide a valuable resource for (re-)producing or enacting the various facets of an individual's social identity; and they often serve as effective and socially acceptable discursive strategies for reconciling conflicting aspects of workplace identity. Finally, workplace narratives may contribute to the gendering of the communities of practice in which they occur, reinforcing, ameliorating, or even subverting aspects of the dominant workplace cultures in which they are told.

NOTES

1   See, for example, Coates (1996, 2003), Johnstone (1990), Riessman (1993), Attanucci (1993), Schiffrin (1996), Holmes (1997b, 1998).
2   But see Olsson (2000).
3   Fletcher (1999: 48).
4   See, for example, Boyce (1995, 1996), Gabriel (1998), Kaye (1996), McCollum (1992).
5   This section draws on Holmes and Marra (2005c).
6   Dyer and Keller-Cohen (2000).
7   Baxter (2003: 147), italics in original.
8   Holmes and Stubbe (2003a: 584–8), and see also example 6.5 below.
9   Holmes (2005b), Holmes and Marra (2005c).
10 See Johnstone (1990), Coates (2003), Holmes (1997b, 1998).
11 Baxter (2003: 139–41).
12 Fletcher (1999: 48).
13 For example, the story of growth from a 'family business', a common theme in the business literature (see Bryson and May 2004), and the significance of such 'birth of the company' stories, sometimes referred to as origin myths in the organizational literature (e.g. Kaye 1996, Fleming 2001, Ready 2002).
14 See Stubbe (2000a, 2000b).
15 See Holmes and Stubbe (2003: ch. 6).
16 See also McElhinny (2003b).
17 I do not discuss definitions of the term 'narrative' or issues of narrative structure here. Labov (1972) is the standard analytical framework in this area, and I use his terms as relevant ('abstract', 'complicating action', 'evaluation', 'coda'). See also *Journal of Narrative and Life History* vol. 7, and Marra and Holmes (2004).
18 See Coates (2003).
19 See Holmes (2005b) for further exemplification of the way Ginette constructs her professional identity through narrative.
20 McRae (2004) describes a similar team in the British context, which she labels the Comco team.
21 See also Stubbe (2000a), Holmes and Stubbe (2003b) and Holmes (2005b) for further illustration of this point.
22 See, for example, Olsson (2000).
23 See Holmes (1998) for a discussion of a similar tendency identified in the stories of some Māori males in the Wellington Corpus of Spoken New Zealand English. Just as Pākehā society conventionally expects women to be modest and self-effacing, so Māori culture values humility, and self-promotion is frowned upon. Stories of amusing failures are common.

24 I am grateful to Meredith Marra for valuable insights on 'what is going on here' based on her familiarity with the relevant team.
25 See Holmes and Stubbe (2003a), for further discussion of this community of practice.
26 See Holmes and Stubbe (2003a, 2003b) for further discussion of Leila's professional persona.
27 See Holmes and Stubbe (2003a, 2003b).
28 See, for example, Schiffrin (1996), Olsson (2000), and Dyer and Keller-Cohen (2000).
29 Dyer and Keller-Cohen (2000: 300).
30 See Baxter (2003).
31 Olsson (2000: 189, 183).
32 Eder (1993: 25).
33 The discussion of this example is taken from Holmes and Schnurr (2004).
34 Tannen (1999: 226); see also Kuhn (1992), Kendall (2004).
35 Kendall (2004: 75).
36 Holmes (2004a); see also Swap et al. (2001).
37 Coates (1996).
38 The term 'abstract' is a component of narrative structure. See note 17.
39 Goffman (1959: 16).
40 Compare Baxter's (2003: 166, 195) discussion of the 'boysy culture' in the dotcom company she researched.
41 Kotthoff (2000).
42 See Holmes (2004a) for the complete narrative as well as more detailed analysis.
43 See Holmes (2004a).
44 Holmes (1988b).
45 See, for example, Coates (2003).

CHAPTER SEVEN

Giving Women the Last Word

'A kind of mad squeamishness prevents women from quantifying the nuisance value of maleness.'

Germaine Greer, quoted in The Bulletin, 9 Sept. 2003: 28

We achieve many different things through our talk, but this book has focused on the contribution that discourse makes to gendering the workplace by exploring the complex ways in which people draw on both feminine and masculine discourse resources to convey gendered stances at work and to construct their gender identities. I have been at pains to challenge the equation of stereotypically feminine ways of talking with women and stereotypically masculine styles of talk with men. The analyses in different chapters have demonstrated that both women and men make use of normatively masculine and feminine discourse strategies and styles according to the demands of the type of interaction, the people they are interacting with, and the immediate discourse context, as well as the norms of their workplace culture. In this concluding chapter, I take a more explicitly political position, exploring the implications of the analyses in this book for women in particular. Despite the fact that many women clearly can and do exploit diverse discursive resources to communicate effectively at work, the reality is that many women continue to experience discrimination, and that many workplaces are not particularly woman-friendly. I argue in this final chapter that it is important to identify ways in which the gendered norms and expectations which pervade many workplaces, including discourse norms, may disadvantage some working women. Social transformation is a legitimate goal for a feminist linguist.[1]

Gender and Communication Skills

I have attempted in the different chapters of this book to demonstrate the enormous diversity in linguistic practices among women and men at work, while also indicating the complex ways in which gender pervades much workplace interaction. Material in different chapters has illustrated the many ways in which workplace discourse provides a resource for indexing gender, contributing to the construction of gender identity as one component of our complex socio-cultural identity.

Context is crucial, of course, as has been evident throughout in the discussion of the many examples analysed. But gender is an important component of that context. At some level, we are always aware of the sex of those we are talking to, and we bring to every interaction our familiarity with societal gender stereotypes and the gendered norms to which women and men are expected to conform. Gender may move into the foreground or retreat into the background at different points in an interaction, but it is an omnipresent influence, and always potentially relevant to the interpretation of the meaning of an interaction. We may use language in ways which index femininity or masculinity at different points in any interaction at work, and the styles of discourse which predominate in a particular community of practice contribute to the impression of a relatively feminine or relatively masculine workplace culture.

Susan Philips argues that current approaches in language and gender analysis do not adequately highlight discursive behaviours which penalize women, or document women's discursive resistance to domination.[2] But by demonstrating the diversity, complexity and richness of workplace discourse, and the ways in which both women and men draw on gendered resources to accomplish their relational and transactional objectives, the analyses in this book have contributed, I hope, to eroding the negative stereotypes which disempower women in some workplace contexts. Another strategy available to those concerned to promote the interests of women, to oppose their relegation to subordinate roles in the workplace, and to help them break through the glass ceiling to senior positions, is to expose and contest the systemic ways in which sexism and discrimination filter into workplace discourse.[3]

In what follows, then, I turn the spotlight on gendered workplace ideologies, contesting assumptions that masculine discourse is most effective in the workplace, and that feminine styles of interaction are inappropriate for some workplace roles. The discussion centres around how the regulatory norms 'that define what kinds of language are possible, intelligible and appropriate resources for performing masculinity and femininity'[4] may disadvantage women in some workplace contexts. The complex reality revealed by detailed analysis of workplace interaction clearly challenges the constraints constructed by such norms. In concluding I suggest ways in which language and gender research may contribute to raising awareness of disadvantage as a precursor to changing this situation.[5]

Feminine Leadership – An Oxymoron?

Stereotypes are problematic and constraining. To what extent, then, does the expectation that they should portray or adopt a feminine as opposed to a more masculine social identity exert pressure on women at work – especially on those in senior management positions in organizations? No one has a problem with women in the workplace as long as they take appropriately subordinate roles and behave in appropriately feminine and subservient ways. Things get trickier when women challenge the status quo by taking positions traditionally associated with men and, as the research reviewed in chapter 2 reports, this is particularly problematic in male-dominated workplaces with pervasive masculinist ideologies.

Many traditional measures of leadership reflect a very authoritarian view of the way management and leadership is most effectively accomplished, and consequently present a relatively masculine profile of the 'best' leaders. As chapter 2 indicated, this research suggests that women with aspirations to leadership are faced with a dilemma – unless they learn to operate in the masculine styles which dominate in so many workplaces, they will not be taken seriously. On the other hand, more feminine ways of interacting at work, although often paid lip-service, and apparently valued when men adopt them as aspects of their management style, are, it is claimed, regarded negatively when adopted by women in many organizations.[6]

Before accepting this pessimistic view of the difficulties for women who aspire to leadership positions, it is worth noting that most of the research which gives weight to the concept of the male hero leader has typically used survey or questionnaire methodology. The data from the Wellington Language in the Workplace (LWP) Project provides a rather more nuanced picture of workplace interaction. Responsiveness to the specific demands of the particular interaction is an important aspect of the management skills displayed by effective managers, female and male, and they make use of a diversity of discursive resources to accomplish both transactional and relational objectives, including ways of interacting that instantiate many different points on the masculine–feminine stylistic dimension. In other words, the reality of workplace interaction indicates that those (women and men) who respond most sensitively to contextual factors and who are most stylistically flexible are likely to be the most effective workplace leaders. Reality is not as black and white or as uncompromising as the leadership and management literature often suggests.

The data from our LWP Project also suggests some alternative avenues for women faced with the classic workplace double bind. Some of the most effective women workers in our database opted to work in women-friendly communities of practice, where predominantly feminine styles of interaction were unmarked and normal, where pre-meeting talk topics included personal and family topics without attracting comment, where humour tended to be collaborative and non-abrasive, and where it was acceptable to instantiate leadership in relatively negotiative and less authoritarian ways. Other women were quite demonstrably ameliorating or even subverting the dominant masculinist workplace culture in which they operated, effectively integrating aspects of more feminine discourse styles in their workplace talk, and establishing the acceptability of more feminine ways of interacting where appropriate. (Moreover, their efforts were often supported by men who shared their preference for normatively feminine ways of interacting.) As suggested in chapter 2, senior women who adopt this approach are also effectively contesting the association of leadership with masculinity. By making use of strategies traditionally associated with male ways of talking when appropriate, women de-gender and re-categorize them as neutral tools of leadership discourse, rather than exclusively male discursive resources. Through their success, they modify the concept of what it means to be an effective leader.[7]

Thirdly, some senior women 'do femininity' quite explicitly and confidently in a variety of discursive ways in their workplace interactions, creating feminine spaces within masculine workplaces, and contesting the view that 'feminine' is a dirty word at work. In a range of ways, and to differing degrees, such women are contesting and troubling the gendered discourse norms which characterize so many workplaces, and which contribute to the glass ceiling they are trying to breach. Our detailed discourse analyses of workplace interactions are thus useful in identifying the complex realities of talk at work, as well as the impressive range of ways in which many women operate effectively in different workplaces, suggesting there are many possible responses to the challenge of potentially discriminatory and disadvantageous discourse patterns.

Relational Work – A Woman's Forte?

As noted at the end of chapter 2, ' "nice", "helpful" and "thoughtful" are not found on many lists of leadership characteristics',[8] but they are characteristics we all appreciate in our colleagues. They are also, of course, characteristics which are stereotypically associated with women. The concept of relational practice, examined in chapter 3, similarly has strong feminine associations. Relational practice (RP) typically consists of backstage, unnoticed and unrewarded behaviours which contribute in a range of subtle ways to the achievement of workplace objectives. Like shopping and housework, such constructive but invisible work is stereotypically regarded as 'women's work'. RP is clearly a gendered concept, feminine both in function and style.

The examples in chapter 3 demonstrate that both women and men engage in RP, and that the association of RP with femininity derives not only from outmoded perceptions of appropriate roles for women at work, but also from traditional and outdated concepts of effective workplace behaviours. The most senior people, female and male, in the workplaces we studied, made skilful use of RP in a wide variety of contexts.

Going further, the analysis in chapter 3 also suggests that behaviours which are considered to count as RP may have been subject to a rather sexist lens; I questioned the absoluteness of the equation of relational practice with a 'feminized' style of discourse, and raised the possibility that manifestations of relational practice may differ in different communities of practice. For some communities of practice more normatively masculine styles of interaction may serve as accepted and standard means of doing RP by creating team, for example. The range of ways of accomplishing RP in diverse communities of practice, and their effect on workplace relationships and structures, is a challenging area for further research, and one which is likely to benefit women. As we begin to identify and value more diverse ways of expressing positive support for others at work, the assumption that RP is primarily 'women's work' may gradually be eroded.

The different ways in which people do RP is one factor which contributes to the construction of particular kinds of workplace culture, and helps shape normative ways of behaving within specific communities of practice. When there is a lack of fit between your preferred interactional style and that of your colleagues, you feel uncomfortable. Certainly there is evidence that many women (as well as some men) find masculinist workplace contexts, where normatively masculine styles of interaction predominate, to be uncomfortable and unwelcoming. One study, for instance, reported that women found it unpleasant working in a male-dominated environment where interpersonal behaviour at senior levels was 'often very aggressive, rude, territorial, status conscious and hostile, with conflict, power struggles and politicking as common features'.[9] Evidence of diversity in ways of doing RP, as documented in chapter 3, is again helpful, since it challenges the presumption that such behaviour is necessary for the successful achievement of transactional workplace objectives.

Women at Work – No Laughing Matter

Humour is a wonderfully flexible interactional strategy which makes an important contribution to relational aspects of workplace interaction. It is also highly valued by prospective employers, who report that a sense of humour is crucial to job success. A 1985 survey of the American Chief Executive Officers of 329 of the Fortune 500 corporations, for example, revealed that 97 per cent identified humour as important to the conduct of business, and considered that 'executives should develop a greater sense of humor, and that in hiring people they should look for a sense of humor'.[10] Another more recent survey similarly indicated that 96 per cent of executives thought people with a sense of humour did better at their jobs than those who had little or no sense of humour.[11]

Chapter 4 indicated that both women and men use humour at work as a rich resource for achieving diverse objectives, including the construction of differently nuanced gender identities. In choices related to propositional orientation (supportive vs. contestive comments) as well as discursive style (more or less collaboratively expressed), humour provides a productive resource for indexing a more normatively masculine or feminine gender identity in different workplace contexts. The acceptability of humour as a welcome way of breaking tension and countering boredom at work means the full range of these discursive resources are readily accessible to both women and men, and indeed humour is a valuable resource for integrating conflicting aspects of a person's social identity at work.

But people do not simply use humour to enact and maintain gender stereotypes, they also exploit its potential for modifying, contesting and subverting them in a range of subtle ways. Thus many men in our data used humour to defuse tensions during or after a confrontational exchange between team members, a normatively feminine role. Conversely, some women used humour to challenge and reject the stereotypical supportive discourse role often assigned to them, constructing in the process a more critical and challenging identity. Humour provides a conduit both for conveying and reinforcing masculine and feminine interactional norms and performing a stereotypical gender identity, but also for challenging and undermining stereotypes.

I have mentioned that normatively masculine or feminine discourse patterns in workplace talk can be problematic for some. Just as ways of doing RP vary from workplace to workplace, so acceptable types of humour may also differ. Masculinist norms with contestive, challenging and even abusive styles of interaction are often manifested through humour; and humour can provide a hard-to-contest conduit for sexism or sexist discourse at work. Such talk more often disadvantages women than men. It is hard to contest because humour is so universally regarded positively; those who complain are dismissed as kill-joys. In other words, the use of humour for such purposes raises serious problems of contestation for those wishing to challenge subtle and not so subtle sexist assumptions in workplace interaction. Analysis of the sort exemplified in chapter 4 is hopefully a useful starting point for those concerned about such issues.

Women the Peacemakers?

Managing negatively affective talk is another challenging area of workplace discourse. In some western countries, including New Zealand, the dominant ideology subscribes to a philosophy which considers peace and harmony as desirable, and regards conflict and confrontation as disagreeable, and even potentially 'species-threatening'.[12] This philosophy, which prevails in many social contexts, could be regarded as gendered.[13] Fletcher's (1999) discussion of relational practice, for example, is predicated on the assumption that conflict avoidance is not only feminine but also desirable in an organization. None the less, there are a number of contexts where argument and contestation are accepted ways of engaging in interaction: e.g. law courts, Parliament or the House of Representatives at certain times, informal interactions in some communities of practice. And, of course, in different cultural groups a range of diverse norms prevail.

The simplifications involved in such generalizations are very apparent when we examine disagreements in workplace interaction. It can be argued that conflict is a positive influence in workplace discussion and that it may facilitate progress towards good workplace decisions.[14] On the other hand, conflict can also be damaging and 'can cripple [an organization's] ability to function in goal-setting, staffing, the conduct of meetings, problem solving and decision making'.[15] The analyses in chapter 5 demonstrated the paramount importance of contextual factors in interpreting the effects of disagreement in workplace interaction, and the complex relationship between different ways of managing conflict, and different workplace social relationships. Confrontations which might cause grave offence in some (typically more feminine) workplace cultures and contexts, could be considered quite acceptable and even positive in terms of their effects in other (typically more masculine) communities of practice.

As noted throughout this book, previous language and gender research suggests that, stereotypically, males thrive on competition, contestation and challenge, while women tend to prefer cooperation, smooth talk, negotiation and peaceful interaction. Chapter 5 indicated that in fact gender lines are anything but clear-cut in relation to ways of managing conflict. Effective employees, both female and male, draw extensively on both normatively masculine and feminine discursive resources and gendered norms to achieve their transactional and relational objectives in different workplace contexts, and such flexibility is undoubtedly advantageous in managing workplace interaction.

From a feminist perspective, then, it is useful to ask whether gendered patterns of handling disagreement and conflict potentially disadvantage women in the workplace. If the wider society values harmonious interaction, surely feminine ways of talking should also be valued in the workplace? The management literature suggests that, in many contexts, masculine norms continue to prevail, 'and women are expected to adjust to this male model if they are to be successful in the workplace'.[16] In male-dominated workplaces, then, with masculine norms of interaction, the feminist question is essentially 'how difficult is it for women to develop skills in adversarial and confrontational ways of responding in discussion?' The analyses of authentic workplace discourse in chapter 5 provide evidence that many women have successfully developed such skills. However, it is also worth noting that current socialization patterns may in fact disadvantage some women.[17] While most boys have the opportunity to acquire normatively feminine discursive skills in schools (which are typically very middle-class institutions),[18] opportunities for practising contestive interaction are not always so readily available to the middle-class girls who typically end up in professional white-collar workplaces.[19] Getting integrated into a community of practice involves learning to handle the appropriate styles of interaction. For some women, joining a team whose preferred style is contestive and challenging may present considerable problems.

On the other hand, management experts draw attention to the fact that many organizations are increasingly adopting more informal, 'collaborative and participative styles ... feminine organizational styles'.[20] The analysis in chapter 5 supported the suggestion that men have opportunities during their socialization to acquire features of more feminine styles of interaction. It would be ironic if the proclaimed general move towards more collaborative styles of interaction, at least in white-collar organizations, helped contribute to the development of an alternative set of regulatory norms which favoured men and disadvantaged women: e.g. by valuing men who extend their discursive range to encompass both feminine and masculine styles, but denigrating women who prefer more feminine styles, styles which have paradoxically been undervalued in the past precisely because of their association with femininity. In this context more extensive analyses of the way people actually use language to manage conflict in the workplace are very valuable to help counter the often misleading impressions provided by survey and interview data.

Women's Workplace Stories?

Workplace stories provide another means for people to emphasize particular facets of their social identities and different dimensions of social meaning – professional status, team solidarity, authority responsibilities, gender category, group affiliations, distinctive workplace culture, and so on. They provide an additional resource for constructing a relatively feminine or relatively masculine gender identity at work, while also contributing to the construction of communities of practice as collegial or competitive, supportive or aggressive, relatively masculine or feminine. Narratives provide a way of reinforcing the accepted workplace ethos through moral tales which indicate the values endorsed by those in power; and they also provide a means of subverting and contesting such values. Examining workplace metaphors in business magazines, for example, Koller draws attention to the continued domination of masculine images in the modern workplace. She points to Connell's discussion of

> the globalized male manager, that is, the – mostly male – executive working for a multinational corporation, as a representative of hegemonic masculinity who has all but replaced the male archetype of the soldier.[21]

She notes that the war metaphor so prevalent in business magazines, 'simultaneously constructs and excludes the outgroup of business-women' (2004: 6).[22] Workplace narratives have similar potential, namely to construct a woman-friendly working environment, or not; and to construct women as an asset in the workplace or to 'create and sustain male advantage in power and prestige'.[23]

The narratives discussed in chapter 6 illustrate the interesting ways in which both women and men draw on normatively masculine and normatively feminine ways of telling stories to construct complex workplace identities. Narrative provides a remarkably adaptable discursive resource for constructing oneself as a hero or a clown, a leader, or a gullible incompetent, depending on the context and the audience. And many people use workplace stories very skilfully to instantiate and accomplish the complexities and ambiguities of their workplace roles.

Where do women's interests lie in relation to this area of workplace discourse? The evidence in chapter 6 suggested that here, as elsewhere, both women and men draw on stereotypically gendered content, as well as different aspects of normatively gendered styles of narration to construct their multi-faceted workplace identities. It seems that many people are very skilled at judging their audience when using narrative as a strategic resource in the workplace, and at integrating components of different narrative types and styles to achieve both their transactional and relational goals. In this area, then, a feminist perspective might raise the issue of how different stories are perceived and evaluated in the context of different workplace cultures and communities of practice. It is possible that people in more feminine workplaces tend to respond less appreciatively to 'narrator as hero' narratives, regarding them as inappropriately self-promoting. Equally, it is possible that employees in more masculinist workplaces regard narratives of incompetence as unprofessional or inappropriately personal. These are obvious areas for further research.

Chapter 6 also suggested that, for some women, workplace anecdotes provide a valuable strategy for dealing with the professional–feminine double bind, providing a means of reconciling potentially conflicting aspects of social identity, and serving as effective vehicles for reconciling the varied and often competing demands of different aspects of their professional roles at work. As chapter 2 indicated, portraying oneself as a successful leader, for example, is perhaps more acceptable to some audiences if the images exploited are reassuringly feminine as well as powerful (e.g. mother, queen). Moreover, workplace narratives often contribute to the gendering of the communities of practice in which they occur, reinforcing or subverting the dominant workplace cultures in which they are told. For those concerned with furthering women's interests in the workplace, narrative provides another discursive strategy for promoting feminist values and challenging sexist norms.

Conclusion

New Zealand organizations are increasingly asking 'what do we need to do differently so that our environment is more welcoming and enables women, and others, to fully participate?'[24] This book has suggested a number of possible answers to this question. A predominantly masculinist workplace culture is not a comfortable environment for many women (or for some men). Women in the United Kingdom who were asked why they left organizations, identified as their most common concern working in a 'male-dominated organizational culture' where power struggles and aggressive behaviour prevailed.[25] The discourse examined in this book has presented a far more differentiated and variegated picture, illustrating that people draw on a wide range of different ways of talking at work in different contexts. None the less it is apparent that the predominance of normatively masculine styles of interaction can at times contribute to making the working environment considerably less comfortable for many women.

Some researchers have argued that as a result of their experiences, women may be more able to adapt to different social contexts than men, that a woman is more easily able to multi-task as a result of the demands made on her in her 'double duty' as professional worker and wife–mother–housekeeper.[26] I have not followed this line of analysis very far in this book. Rather, I have provided evidence of the importance for both women and men of access to, and skill in drawing on, diverse discourses and integrating aspects of normatively masculine and normatively feminine styles of interaction, as appropriate, in different workplace contexts. Sinclair suggests that women

> may well prove, in a comprehensive analysis of influence strategies, to be bigendered in their approach. That is they learn an array of influence strategies depending on the context, who they are working with, how much power they have and whether influencing upwards or downwards ... women typically move across several sub-cultures ... they are sensitive to local 'currencies'.[27]

This suggestion has appeal, but again requires further research, especially in the form of the analysis of interaction in real-life workplace contexts. The analysis in this book demonstrates that the relevant skills are best regarded as gendered resources which both women and men use in complex ways according to their experience and verbal competence. Certainly, effective female leaders demonstrate a wide range of discursive skills; but so do effective male leaders.

In conclusion, then, documenting variation and diversity in language and discourse is a valuable starting position for those who would challenge pervasive and disabling patterns. But it is important to ask also, 'what next?' Judith Baxter argues that feminist researchers have a responsibility to work for the benefit of women, and that feminist analysis should be 'transformative', representing 'the complexities and ambiguities of female experience'.[28] Thus, while her analysis of boardroom talk focuses on 'the considerable achievement' of a single woman, Sarah, in the 'otherwise all-male environment' of a dotcom company's senior management team, Baxter also critiques Sarah's use of a 'stereotypically masculinized style of engagement', which contributes to 'the discourse of masculinization within the company culture'.[29]

The analyses in this book have hopefully contributed to documenting the complexities of people's interactions at work, illustrated diversity in the discourse of both women and men, and demonstrated especially the multiplicity of approaches taken by effective women in management roles. Leaders come in a variety of shapes and sizes; and they demonstrate a wide range of discursive skills in meeting the challenges of different workplace cultures, and the specific interactional contexts within them. Hopefully, our research will assist in challenging the straitjacket of stereotypes which have generated apprehension and suspicion of women who do not conform to the expected mould. In this context, I suggest yet another interpretation of Sarah's (Baxter's) use of 'masculinist' discourse. She could be regarded as making strategic use of types of discourse which are more likely to elicit respect, and to her being treated seriously, a gendered discourse well adapted to her workplace environment. Sarah's strategy could be regarded as an effective first step towards change from within her organization – contestation and challenge can follow once one has the ears and attention of those with influence.

Susan Philips provides another answer to the question 'what next?', an answer which could also serve as the next step for women in Sarah's position. Philips proposes that we should build on ways of doing things which benefit women, arguing that we should 'enhance, elaborate, and build on the gender ideologies that are most enabling of women'.[30] In the Tongan context that Philips studied, this meant making use of the high traditional status of the older sister to enhance the status of the role of wife, a strategy effectively used by Queen Salote, who was regarded with great respect throughout the society. This strategy was apparent in the discourse behaviour of some of the successful women discussed in earlier chapters of this book, women who espoused and enacted roles such as queen and mother, roles which acceptably integrate power with femininity in the wider society.

In the context of this book, I further interpret Philips' suggestion as an argument for promoting the positive aspects of normatively feminine talk, a discourse style used by both men and women in different contexts, as I have demonstrated, but stereotypically associated with women. This association can work to women's advantage, and especially to the benefit of those in less senior positions where subordinate status lines up with a style traditionally associated with weakness and compromise. Arguments that we are currently experiencing a global shift towards flatter management structures, and 'a new emphasis on co-operation, teamwork, intuition and creativity',[31] suggest that the timing for promoting the positive aspects of normatively feminine talk may be particularly auspicious.[32] Research which demonstrates the valuable role of certain aspects of normatively feminine discourse in workplace interaction can help erode associations of seniority with masculinity, and establish associations of effectiveness with femininity. Hopefully, this book will contribute to this process.

NOTES

1   See Baxter (2003), Sunderland (2004).
2   Philips (2003).
3   See Martín Rojo (1997), Tannen (1994b), Olsson and Walker (2003), Cameron (2003), McConnell-Ginet (2003), McElhinny (2003a), Talbot (2003). Schnurr (forthcoming) reviews the literature on ways in which men in some workplaces create all-male groups, thus reinforcing their hegemonic status; women in such workplaces simply cannot access all the influential processes available to their male colleagues.
4   Cameron (1997: 49).
5   See Sunderland (2004: 215) for a similar approach in a wider social context.
6   See Crawford (1995), Martín Rojo and Estaban (2003), Kendall (2004).
7   Wodak (2005: 106) identifies the structure of the organization as a relevant constraint in this respect. She suggests that the 'more open and less organized' structure of the European Union makes it possible for female politicians to negotiate their gender identities and political identities in a range of different ways which are not possible in more rigidly structured institutions.
8   Fletcher (1999: 115).
9   Hanson (1997: 2).
10   Nolan (1986: 28).

11 *Personnel Journal* 71 (June 1992): 64.
12 Grimshaw (1990: ix, 1); see also Labov (1990).
13 Tannen (1999); and possibly also classist: see Mills (2003).
14 Lewis et al. (1997).
15 Ibid., 275.
16 Berryman-Fink (1997: 266).
17 See e.g. Sheldon (1990), Sheldon and Johnson (1998).
18 See e.g. Freed (1996), Maybin (2002).
19 But see Baxter (2003) for an alternative perspective.
20 Berryman-Fink (1997: 266). See also Cameron (2000), Candlin, Maley and Sutch (1999), McRae (2004).
21 Koller (2004: 5), paraphrasing Connell (1998).
22 Koller (2004: 6).
23 McConell-Ginet (2000: 263).
24 Hanson (1997: 2).
25 Ibid., 3.
26 Martín Rojo (1997: 234).
27 Sinclair (1998: 128). See Bunker (1990), Perrault and Irwin (1996) and Case (1991, 1995) for further support for this position.
28 Baxter (2003: 56).
29 Ibid., 150.
30 Philips (2003: 271–2).
31 Niven (1993: 53).
32 See also Ferrario (1994), Olsson (1996), Bass (1998), Parry and Proctor (2000).

Appendix: Transcription Conventions

yes	Underscore indicates emphatic stress
[laughs] : :	Paralinguistic features in square brackets, colons indicate start/finish
+	Pause of up to one second
(3)	Pause of specified number of seconds
xx /xxxx\ xx	Simultaneous speech
(hello)	Transcriber's best guess at an unclear utterance
( )	Unintelligible word or phrase
?	Rising or question intonation
-	Incomplete or cut-off utterance
. . .	Section of transcript omitted
XM/XF	Unidentified Male/Female
[voc]	Untranscribable noises
[*comments*]	Editorial comments italicized in square brackets

All names used in examples are pseudonyms.

References

Ainsworth-Vaughn, Nancy 1992. Topic transitions in physician–patient interviews: Power, gender and discourse change. *Language in Society* 21(3): 409–26.

Akande, Adebowale 1994. The glass ceiling: Women and mentoring in management and business. *Journal of Workplace Learning* 6: 21–8.

Alvesson, Mats and Yvonne Due Billing 1997. *Understanding Gender and Organizations.* London: Sage.

Aries, Elizabeth 1996. *Men and Women in Interaction.* Oxford: Oxford University Press.

Ashford, Susan J. and L. L. Cummings 1983. Feedback as an individual resource: Personal strategies of creating information. *Organizational Behavior and Human Performance* 32: 370–98.

Astin, Helen S. and Carole Leland 1991. *Women of Influence, Women of Vision.* San Francisco: Jossey-Bass.

Atkinson, J. Maxwell 1979. Sequencing and shared attentiveness to court proceedings. In George Psathas (ed.), *Everyday Language: Studies in Ethnomethodology.* New York: Irvington Press, 257–86.

Attanucci, Jane S. 1993. Time characterization of mother–daughter and family–school relations: Narrative understandings of adolescence. *Journal of Narrative and Life History* 3: 99–116.

Austin, Paddy 1990. Politeness revisited – The dark side. In Allan Bell and Janet Holmes (eds.), *New Zealand Ways of Speaking English.* Clevedon, Avon: Multilingual Matters, 277–93.

Bargiela-Chiappini, Francesca and Sandra J. Harris 1996. Interruptive strategies in British and Italian management meetings. *Text* 16(3): 269–97.

Bargiela-Chiappini, Francesca and Sandra J. Harris 1997. *Managing Language: The Discourse of Corporate Meetings.* Amsterdam: John Benjamins.

Barretta-Herman, Angeline 1990. The effective social service staff meeting. In Frank X. Sligo (ed.), *Business Communication: New Zealand Perspectives.* Palmerston North, NZ: Software Technology NZ Ltd., 136–46.

Bass, Bernard M. 1998. *Transformational Leadership: Industrial, Military, and Educational Impact*. London and Mahwah, NJ: Lawrence Erlbaum.

Bass, Bernard M. and Bruce J. Avolio 1994. *Improving Organizational Effectiveness Through Transformational Leadership*. Thousand Oaks, CA: Sage.

Baxter, Judith 2003. *Positioning Gender in Discourse: A Feminist Methodology*. Basingstoke: Palgrave Macmillan.

Beck, Dominique M. 1999. Managing discourse, self and others: Women in senior management positions. Unpublished PhD thesis, University of Western Sydney, Nepean.

Beebe, Leslie M. and Martha Clark Cummings 1996. Natural speech act data versus written questionnaire data: How data collection method affects speech act performance. In Susan Gass and Joyce Neu (eds.), *Speech Acts Across Cultures: Challenges to Communication in a Second Language*. Berlin/New York: Mouton de Gruyter.

Beebe, Leslie M., Tomoko Takahashi and Robin Uliss-Weltz 1990. Pragmatic transfer in ESL refusals. In Robin Scarcella, Stephen D. Krashen and Elaine Anderson (eds.), *On the Development of Communicative Competence in a Second Language*. Cambridge, MA: Newbury House, 55–73.

Bell, Arthur 1990. *Mastering the Meeting Maze: How to Plan, Lead, and Participate in More Effective Meetings*. Reading, MA: Addison-Wesley.

Bell, Allan and Georgina Major 2004. 'Yeah right': Voicing kiwi masculinity. Paper presented at the NZ Language and Society Conference, Massey University, Palmerston North, Sept. 2004.

Bellinger, David 1979. Changes in the explicitness of mother's directives as children age. *Journal of Child Language* 6: 443–58.

Bellinger, David and Jean Berko Gleason 1982. Sex differences in parental directives to young children. *Sex Roles* 8: 1123–39.

Bergvall, Victoria L. 1996. Constructing and enacting gender through discourse: Negotiating multiple roles as female engineering students. In Victoria L. Bergvall, Janet M. Bing and Alice F. Freed (eds.), *Rethinking Language and Gender Research: Theory and Practice*. New York: Longman, 173–201.

Bergvall, Victoria L., Janet M. Bing and Alice F. Freed (eds.) 1996. *Rethinking Language and Gender Research: Theory and Practice*. New York: Longman.

Berryman-Fink, Cynthia 1997. Gender issues: Management style, mobility, and harassment. In Peggy Yuhas Byers (ed.), *Organizational Communication: Theory and Behavior*. Needham Heights, MA: Allyn and Bacon, 259–83.

Besson, Amber L., Michael E. Roloff and Gaylene D. Paulson 1998. Preserving face in refusal situations. *Communication Research* 25: 183–99.

Blake, Robert R. and Jane S. Mouton 1978. *The New Managerial Grid*. Houston: Gulf Publishing.

Bloch, Susan 1993. The mentor as counsellor. *Employee Counselling Today* 5(3): 9.

Blum-Kulka, Shoshana, Juliane House and Gabriele Kasper (eds.) 1989. *Cross-Cultural Pragmatics: Requests and Apologies*. Norwoood, NJ: Ablex.

Boden, Deirdre 1994. *The Business of Talk: Organizations in Action*. Cambridge, UK: Polity Press.

Bordo, Susan 1990. Feminism, postmodernism, and gender scepticism. In Linda Nicholson (ed.), *Feminism/Postmodernism*. New York: Routledge, 133–56.

Boyce, Mary E. 1995. Collective centring and collective sense making in the stories and story telling of one organization. *Organization Studies* 16(1): 107–37.

Boyce, Mary E. 1996. Organisational story and story telling: A critical review. *Journal of Organisational Change Management* 9(5): 5–26.

Brewer, Neil, Patricia Mitchell and Nathan Weber 2002. Gender role, organizational status, and conflict management styles. *International Journal of Conflict Management* 13(1): 78–94.

Brewis, Joanna 2001. Telling it like it is? Gender, language and organizational theory. In Robert Westwood and Stephen Linstead (eds.), *The Language of Organization*. London: Sage, 283–309.

Brown, Penelope and Stephen C. Levinson 1987. *Politeness: Some Universals in Language Usage*. Cambridge: Cambridge University Press.

Bryson, Jane and Robyn May 2004. Good life in the bleak house. Paper presented at AIRAANZ Conference, Griffith University, Brisbane, Feb. 2004.

Bublitz, Wolfram 1988. *Supportive Fellow-Speakers and Co-operative Conversations: Discourse Topics and 'Recipient Action' in a Particular Type of Everyday Conversation*. Amsterdam: John Benjamins.

Bucholtz, Mary, A. C. Liang and Laurel A. Sutton 1999. *Reinventing Identities: The Gendered Self in Discourse*. Oxford: Oxford University Press.

Bunker, Barbara Benedict 1990. Appreciating diversity and modifying organizational cultures: men and women at work. In Suresh Srivasta, David L. Cooperrider and Associates (eds.), *Appreciative Management and Leadership: The Power of Positive Thought and Action in Organizations*. San Francisco: Jossey-Bass, 126–49.

Burke, Ronald J. and Carol McKeen 1990. Mentoring in organizations: Implications for women. *Journal of Business Ethics* 9: 317–32.

Butler, Judith 1990. *Gender Trouble: Feminism and the Subversion of Identity*. New York: Routledge.

Caldwell, Brian J. and E. M. A. Carter (eds.) 1992. *The Return of the Mentor: Strategies for Workplace Learning*. London and Washington, DC: Falmer Press.

Cameron, Deborah 1992. *Feminism and Linguistic Theory* (2nd ed). New York: St. Martin's Press.

Cameron, Deborah 1996. The language–gender interface: Challenging co-optation. In Victoria L. Bergvall, Janet M. Bing and Alice F. Freed (eds.), *Rethinking Language and Gender Research: Theory and Practice*. New York: Longman, 31–53.

Cameron, Deborah 1997. Performing gender identity: Young men's talk and the construction of heterosexual masculinity. In Sally Johnson and Ulrike Hanna Meinhof (eds.), *Language and Masculinity*. Oxford: Blackwell, 47–65.

Cameron, Deborah 2000. *Good To Talk? Living and Working in a Communication Culture*. London and Thousand Oaks, CA: Sage.

Cameron, Deborah 2003. Gender and language ideologies. In Janet Holmes and Miriam Meyerhoff (eds.), *Handbook of Language and Gender*. Oxford: Blackwell, 447–67.

Cameron, Deborah and Don Kulick 2003. *Language and Sexuality*. Cambridge: Cambridge University Press.

Candlin, Christopher N., Yon Maley and Heather Sutch 1999. Industrial instability and the discourse of enterprise bargaining. In Srikant Sarangi and Celia Roberts (eds.), *Talk, Work and Institutional Order: Discourse in Medical, Mediation and Management Settings*. Berlin and New York: Mouton de Gruyter, 323–50.

Carr-Ruffino, Norma 1993. *The Promotable Woman: Advancing Through Leadership Skills*. Belmont, CA: Wadsworth.

Case, Susan Schick 1988. Cultural differences, not deficiencies: An analysis of managerial women's language. In Suzanna Rose and Laurie Larwood (eds.), *Women's Careers: Pathways and Pitfalls*. New York: Praeger, 41–63.

Case, Susan Schick 1991. Wide verbal repertoire speech: Gender, language and managerial influence. *Women's Studies International Forum* 16(3): 271–90.

Case, Susan Schick 1995. Gender, language and the professions: Recognition of wide-verbal-repertoire speech. *Studies in the Linguistic Sciences* 25(2): 149–92.

Caudron, Shari 1992. Humor is healthy in the workplace. *Personnel Journal* 71 (June): 63–8.

Chan, Angela forthcoming. Small talk in business meetings in Hong Kong and New Zealand. Unpublished PhD thesis, Victoria University of Wellington, Wellington, NZ.

Chase, Susan E. 1988. Making sense of 'the woman who becomes a man'. In Alexandra Dundas Todd and Sue Fisher (eds.), *Gender and Discourse: The Power of Talk*. Advances in Discourse Processes 30. Norwood, NJ: Ablex, 275–95.

Chen, Xing, Lei Ye and Yanyin Zhang 1995. Refusing in Chinese. In Gabriele Kasper (ed.), *Pragmatics of Chinese as Native and Target Language*. Honolulu, HI: University of Hawai'i, Second Language Teaching & Curriculum Center, 119–63.

Clayman, Steven 2002. Disagreements and third parties: Dilemmas of neutralism in panel news interviews. *Journal of Pragmatics* 34: 1385–1402.

Clutterbuck, David 1992. *Mentoring*. Henley-on-Thames: Henley Distance Learning.

Coates, Jennifer 1989. Gossip revisited: Language in all-female groups. In Jennifer Coates and Deborah Cameron (eds.), *Women in their Speech Communities: New Perspectives on Language and Sex*. London: Longman, 94–122.

Coates, Jennifer 1996. *Women Talk*. Oxford: Blackwell.

Coates, Jennifer 1997. One-at-a-time: The organization of men's talk. In Sally Johnson and Urike Hanna Meinhof (eds.), *Language and Masculinity*. Oxford: Blackwell, 107–29.

Coates, Jennifer (ed.) 1998. *Language and Gender: A Reader*. Oxford: Blackwell.

Coates, Jennifer 2003. *Men Talk*. Oxford: Blackwell.

Cohen, Andrew D. and Elite Olshtain 1981. Developing a measure of sociocultural competence: The case of apology. *Language Learning* 31(1): 113–34.

Connell, Robert W. 1987. *Gender and Power: Society, the Person and Sexual Politics*. Stanford: Stanford University Press.

Connell, Robert W. 1988. Maculinities and globalization. *Men and Masculinities* 1: 3–23.

Cook-Gumperz, Jenny 1995. Reproducing the discourse of mothering: How gendered talk makes gendered lives. In Kira Hall and Mary Bucholtz (eds.), *Gender Articulated: Language and the Socially Constructed Self*. London: Routledge, 401–20.

Coser, Rose Laub 1960. Laughter among colleagues. A study of social functions of humor among the staff of a mental hospital. *Psychiatry* 23: 81–95.

Coupland, Justine 2000. *Small Talk*. London: Longman.

Craig, D. and M. K. Pitts 1990. The dynamics of dominance in tutorial discussions. *Linguistics* 28: 125–38.

Crawford, Mary 1989. Humor in conversational context: Beyond biases in the study of gender and humor. In Rhonda K. Unger (ed.), *Representations: Social Constructions of Gender*. Amityville, NY: Baywood, 155–66.

Crawford, Mary 1995. *Talking Difference: On Gender and Language*. London and Thousand Oaks, CA: Sage.

Crawford, Mary and Diane Gressley 1991. Creativity, caring and context – Women's and men's accounts of humor preferences and practices. *Psychology of Women Quarterly* 15(2): 217–31.

Cuff, E. C. and Wes Sharrock 1985. Meetings. In Teun A. van Dijk (ed.), *Handbook of Discourse Analysis*, Vol. 3: *Discourse and Dialogue*. London: Academic Press, 149–59.

Daly, Nicola, Janet Holmes, Jonathan Newton and Maria Stubbe 2004. Expletives as solidarity signals in FTAs on the factory floor. *Journal of Pragmatics* 36(5): 945–64.

Darling, John R. and W. Earl Walker 2001. Effective conflict management: Use of the behavioral style model. *Leadership and Organization Development Journal* 22(5): 230–42.

Drew, Paul and John Heritage (eds.) 1992. *Talk at Work*. Cambridge: Cambridge University Press.

Dwyer, Judith 1993. *The Business Communication Handbook*. New York: Prentice-Hall.

Dyer, Judith and Deborah Keller-Cohen 2000. The discursive construction of professional self through narratives of personal experience. *Discourse Studies* 2(3): 283–304.

Dymock, Darryl 1999. Blind date: A case study of mentoring as workplace training. *Journal of Workplace Learning* 11(8): 312–17.

Eakins, Barbara Westbrook and R. Gene Eakins 1979. Verbal turn-taking and exchanges in faculty dialogue. In Betty Lou Dubois and Isabel Crouch (eds.), *The Sociology of the Languages of American Women*. San Antonio, TX: Trinity University Press, 53–62.

Eckert, Penelope 2000. *Language Variation as Social Practice*. Oxford: Blackwell.

Eckert, Penelope and Sally McConnell-Ginet 1992. Communities of practice: Where language, gender and power all live. In Kira Hall, Mary Bucholtz and Birch Moonwomon (eds.), *Locating Power: Proceedings of the Second Berkeley Women and Language Conference*. Berkeley, April 1992. University of California: Berkeley Women and Language Group, 89–99.

Eckert, Penelope and Sally McConnell-Ginet 1995. Constructing meaning, constructing selves: Snapshots of language, gender, and class from Belten High. In Kira Hall and Mary Bucholtz (eds.), *Gender Articulated: Language and the Socially Constructed Self*. London: Routledge, 469–507.

Eckert, Penelope and Sally McConnell-Ginet 2003. *Language and Gender*. Cambridge: Cambridge University Press.

Edelsky, Carole 1981. Who's got the floor? *Language in Society* 10: 383–421.

Eder, Donna 1993. 'Go get ya a French!': Romantic and sexual teasing among adolescent girls. In Deborah Tannen (ed.), *Gender and Conversational Interaction*. Oxford: Oxford University Press, 17–31.

Edley, Nigel and Margaret Wetherell 1997. Jockeying for position: The construction of masculine identities. *Discourse and Society* 8(2): 203–17.

Edmonson, Willis 1981. *Spoken Discourse*. London: Longman.

Ehrich, Lisa Catherine 1994. Mentoring and networking for women educators. *Women in Management Review* 9(3): 4–10.

Ervin-Tripp, Susan and Martin Lampert 1992. Gender differences in the construction of humorous talk. In Kira Hall, Mary Bucholtz and Birch Moonwomon (eds.), *Locating Power: Proceedings of the Second Berkeley Women and Language Conference April 4 and 5 1992*, Vol. 1. University of California, Berkeley Women and Language Group, 108–17.

Fairclough, Norman L. 1989. *Language and Power*. Essex, UK: Longman.

Fairclough, Norman L. (ed.) 1992. *Critical Language Awareness*. London: Longman.

Feather, Norman T. 1996. Values, deservingness and attitudes toward high achievers: Research in tall poppies. In Clive S. R. Seligman, James M. Olson and Mark P. Zanna (eds.), *The Psychology of Values. The Ontario Symposium*, Vol. 8. Mahwah, NJ: Erlbaum, 215–51.

Ferrario, Margaret 1994. Women as managerial leaders. In Marilyn Davidson and Ronald Burke (eds.), *Women in Management: Current Research Issues.* London: Paul Chapman, 110–25.

Firth, Alan (ed.) 1995. *The Discourse of Negotiation: Studies of Language in the Workplace.* Oxford: Pergamon.

Fisher, B. Aubrey and Donald G. Ellis 1990. *Small Group Decision Making: Communication and the Group Process.* New York: McGraw-Hill.

Fishman, P. M. 1977. Interactional shitwork. *Heresies* 2: 99–101.

Fleming, David 2001. Narrative leadership: Using the power of stories. *Strategy & Leadership* 29(4): 34–6.

Fletcher, Joyce K. 1999. *Disappearing Acts: Gender, Power, and Relational Practice at Work.* Cambridge, MA: MIT Press.

Folkes, Valerie 1982. Communicating the reasons for social rejection. *Journal of Social Psychology* 18: 235–52.

Freed, Alice F. 1996. Language and gender research in an experimental setting. In Victoria L. Bergvall, Janet M. Bing and Alice F. Freed (eds.), *Rethinking Language and Gender Research: Theory and Practice.* New York: Longman, 54–76.

Freed, Alice 2003. Epilogue: Reflections on language and gender research. In Janet Holmes and Miriam Meyerhoff (eds.), *Handbook of Language and Gender.* Oxford: Blackwell, 699–721.

Freed, Alice 2004. *Sex* or *gender*: Still a conundrum in language and gender research. Paper presented at 3rd Biennial Conference of the International Gender and Language Association, Ithaca, NY.

Gabriel, Yiannis 1998. Stories and sense-making. In David Grant, Tom Keenoy and Cliff Oswick (eds.), *Discourse and Organization.* London: Sage, 84–103.

Gal, Susan 1991. Between speech and silence: The problematics of research on language and gender. In Micaela di Leonardo (ed.), *Gender at the Crossroads of Knowledge.* Berkeley: University of California Press, 180–201.

Gardner, John and Deborah Terry 1996. Communication, leadership and organisational change. In Ken Parry (ed.), *Leadership Research and Practice: Emerging Themes and New Challenges.* South Melbourne, Vic.: Pitman, 153–61.

Garfinkel, Harold 1967. *Studies in Ethnomethodology.* Englewood Cliffs, NJ: Prentice-Hall.

Gass Susan and Noel Houck 1999. *Interlanguage Refusals: A Cross-cultural Study of Japanese-English.* Berlin/New York: Morton de Gruyter.

Gilligan, Carol 1982. *In a Different Voice.* Cambridge, MA: Harvard University Press.

Goffman, Erving 1959. *Presentation of Self in Everyday Life.* New York: Anchor Books.

Goffman, Erving 1967. *Interaction Ritual: Essays on Face to Face Behavior.* New York: Anchor Books.

Goffman, Erving 1974. *Frame Analysis.* New York: Harper and Row.

Goleman, Daniel 1995. *Emotional Intelligence*. New York: Bantam Books.

Grant, Jan 1988. Women as managers: What they can offer to organization. *Organizational Dynamics* (Spring): 56–63.

Grey, C. 1995. Review article: Gender as a grid of intelligibility. *Gender, Work and Organization* 2(1): 46–50.

Grimshaw, Allen D. 1990. Introduction. In Allen D. Grimshaw (ed.), *Conflict Talk: Sociolinguistic Investigations of Arguments in Conversations*. Cambridge: Cambridge University Press, 1–20.

Gumperz, John J. 1982. *Discourse Strategies*. Cambridge: Cambridge University Press.

Gumperz, John J. 1992. Interviewing in intercultural situations. In Paul Drew and John Heritage (eds.), *Talk at Work*. Cambridge: Cambridge University Press, 302–27.

Gumperz, John J. 2001a. Contextualization and ideology in intercultural communication. In Also di Luzio, Susanne Günthner and Frances Orletti (eds.), *Culture in Communication: Analyses of Intercultural Situations*. Amsterdam: John Benjamins, 35–53.

Gumperz, John J. 2001b. Interactional sociolinguistics: A personal perspective. In Deborah Schiffrin, Deborah Tannen and Heidi E. Hamilton (eds.), *The Handbook of Discourse Analysis*. Oxford: Blackwell, 215–28.

Gunnarsson, Britt-Louise 2001. Academic women in the male university field: Communicative practices at postgraduate seminars. In Bettina Baron and Helga Kotthoff (eds.), *Gender in Interaction*. Amsterdam: John Benjamins, 247–81.

Hackman, Michael Z. and Craig E. Johnson 2000. *Leadership: A Communication Perspective*. Prospect Heights, IL: Waveland.

Hall, Kira 1995. Lip service on the fantasy lines. In Kira Hall and Mary Bucholtz (eds.), *Gender Articulated: Language and the Socially Constructed Self*. New York: Routledge, 183–216.

Hall, Kira 2003. Exceptional speakers: Contested and problematized gender identities. In Miriam Meyerhoff and Janet Holmes (eds.), *Handbook of Language and Gender*. Oxford: Blackwell, 352–80.

Hall, Kira and Mary Bucholtz (eds.) 1995. *Gender Articulated: Language and the Socially Constructed Self*. New York: Routledge.

Hanak, Irmi 1998. Chairing meetings: Turn and topic control in development communication in rural Zanzibar. *Discourse and Society* 9(1): 33–56.

Hanson, Margaret 1997. Why women leave organisations, and what organisations are doing about it. Report by Top Drawer Consultants.

Harris, Thomas E. 2002. *Applied Organizational Communication* (2nd ed). Mahwah, NJ: Lawrence Erlbaum.

Harris, Sandra J. 2003. Politeness and power: Making and responding to 'requests' in institutional settings. *Text* 21(1): 27–52.

Harvey, Lynda 1997. A genealogical exploration of gendered genres in IT cultures. *Information Systems Journal* 7(2): 153–72.

Hay, Jennifer 1994. Jocular abuse patterns in mixed-group interactions. *Wellington Working Papers in Linguistics* 6: 26–55.

Hay, Jennifer 1995. Gender and humor: Beyond a joke. Unpublished Master's thesis, Victoria University of Wellington, Wellington, NZ.

Hay, Jennifer 2002. Male cheerleaders and wanton women: Humour among New Zealand friends. *Te Reo* 45: 3–36.

Heaney, Liam F. 2001. A question of management: Conflict, pressure and time. *The International Journal of Educational Management* 15(4): 197–203.

Hearn, Jeff and P. Wendy Parkin 1989. Women, men, and leadership: A critical review of assumptions, practices, and change in the industrialized nations. In Nancy Adler and Dafna Izraeli (eds.), *Women in Management Worldwide*. London: M. E. Sharpe, 17–40.

Heifertz, Ronald 1998. Values in leadership. In Gill Robinson Hickman (ed.), *Leading Organizations: Perspectives for a New Era*. London: Sage, 343–56.

Heifertz, Ronald and Donald Laurie 2001. The work of leadership. *Harvard Business Review. Special Issue on Leadership* 79(11): 131–40.

Heilman, Madeline E., Caryn J. Block, Richard F. Martell and Michael C. Simon 1989. Has anything changed? Current characterizations of men, women, and managers. *Journal of Applied Psychology* 74(6): 935–42.

Herbert, Robert K. 1990. Sex-based differences in compliment behavior. *Language in Society* 19: 201–24.

Heritage, John 1984. *Garfinkel and Ethnomethodology*. Cambridge, UK: Polity Press.

Heritage, John 1998. Oh-prefaced responses to inquiry. *Language in Society* 27(3): 291–334.

Heritage, John 2002. The limits of questioning: Negative interrogatives and hostile question content. *Journal of Pragmatics* 34: 1427–46.

Hofstede, Geert 1980. *Culture's Consequences: International Differences in Work-Related Values*. Newbury Park, CA: Sage.

Holmes, Janet 1984. Modifying illocutionary force. *Journal of Pragmatics* 8(3): 345–65.

Holmes, Janet 1987. Hedging, fencing and other conversational gambits: An analysis of gender differences in New Zealand speech. In Anne Pauwels (ed.), *Women and Language in Australian and New Zealand Society*. Sydney: Australian Professional Publications, 59–79.

Holmes, Janet 1988a. Paying compliments: A sex-preferential positive politeness strategy. *Journal of Pragmatics* 12(3): 445–65.

Holmes, Janet 1988b. *Of course*: a pragmatic particle in New Zealand women's and men's speech. *Australian Journal of Linguistics* 8(1): 49–74.

Holmes, Janet 1990. Apologies in New Zealand English. *Language in Society* 19(2): 155–99. Reprinted in Jenny Cheshire and Peter Trudgill (eds.), *Reader in Sociolinguistics*. London: Edward Arnold.

Holmes, Janet 1992. Women's talk in public contexts. *Discourse and Society* 3(2): 131–50.

Holmes, Janet 1993. New Zealand women are good to talk to: An analysis of politeness strategies in interaction. *Journal of Pragmatics* 20: 91–116.

Holmes, Janet 1995. *Women, Men and Politeness*. London: Longman.

Holmes, Janet 1996. Women's role in language change: A place for quantification. In Natasha Warner, Jocelyn Ahlers, Leela Bilmes, Monica Oliver, Suzanne Wertheim and Melinda Chen (eds.), *Gender and Belief Systems: Proceedings of the Fourth Berkeley Women and Language Conference, April 19–21, 1996*. University of California, Berkeley Women and Language Group, 313–30.

Holmes, Janet 1997a. Women, language and identity, *Journal of Sociolinguistics* 2(1): 195–223.

Holmes 1997b. Story-telling in New Zealand women's and men's talk. In Ruth Wodak (ed.), *Gender, Discourse and Ideology*. London: Sage, 263–93.

Holmes, Janet 1998. Why tell stories? Contrasting themes and identities in the narratives of Maori and Pakeha women and men. *Journal of Asian Pacific Communication* 8(1): 1–29.

Holmes, Janet 2000a. Women at work: Analysing women's talk in New Zealand workplaces. *Australian Review of Applied Linguistics (ARAL)* 22(2): 1–17.

Holmes, Janet 2000b. Doing collegiality and keeping control at work: Small talk in government departments. In Justine Coupland (ed.), *Small Talk*. London: Longman, 32–61.

Holmes, Janet 2000c. Politeness, power and provocation: How humour functions in the workplace. *Discourse Studies* 2(2): 159–85.

Holmes, Janet 2004a. Story-telling at work: One resource for integrating personal, professional and social identities. Paper presented at SS15. (To appear in *Discourse Studies*.)

Holmes, Janet 2005a. Leadership talk: How do leaders 'do mentoring', and is gender relevant? (To appear in special issue of *Journal of Pragmatics*, edited by Karin Aijmer and Anna-Brit Stenstrom.)

Holmes, Janet 2005b. Workplace narratives, professional identity and relational practice. In Anna De Fina, Deborah Schiffrin and Michael Bamberg (eds.), *Discourse and Identity*. Cambridge: Cambridge University Press.

Holmes, Janet 2005c. Power and discourse at work: Is gender relevant? In Michelle Lazar (ed.), *Feminist Critical Discourse Analysis*. London: Palgrave, 31–60.

Holmes 2005d. Sharing a laugh: pragmatic aspects of humor and gender in the workplace. (To appear in special issue of *Journal of Pragmatics* edited by Helga Kotthoff.)

Holmes, Janet (forthcoming). The glass ceiling: Does talk contribute? Gendered discourse in the New Zealand workplace. Plenary paper presented at the Conference of the Australia and New Zealand Communication Association, Christchurch, 4–7 July 2005.

Holmes, Janet, Louise Burns, Meredith Marra, Maria Stubbe and Bernadette Vine 2003. Women managing discourse in the workplace. *Women and Management Review* 18(8): 414–24.

Holmes, Janet and Georgina Major 2003. Nurses communicating on the ward: The human face of hospitals. *Kai Tiaki: Nursing New Zealand* 8(11): 14–16.

Holmes, Janet and Meredith Marra 2002a. Humour as a discursive boundary marker in social interaction. In Anna Duszak (ed.), *Us and Others: Social Identities across Languages, Discourses and Cultures*. Amsterdam: John Benjamins, 377–400.

Holmes, Janet and Meredith Marra 2002b. Having a laugh at work: How humour contributes to workplace culture. *Journal of Pragmatics* 34: 1683–1710.

Holmes, Janet and Meredith Marra 2002c. Over the edge? Subversive humour between colleagues and friends. *Humor* 15(1): 1–23.

Holmes, Janet and Meredith Marra 2004. Relational practice in the workplace: Women's talk or gendered discourse? *Language in Society* 33: 377–98.

Holmes, Janet and Meredith Marra 2005a. Communicating in a diverse workplace: gender and identity. In Frank X. Sligo and Ralph Bathurst (eds.), *Communication in the New Zealand Workplace: Theory and Practice*. Palmerston North, NZ: Software Technology NZ Ltd., 71–82.

Holmes, Janet and Meredith Marra 2005b. Leadership and managing conflict in meetings. *Pragmatics* 4(4).

Holmes, Janet and Meredith Marra 2005c. Narrative and the construction of professional identity in the workplace. In Joanna Thornborrow and Jennifer Coates (eds.), *The Sociolinguistics of Narrative: Theory, Context and Culture in Oral Story-telling*. Amsterdam: John Benjamins, 193–213.

Holmes, Janet and Meredith Marra forthcoming. Queen Clara: Managing professional and gender identity conflict.

Holmes, Janet, Meredith Marra and Louise Burns 2001. Women's humour in the workplace: A quantitative analysis. *Australian Journal of Communication* 28(1): 83–108.

Holmes, Janet and Miriam Meyerhoff 2003a. *Handbook of Language and Gender*. Oxford: Blackwell.

Holmes, Janet and Miriam Meyerhoff 2003b. Different voices, different views: An introduction to current research in language and gender. In Janet Holmes and Miriam Meyerhoff (eds.), *Handbook of Language and Gender*. Oxford: Blackwell, 1–17.

Holmes, Janet and Stephanie Schnurr 2004. Doing femininity at work: More than just relational practice. Paper presented at 3rd Biennial Conference of the International Gender and Language Association, Ithaca, NY.

Holmes, Janet and Stephanie Schnurr 2005. Politeness, humour and gender in the workplace: Negotiating norms and identifying contestation. *Journal of Politeness* 1(1): 121–49.

Holmes, Janet and Maria Stubbe 2001. Managing conflict at work. Paper presented at Colloquium on Researching the Discourse of Workplace and Professional Settings, AAAL 2000, St. Louis, MO, USA.

Holmes, Janet and Maria Stubbe 2003a. 'Feminine' workplaces: Stereotypes and reality. In Janet Holmes and Miriam Meyerhoff (eds.), *Handbook of Language and Gender*. Oxford: Blackwell, 573–99.

Holmes, Janet and Maria Stubbe 2003b. *Power and Politeness in the Workplace: A Sociolinguistic Analysis of Talk at Work*. London: Longman.

Holmes, Janet, Maria Stubbe and Bernadette Vine 1999. Constructing professional identity: 'Doing power' in policy units. In Srikant Sarangi and Celia Roberts (eds.), *Talk, Work and Institutional Order: Discourse in Medical, Mediation and Management Settings*. Berlin and New York: Mouton de Gruyter, 351–85.

Hopper, Robert and Curtis LeBaron 1998. How gender creeps into talk. *Research on Language and Social Interaction* 31(1): 59–74.

Houck, Noel and Susan M. Gass 1996. Non-native refusals: A methodological perspective. In Susan M. Gass and Joyce Neu (eds.), *Speech Acts Across Cultures*. New York: Mouton de Gruyter, 46–63.

Houtkoop, Hanneke 1987. *Establishing Agreement: An Analysis of Proposal–Acceptance Sequences*. Dordrecht: Foris Publications.

Ivanic, Roz 1998. *Writing and Identity: The Discoursal Construction of Identity in Academic Writing*. Amsterdam: John Benjamins.

Jackson, Brad and Ken Parry 2001. *The Hero Manager: Learning from New Zealand's Top Chief Executives*. Auckland: Penguin.

Jacobs, Scott 2002. Maintaining neutrality in third-party dispute mediation. *Journal of Pragmatics* 34: 1403–26.

James, Deborah and Sandra Clarke 1992. Interruptions, gender and power: A critical review of the literature. In Kira Hall, Mary Bucholtz and Birch Moonwomon (eds.), *Locating Power: Proceedings of the Second Berkeley Women and Language Conference, April 4 and 5, 1992*, Vol. 2. University of California, Berkeley Women and Language Group, 286–99. Also in Deborah Tannen (ed.) 1993. *Gender and Conversational Interaction*. Oxford: Oxford University Press, 231–80.

James, Deborah and Janice Drakich 1993. Understanding gender differences in amount of talk. In Deborah Tannen (ed.), *Gender and Conversational Interaction*. Oxford: Oxford University Press, 281–312.

Jenkins, Mercilee M. 1985. What's so funny? Joking among women. In Noelle Caskey, Sue Bremner and Birch Moonwomon (eds.), *Proceedings of the First Berkeley Women and Language Conference*. University of California, Berkeley Women and Language Group, 131–51.

Johnson Sally 1997. Theorizing language and masculinity: A feminist perspective. In Sally Johnson and Ulrike Meinhoff (eds.), *Language and Masculinity*. London: Blackwell, 8–26.

Johnson, Donna M. and Duane H. Roen 1992. Complimenting and involvement in peer reviews: Gender variation. *Language in Society* 21: 27–57.

Johnstone, Barbara 1990. *Stories, Community, and Place.* Bloomington: Indiana University Press.

Johnstone, Barbara 1993. Community and contest: Midwestern men and women creating their worlds in conversational story-telling. In Deborah Tannen (ed.), *Gender and Conversational Interaction.* Oxford: Oxford University Press, 62–80.

Jones, Deborah 2000. Gender trouble in the workplace: 'Language and gender' meets 'feminist organisational communication'. In Janet Holmes (ed.), *Gendered Speech in Social Context: Perspectives from Gown & Town.* Wellington: Victoria University Press, 192–210.

Kakavá, Christina 2002. Opposition in Modern Greek discourse. *Journal of Pragmatics* 34: 1537–68.

Kangasharju, Helena 2002. Alignment in disagreement. *Journal of Pragmatics* 34: 1447–72.

Karsten, Margaret Foegen 1994. *Management and Gender.* Westport, CT: Quorum Books.

Kaufmann, Anita 2002. Negation prosody in British English. *Journal of Pragmatics* 34: 1473–94.

Kaye, Michael 1996. *Myth Makers and Story-tellers.* Sydney: Business and Professional Publishing. Pty. Ltd.

Kendall, Shari 2003. Creating gendered demeanours of authority at work and at home. In Janet Holmes and Miriam Meyerhoff (eds.), *Handbook of Language and Gender.* Oxford: Blackwell, 600–23.

Kendall, Shari 2004. Framing authority: Gender, face and mitigation at a radio network. *Discourse and Society* 15(1): 55–79.

Kendall, Shari and Deborah Tannen 1997. Gender and language in the workplace. In Ruth Wodak (ed.), *Gender and Discourse.* London: Sage, 81–105.

Kiesling, Scott 2001. 'Now I gotta watch what I say': Shifting constructions of gender and dominance in discourse. *Journal of Linguistic Anthropology* 11: 250–73.

Kitzinger, Celia 2002. Doing feminist Conversational Analysis. In Paul McIlvenny (ed.), *Talking Gender and Sexuality.* Amsterdam: John Benjamins, 163–93.

Kline, Susan L. and Cathy H. Floyd 1990. On the art of saying no: The influence of social cognitive development on messages of refusal. *Western Journal of Speech Communication* 54: 454–72.

Knippen, Jay T. and Thad B. Green 1999. Handling conflicts. *The Journal of Workplace Learning* 11(1): 27–32.

Koller, Veronika 2004. Business women and war metaphors: 'Possessive, jealous and pugnacious'? *Journal of Sociolinguistics* 8(1): 3–22.

Kotthoff, Helga 1999. Coherent keying in conversational humour: Contextualising joint fictionalisation. In Wolfram Bublitz, Uta Lenk and Elija Ventola (eds.), *Coherence in Spoken and Written Discourse*. Amsterdam/Philadelphia: John Benjamins, 125–50.

Kotthoff, Helga 2000. Gender and joking: On the complexities of women's image politics in humorous narratives. *Journal of Pragmatics* 32: 55–80.

Kotthoff, Helga forthcoming. Introduction. (To appear in *Journal of Pragmatics*.)

Kram, Kathy 1988. *Mentoring at Work: Developmental Relationships in Organizational Life*. Lanham, MD: University Press of America. (Originally published by Glenview, IL: Scott Foresman, 1985.)

Kuhn, Elisabeth D. 1992. Playing down authority while getting things done: Women professors get help from the institution. In Kira Hall, Mary Bucholtz and Birch Moonwomon (eds.), *Locating Power: Proceedings of the Second Berkeley Women and Language Conference, April 4 and 5, 1992*, Vol. 1. University of California, Berkeley Women and Language Group, 318–25.

Kuiper, Koenraad 1991. Sporting formulae in New Zealand English: Two models of male solidarity. In Jenny Cheshire (ed.), *English Around the World. Sociolinguistics Perspectives*. Cambridge: Cambridge University Press, 200–9.

Labov, Teresa 1990. Ideological themes in reports of interracial conflict. In Allen D. Grimshaw (ed.), *Conflict talk: Sociolinguistic Investigations of Arguments in Conversations*. Cambridge: Cambridge University Press, 139–59.

Labov, William 1972. The transformation of experience in narrative syntax. In *Language in the Inner City: Studies in the Black English Vernacular*. Philadelphia: University of Pennsylvania Press, 354–96.

Lakoff, Robin 1975. *Language and Woman's Place*. New York: Harper and Row.

Lakoff, Robin Tolmach 1990. *Talking Power: The Politics of Language in Our Lives*. New York: Basic Books.

Lampert, Martin D. 1996. Studying gender differences in the conversational humor of adults and children. In Dan Isaac Slobin, Julie Gerhardt, Amy Kyratzis and Jiansheng Guo (eds.), *Social Interaction, Social Context and Language: Essays in Honor of Susan Ervin-Tripp*. Mahwah, NJ: Lawrence Erlbaum, 579–95.

Levinson, Stephen C. 1979. Activity types and language. *Linguistics* 17(5/6): 365–99.

Levinson, Stephen C. 1983. *Pragmatics*. Cambridge, UK: Cambridge University Press.

Lewis, Dianne S., Erica French and Peter Steane 1997. A culture of conflict. *Leadership and Organization Development Journal* 18(6): 275–82.

Litosseliti, Lia and Jane Sunderland (eds.) 2002. *Gender, Identity and Discourse Analysis*. Philadelphia, PA: John Benjamins.

Locher, Miriam 2004. *Power and Politeness in Action: Disagreements in Oral Communication*. Berlin: Mouton de Gruyter.

McCollum, Marion 1992. Organizational stories in a family owned business. *Family Business Review* 5(1): 3–24.

McConnell-Ginet, Sally 2000. Breaking through the 'glass ceiling': Can linguistic awareness help? In Janet Holmes (ed.), *Gendered Speech in Social Context: Perspectives from Gown & Town*. Wellington: Victoria University Press, 259–82.

Macdonald, Lindsay 2002. Nurse talk: Features of effective verbal communication used by expert district nurses. Unpublished MA thesis, Victoria University of Wellington, Wellington, NZ.

McElhinny, Bonnie S. 1995. Challenging hegemonic masculinities: Female and male police officers handling domestic violence. In Kira Hall and Mary Bucholtz (eds.), *Gender Articulated: Language and the Socially Constructed Self*. London: Routledge, 217–43.

McElhinny, Bonnie 2003a. Theorizing gender in sociolinguistics and linguistic anthropology. In Janet Holmes and Miriam Meyerhoff (eds.), *Handbook of Language and Gender*. Oxford: Blackwell, 21–42.

McElhinny, Bonnie 2003b. Fearful, forceful agents of the law: Ideologies about language and gender in police officer's narratives about the use of physical force. *Pragmatics* 13(2): 253–84.

McLaughlin, Margaret 1984. *Conversation: How Talk is Organized*. Beverly Hills: Sage.

McRae, Susan S. 2004. Language, Gender and Status in the Workplace: The Discourse of Disagreement in Meetings. PhD thesis, Open University, UK.

Maier, Mark 1997. Gender equity, organizational transformation and challenger. *Journal of Business Ethics* 16(9): 943–62.

Marra, Meredith 1998. Okay we'll start now I think: The boundaries of meetings: Opening and closing sequences, and framing devices. Unpublished MA paper, Victoria University of Wellington, Wellington, NZ.

Marra, Meredith 2003. Decisions in New Zealand business meetings. Unpublished PhD thesis, Victoria University of Wellington, Wellington, NZ.

Marra, Meredith and Janet Holmes 1999. Subverting the system – How humour can help. *Proceedings of 11th National Annual Conference of the New Zealand Communication Association*, 53–8.

Marra, Meredith and Janet Holmes 2004. Workplace narratives and business reports: Issues of definition. *Text* 24(1): 59–78.

Marra, Meredith, Stephanie Schnurr and Janet Holmes forthcoming. Effective leadership in New Zealand workplaces: Balancing gender and role. In Judith Baxter and Allyson Jule (eds.), *Speaking Out: The Female Voice in Public Contexts*.

Marshall, Judi 1984. *Women Managers: Travellers in a Male World*. London: John Wiley.

Marshall, Judi 1993. Organisational cultures and women managers: Exploring the dynamics of resilience. *Applied Psychology: An International Review* 42(4): 313–22.

Marshall, Judi 1995. *Women Managers Moving On: Exploring Career and Life Choices*. London: Routledge.

Martín Rojo, Luisa 1997. The politics of gender: Agency and self-reference in women's discourse. *Belgian Journal of Linguistics* 11: 231–54.

Martín Rojo, Luisa 1998. Intertextuality and the construction of a new female identity. In Mercedes Bengoechea and Ricardo J. Sola Buil (eds.), *Intertextuality/Intertextualidad*. Alcalá de herares: Universidad de Alcalá de Herar.

Martín Rojo, Luisa and Conception Gomez Esteban 2003. Discourse at work: When women take on the role of manager. In Gilbert Weiss and Ruth Wodak (eds.), *Critical Discourse Analysis: Theory and Interdisciplinarity*. New York: Palgrave Macmillan, 241–71.

Martín Rojo, Luisa and Conception Gomez Esteban 2005. The gender of power: The female style in labour organizations. In Michelle Lazar (ed.), *Feminist Critical Discourse Analysis*. London: Palgrave, 61–89.

Maybin, Janet 2002. 'What's the hottest part of the Sun? Page 3!' Children's exploration of adolescent gender identities through informal talk. In Lia Litosseliti and Jane Sunderland (eds.), *Gender, Identity and Discourse Analysis*. Philadelphia, PA: John Benjamins, 257–73.

Meyerhoff, Miriam and Nancy Niedzielski 1994. Resistance to creolization: An intergroup account. *Language and Communication* 14(4): 313–30.

Miller Jean B. and Irene Stiver 1997. *The Healing Connection*. Boston: Beacon Press.

Mills, Sara 1999. Discourse competence: Or, how to theorize strong women speakers. In Christina Hendricks and Kelly Oliver (eds.), *Language and Liberation: Feminism, Philosophy, and Language*. Albany, NY: State University of New York Press, 81–97.

Mills, Sara 2003. *Gender and Politeness*. Cambridge, UK: Cambridge University Press.

Morand, David A. 1996a. Dominance, deference, and egalitarianism in organizational interaction: A sociolinguistic analysis of power and politeness. *Organization Science* 7(5): 544–56.

Morand, David A. 1996b. Politeness as a universal variable in cross-cultural managerial communication. *International Journal of Organizational Analysis* 4(1): 52–74.

Morand, David A. 2000. Language and power. *Journal of Organizational Behaviour* 21(3): 235–48.

Morris, Michael W., Katherine Y. Williams, Kwok Leung and Richard Larrick 1998. Conflict management style: Accounting for cross-national differences. *Journal of International Business Studies* 29(4): 729–47.

Morrison, Anthea forthcoming. Refusals: the influence of context, gender and culture on how they are accomplished. Unpublished MA thesis, Victoria University of Wellington, Wellington, NZ.

Morrison, Anthea and Janet Holmes 2003. Eliciting refusals: A methodological challenge. *Te Reo* 46: 47–66.

Morrison, Ann M., Randall P. White, Ellen Van Velsor and the Center for Creative Leadership 1987. *Breaking the Glass Ceiling: Can Women Reach the Top of America's Largest Corporations?* Reading, MA: Addison-Wesley.

Mouly, Suchitra and Jayram Sankara 2002. The enactment of envy within organizations. *The Journal of Applied Behavioural Science* 38(1): 36–56.

Niven, Christine 1993. Women: The road ahead. *Management* (Nov.): 50–3.

Nolan, Maria 1986. Success can be a laughing matter. *Data Management* 24: 28–9.

Northhouse, Peter G. 2001. *Leadership Theory and Practice* (2nd ed). Thousand Oaks, CA: Sage.

Ochs, Elinor 1992. Indexing gender. In Alessandro Duranti and Charles Goodwin (eds.), *Rethinking Context: Language as an Interactive Phenomenon.* Cambridge, UK: Cambridge University Press, 335–58.

Ochs, Elinor 1993. Constructing social identity: A language socialization perspective. *Research on Language and Social Interaction* 26(3): 287–306.

Olsson, Su 1996. A takeover? Competencies, gender and the evolving discourses of management. In Su Olsson and Nicole Stirton (eds.), *Women and Leadership: Power and Practice.* Palmerston North: Massey University Press, 359–78.

Olsson, Su 2000. The 'Xena' paradigm: Women's narratives of gender in the workplace. In Janet Holmes (ed.), *Gendered Speech in Social Context.* Wellington, NZ: Victoria University Press, 178–91.

Olsson, Su and Nicole Stirton (eds.) 1996. *Women and Leadership: Power and Practice.* Palmerston North: Massey University Press.

Olsson, Su and Robyn Walker 2003. 'The wo-men and the boys': Patterns of identification and differentiation in senior women executives representations of career identity. In Caroline Hatcher, Terry Flew and Joanne Jacobs (eds.), *Proceedings of ANZCA 03.* Brisbane: Queensland University of Technology, Brisbane Graduate School of Business.

Parry, Ken 2000. Women behaving as leaders. *Management* 47(5): 25–7.

Parry, Ken (ed.) 2001. *Leadership in the Antipodes: Findings, Implications and a Leader Profile.* Wellington, NZ: Institute of Policy Studies Centre for the Study of Leadership.

Parry, Ken 2003. Leadership, culture and a feminised workplace. Paper presented at Leadership Communication and Culture Forum. Wellington Turnbull House, March 2003.

Parry, Ken and James Meindl 2001. Models, methods, and triangulation. Researching the social processes in our society. In Ken Parry and James Meindl (eds.), *Grounding Leadership Theory and Research: Issues, Perspectives, and Methods.* Greenwich: Information Age, 199–221.

Parry, Ken and Sarah Proctor 2000. *The New Zealand Leadership Survey, 1999*. Wellington, NZ: Centre for the Study of Leadership, Victoria University of Wellington.

Pearson, Bethyl A. 1988. Power and politeness in conversation: Encoding of face-threatening acts at Church business meetings. *Anthropological Linguistics* 30: 68–93.

Pearson, Judy, Lynn Turner and William Todd-Mancillas 1991. *Gender and Communication* (2nd ed). Dubuque, IA: William Brown.

Peeters, Bert 2004. 'Thou shalt not be a tall poppy': Describing an Australian communicative (and behavioral) norm. *Intercultural Pragmatics* 1(1): 71–92.

Perrault, Michael R. and Janet K. Irwin 1996. *Gender Differences at Work: Are Men and Women Really that Different?: Analysis and Findings from a Study of Women and Men*. Agoura Hills, CA: Advanced Teamware Inc.

Philips, Susan U. 2003. The power of gender ideologies in discourse. In Janet Holmes and Miriam Meyerhoff (eds.), *Handbook of Language and* Gender. Oxford: Blackwell, 252–76.

Plester, Barbara Anne 2003. *Work Hard – Play Hard: Using Humour at Work*. Unpublished MA thesis, Massey University, Auckland, NZ.

Pomerantz, Anita 1978. Compliment responses: notes on the co-operation of multiple constraints. In Jim Schenkein (ed.), *Studies in the Organisation of Conversational Interaction*. New York: Academic Press, 79–112.

Pomerantz, Anita 1984. Agreeing and disagreeing with assessments: Some features of preferred/dispreferred turn shapes. In J. Maxwell Atkinson and John Heritage (eds.), *Structures of Social Action*. Cambridge: Cambridge University Press, 57–101.

Proctor-Thomson, Sarah B. and Ken Parry 2001. What the best leaders look like. In Ken Parry (ed.), *Leadership in the Antipodes: Findings, Implications and a Leader Profile*. Wellington, NZ: Institute of Policy Studies Centre for the Study of Leadership, 166–91.

Putnam, Linda L. 1992. Rethinking the nature of groups in organizations. In Robert S. Cathcart and Larry A. Samovar (eds.), *Small Group Communication*. Dubuque, IA: William Brown.

Ready, Douglas 2002. How storytelling builds next-generation leaders. *MIT Sloan Management Review* 43(4): 63–9.

Riessman, Catherine 1993. *Narrative Analysis*. London: Sage.

Robert, Henry H. 1967. *Robert's Rules of Order*. New Jersey: Fleming H. Revell.

Romaine, Suzanne 1999. *Communicating Gender*. Mahwah, NJ: Lawrence Erlbaum.

Rosener, Judy B. 1990. Ways women lead. *Harvard Business Review* (Nov./Dec.): 119–23.

Sacks, Harvey 1987. On the preferences for agreement and contiguity in sequences in conversation. In Graham Button and John R. E. Lee (eds.), *Talk and Social Organisation*. Exeter: Multilingual Matters Ltd., 58–66.

Saeki, Mimako and Barbara J. O'Keefe 1994. Refusals and rejections: Designing messages to serve multiple goals. *Human Communication Research* 21: 67–102.

Sala, Fabio 2000. Relationship between executives' spontaneous use of humour and effective leadership. *Dissertations Abstracts International Section B. The Sciences and Engineeering* 61 (3-B) (Sept.): 1683.

Sarangi, Srikant and Stefaan Slembrouck 1996. *Language, Bureaucracy and Social Control*. London: Longman.

Sasaki, Miyuki 1998. Investigating EFL students' production of speech acts: A comparison of production questionnaires and role plays. *Journal of Pragmatics* 30: 457–84.

Scheerhorn, Dirk R. 1989. Minding your P's and Q's in interpersonal decision-making: The politeness of messages as a consequent of decisional and relational goals. Unpublished PhD thesis, University of Iowa.

Schegloff, Emmanuel, Gail Jefferson and Harvey Sacks 1977. The preference for self-correction in the organisation of repair in conversation. *Language* 53(2): 361–82.

Schein, Virginia E. 1973. The relationship between sex role stereotypes and requisite management characteristics. *Journal of Applied Psychology* 57(2): 95–100.

Schein, Virginia E. 1975. The relationship between sex role stereotypes and requisite management characteristics among female managers. *Journal of Applied Psychology* 60(3): 34–44.

Schiffrin, Deborah 1994. *Approaches to Discourse*. Oxford: Blackwell.

Schiffrin, Deborah 1996. Narrative as self-portrait: Sociolinguistic constructions of identity. *Language in Society* 25: 167–203.

Schnurr, Stephanie forthcoming. Leadership, humour and gender: An analysis of workplace discourse. Unpublished PhD thesis, Victoria University of Wellington, Wellington, NZ.

Schwartzman, Helen B. 1989. *The Meeting: Gatherings in Organizations and Communities*, New York and London: Plenum Press.

Sheldon, Amy 1990. Pickle fights: Gendered talk in preschool disputes. *Discourse Processes* 13: 5–31.

Sheldon, Amy and Diane Johnson 1994. Preschool negotiators: Linguistic differences in how girls and boys regulate the expressing of dissent in same-sex groups. In Jenny Cheshire and Peter Trudgill (eds.), *The Sociolinguistic Reader*, Vol. 2, *Gender and Discourse*. London: Arnold, 76–98.

Sinclair, Amanda 1998. *Doing Leadership Differently: Gender, Power and Sexuality in a Changing Business Culture*. Melbourne: Melbourne University Press.

Smith, Peter and Mark Peterson 1988. *Leadership, Organizations and Culture*. London: Sage.

Sollitt-Morris, Lynette 1996. Language, gender and power relationships: The enactment of repressive discourse in staff meeting as of two subject departments in a New Zealand secondary school. Unpublished PhD thesis, Victoria University of Wellington, Wellington, NZ.

Spencer-Oatey, Helen 1992. Pragmatic competence and cross-cultural communication. An Analysis of communication between speakers of English and Chinese. Unpublished PhD thesis, Lancaster University, Lancaster, UK.

Spencer-Oatey, Helen 2000. Rapport management: A framework for analysis. In H. Spencer-Oatey (ed.), *Culturally Speaking*. London: Continuum.

Stalpers, Judith 1995. The expression of disagreement. In Konrad Ehlich and Johannes Wagner (eds.), *Discourse of Business Negotiation*. Berlin: Mouton de Gruyter.

Stanworth, Michelle 1983. *Gender and Schooling*. London: Hutchinson.

Stedman, Michael 2002. Belief and vision. *New Zealand Management* 49(10): 22–3.

Still, Leonie 1996. Women as leaders: The cultural dilemma. In Su Olsson and Nicole Stirton (eds.), *Women and Leadership: Power and Practice*. Conference Proceedings. Palmerston North: Massey University, 63–76.

Stodgill, Ralph 1997. Leadership, membership, organization. In Keith Grint (ed.), *Leadership: Classical, Contemporary, and Critical Approaches*. Oxford: Oxford University Press, 112–25.

Stokoe, Elizabeth H. and Janet Smithson 2002. Gender and sexuality in talk-in-interaction: Considering conversation analytic perspectives. In Paul McIlvenny (ed.), *Talking Gender and Sexuality: Conversation, Performativity and Discourse in Interaction*. Amsterdam: John Benjamins, 79–109.

Stokoe, Elizabeth H. and Ann Weatherall 2002. Gender, language, conversation analysis and feminism. *Discourse & Society* 13: 707–13.

Stubbe, Maria 1991. Talking at cross-purposes?: The effect of gender on New Zealand primary school children's interaction strategies in pair discussions. Unpublished MA thesis, Victoria University of Wellington, Wellington, NZ.

Stubbe, Maria 1999. Just joking and playing silly buggers: Humour and team-building on a factory production line. Paper presented at NZ Linguistics Society Conference, Massey, 24–6 Nov. 1999.

Stubbe, Maria 2000a. Talk that works: Evaluating communication in a factory production team. *New Zealand English Journal* 14: 55–65.

Stubbe, Maria 2000b. 'Just do it . . . !': Discourse strategies for 'getting the message across' in a factory production team. In John Henderson (ed.), *Proceedings of the 1999 Conference of the Australian Linguistic Society*; www.arts.uwa.edu.au/LingWWW/als99/proceedings.

Stubbe, Maria 2001. From office to production line: Collecting data for the Wellington Language in the Workplace Project. *Language in the Workplace Occasional Papers* 2. Wellington, NZ.

Sunderland, Jane 2004. *Gendered Discourses*. London: Palgrave Macmillan.

Swacker, Marjorie 1979. Women's verbal behaviour at learned and professional conferences. In Betty Dubois and Isabel Creuch (eds.), *The Sociology of the Languages of American Women*. San Antonio: Trinity University, 155–9.

Swann, Joan 1992. *Girls, Boys and Language*. Oxford, New York: Blackwell.

Swann, Joan 2002. Yes, but is it gender? In Lia Litosseliti and Jane Sunderland (eds.), *Gender, Identity and Discourse Analysis*. Philadelphia, PA: John Benjamins, 43–67.

Swann, Joan 2003. Schooled language: Educational policy and practice. In Janet Holmes and Miriam Meyerhoff (eds.), *Handbook of Language and Gender*. Oxford: Blackwell, 624–44.

Swap, Walter, Dorothy Leonard, Mimi Shields and Lisa Abrams 2001. Using mentoring and storytelling to transfer knowledge in the workplace. *Journal of Management Information Systems* 18: 95–114.

Takahashi, Tomoko and Leslie M. Beebe 1987. The development of pragmatic competence by Japanese learners of English. *JALT Journal* 8: 131–55.

Talbot, Mary 1998. *Language and Gender: An Introduction*. Cambridge, UK and Malden, MA: Polity Press.

Talbot, Mary 2003. Gender stereotypes: Reproduction and challenge. In Janet Holmes and Miriam Meyerhoff (eds.), *Handbook of Language and Gender*. Oxford: Blackwell, 468–86.

Tannen, Deborah (ed.) 1993. *Gender and Conversational Interaction*. Oxford: Oxford University Press.

Tannen, Deborah 1994a. *Gender and Discourse*. London: Oxford University Press.

Tannen, Deborah 1994b. *Talking from 9 to 5*. London: Virago Press.

Tannen, Deborah 1999. *The Argument Culture: Moving from Debate to Dialogue*. New York: Ballantine.

Taylor, Talbot J. and Deborah Cameron 1987. *Analysing Conversation: Rules and Units in the Structure of Talk*. Exeter, UK: Pergamon Press.

Thimm, Caja, Sabine C. Koch and Sabine Schey 2003. Communicating gendered professional identity. In Janet Holmes and Miriam Meyerhoff (eds.), *Handbook of Language and Gender*. Oxford: Blackwell, 528–49.

Thomas, Jenny 1985. The language of power. *Journal of Pragmatics* 9: 765–83.

Thomas, Jenny 1995. *Meaning in Interaction*. London: Longman.

Tjosvold, Dean, Valerie Dann and Choy Wong 1992. Managing conflict between departments to serve customers. *Human Relations* 45(10): 325–37.

Trauth, Eileen 2002. Odd girl out: An individual differences perspective on women in the IT profession. *Information Technology & People* 15(2): 98–118.

Turnbull, William 2001. An appraisal of pragmatic elicitation techniques for the social psychological study of talk: The case of request refusals. *Pragmatics* 11(1): 31–61.

Turner, Roy 1972. Some formal properties of therapy talk. In David Sudnow (ed.), *Studies in Social Interaction*. New York: Free Press, 367–96.

Vine, Bernadette 2001. Workplace language and power: Directives, requests and advice. Unpublished PhD thesis, Victoria University, Wellington, NZ.

Vine, Bernadette 2004. Getting things done at work: The discourse of power in workplace interaction. Amsterdam/Philadelphia: John Benjamins.

Vera, Dusya and Mary Crossan 2004. Strategic leadership and organizational learning. *The Academy of Management Review* 29(2): 222–40.

Watts, Richard 2003. *Politeness*. Cambridge, UK: Cambridge University Press.

Weatherall, Ann 2000. Gender relevance in talk in interaction and discourse. *Discourse & Society* 11: 290–2.

Weigel, M. Margaret and Ronald M. Weigel 1985. Directive use in a migrant agricultural community. *Language in Society* 14(1): 63–79.

Wenger, Etienne 1998. *Communities of Practice: Learning, Meaning, and Identity*. Cambridge, UK and New York: Cambridge University Press.

West, Candace 1984. When the doctor is a lady: Power, status and gender in physician–patient dialogues. *Symbolic Interaction* 7(1): 87–106.

West, Candace 1995. Women's competence in conversation. *Discourse & Society* 6(1): 107–31.

West, Candace and Sarah Fenstermaker 1995. Doing Difference. *Gender & Society* 9: 8–37.

West, Candace and Sarah Fenstermaker 2002. Accountability in action: The accomplishment of gender, race and class in a University of California Board of Regents. *Discourse & Society* 13: 537–63.

Willing, Ken 1992. *Talking it Through: Clarification and Problem Solving in Professional Work*. Sydney, NSW: National Centre for English Language Teaching and Research, Macquarie University.

Wodak, Ruth 1995. Power, discourse and styles of female leadership in school committee meetings. In David Corson (ed.), *Discourse and Power in Educational Organisations*. Cresskill, NJ: Hampton.

Wodak, Ruth 1996. *Disorders of Discourse*. London: Longman.

Wodak, Ruth 1997. 'I know, we won't revolutionize the world with this, but . . .': Styles of female leadership in institutions. In Helga Kotthoff and Ruth Wodak (eds.), *Communicating Gender in Context*. Amsterdam: Benjamins, 335–70.

Wodak, Ruth 1999. Critical Discourse Analysis at the End of the 20th Century. *Research on Language and Social Interaction* 32 (1&2): 185–93.

Wodak, Ruth 2003. Multiple identities: The roles of female parliamentarians in the EU parliament. In Janet Holmes and Miriam Meyerhoff (eds.), *Handbook of Language and Gender*. Oxford: Blackwell, 671–98.

Wodak, Ruth 2005. Gender mainstreaming and the European Union. In Michelle Lazar (ed.), *Feminist Critical Discourse Analysis*. London: Palgrave, 90–113.

Wood, Julia T. 2000. *Gendered Lives: Communication, Gender, and Culture* (3rd ed.). Belmont, CA: Wadsworth.

Wootton, Anthony J. 1981. The management of grantings and rejections by parents in request sequences. *Semiotica* 37: 59–89.

Yaegar-Dror, Malcah 2002. Introduction. *Journal of Pragmatics* 34: 1333–43.

Williams, E. A., G. W. Butt, C. Gray, S. Leach, A. Marr and A. Soares 1998. Mentors' use of dialogue within a secondary initial teacher education partnership. *Educational Review* 50(3): 225–39.

Zeus, Perry and Suzanne Skiffington 2002. *The Coaching at Work Toolkit: A Complete Guide to Techniques and Practices.* Sydney: McGraw-Hill.

Index